Mass Religious Ritual and Intergroup Tolerance

Under what conditions does in-group pride facilitate out-group tolerance? And what are the causal linkages between intergroup tolerance and socialization in religious rituals? This book examines how Muslims from Russia's North Caucuses returned from the Hajj pilgrimage to Mecca both more devout as Muslims and more tolerant of outgroups. Drawing on prominent theories of identity and social capital, the authors resolve seeming contradictions between the two literatures by showing the effects of religious rituals that highlight within-group diversity at the same time that they affirm the group's common identity. This theory is then applied to explain why social integration of Muslim immigrants has been more successful in the United States than in Europe and how the largest Hispanic association in the United States defied the clash of civilizations theory by promoting immigrants' integration into America's social mainstream. This book offers insights into Islam's role in society and politics and the interrelationships between religious faith, immigration and ethnic identity, and tolerance that will be relevant to both scholars and practitioners.

Mikhail A. Alexseev is a professor of political science at San Diego State University. He is the author of *Immigration Phobia and the Security Dilemma* (2006), *Center–Periphery Conflict in Post-Soviet Russia* (1999), and *Threat Assessment, Intelligence, and Global Struggle* (1997).

Sufian N. Zhemukhov is a senior research associate at George Washington University. He is the coauthor of *Putin's Olympics: The Sochi Games and the Evolution of Twenty-First Century Russia* (2017, with Robert Orttung).

Cambridge Studies in Social Theory, Religion, and Politics

Editors

David C. Leege, *University of Notre Dame*
Kenneth D. Wald, *University of Florida, Gainesville*
Richard L. Wood, *University of New Mexico*

The most enduring and illuminating bodies of late nineteenth-century social theory – by Marx, Weber, Durkheim, and others – emphasized the integration of religion, polity, and economy through time and place. Once a staple of classic social theory, however, religion gradually lost the interest of many social scientists during the twentieth century. The recent emergence of phenomena such as Solidarity in Poland, the dissolution of the Soviet empire, various South American, southern African, and South Asian liberation movements, the Christian right in the United States, and Al Qaeda have reawakened scholarly interest in religiously based political conflict. At the same time, fundamental questions are once again being asked about the role of religion in stable political regimes, public policies, and constitutional orders. The series *Cambridge Studies in Social Theory, Religion, and Politics* will produce volumes that study religion and politics by drawing on classic social theory and more recent social scientific research traditions. Books in the series offer theoretically grounded, comparative, empirical studies that raise "big" questions about a timely subject that has long engaged the best minds in social science.

Titles in the Series

Mikhail A. Alexseev and Sufian N. Zhemukhov, *Mass Religious Ritual and Intergroup Tolerance: The Muslim Pilgrims' Paradox*

Luke Bretherton, *Resurrecting Democracy: Faith, Citizenship, and the Politics of a Common Life*

David E. Campbell, John C. Green, and J. Quin Monson, *Seeking the Promised Land: Mormons and American Politics*

Ryan L. Claassen, *Godless Democrats and Pious Republicans? Party Activists, Party Capture, and the "God Gap"*

Paul A. Djupe and Christopher P. Gilbert, *The Political Influence of Churches*

Joel S. Fetzer and J. Christopher Soper, *Muslims and the State in Britain, France, and Germany*

François Foret, *Religion and Politics in the European Union: The Secular Canopy*

Jonathan Fox, *A World Survey of Religion and the State*

Jonathan Fox, *Political Secularism, Religion, and the State: A Time Series Analysis of Worldwide Data*

Anthony Gill, *The Political Origins of Religious Liberty*

Brian J. Grim and Roger Finke, *The Price of Freedom Denied: Religious Persecution and Conflict in the 21st Century*

Kees van Kersbergen and Philip Manow, editors, *Religion, Class Coalitions, and Welfare States*

Karrie J. Koesel, *Religion and Authoritarianism: Cooperation, Conflict, and the Consequences*

Ahmet T. Kuru, *Secularism and State Policies toward Religion: The United States, France, and Turkey*

Damon Maryl, *Secular Conversions: Political Institutions and Religious Education in the United States and Australia, 1800–2000*

Jeremy Menchik, *Islam and Democracy in Indonesia: Tolerance without Liberalism*

Pippa Norris and Ronald Inglehart, *Sacred and Secular: Religion and Politics Worldwide*

Amy Reynolds, *Free Trade and Faithful Globalization: Saving the Market*

Sadia Saeed, *Politics of Desecularization: Law and the Minority Question in Pakistan*

David T. Smith, *Religious Persecution and Political Order in the United States*

Peter Stamatov, *The Origins of Global Humanitarianism: Religion, Empires, and Advocacy*

Mass Religious Ritual and Intergroup Tolerance

The Muslim Pilgrims' Paradox

MIKHAIL A. ALEXSEEV

San Diego State University

SUFIAN N. ZHEMUKHOV

George Washington University, Washington, DC

CAMBRIDGE
UNIVERSITY PRESS

CAMBRIDGE
UNIVERSITY PRESS

University Printing House, Cambridge CB2 8BS, United Kingdom

One Liberty Plaza, 20th Floor, New York, NY 10006, USA

477 Williamstown Road, Port Melbourne, VIC 3207, Australia

4843/24, 2nd Floor, Ansari Road, Daryaganj, Delhi – 110002, India

79 Anson Road, #06–04/06, Singapore 079906

Cambridge University Press is part of the University of Cambridge.

It furthers the University's mission by disseminating knowledge in the pursuit of
education, learning, and research at the highest international levels of excellence.

www.cambridge.org
Information on this title: http://www.cambridge.org/9781107191853
DOI: 10.1017/9781108123716

First published 2017

Printed in the United States of America by Sheridan Books, Inc.

A catalogue record for this publication is available from the British Library.

Library of Congress Cataloging-in-Publication Data
NAMES: Alexseev, Mikhail A., 1963– author.
TITLE: Mass religious ritual and intergroup tolerance : the Muslim pilgrims'
paradox / Mikhail A. Alexseev, San Diego State University, Sufian N. Zhemukhov,
George Washington University, Washington DC.
DESCRIPTION: New York : Cambridge University Press, 2017. | Series: Cambridge studies
in social theory, religion, and politics | Includes bibliographical references and index.
IDENTIFIERS: LCCN 2017012132 | ISBN 9781107191853 (alk. paper)
SUBJECTS: LCSH: Muslim pilgrims and pilgrimages – Saudi Arabia – Mecca. | Pilgrims
and pilgrimages – Psychology. | Psychology, Religious. | Rites and .
ceremonies – Psychological aspects.
CLASSIFICATION: LCC BP187.3 .A397 2017 | DDC 297.3/524–DC23
LC record available at https://lccn.loc.gov/2017012132

ISBN 978-1-107-19185-3 Hardback

For our parents,
Anatoly & Lyudmila
and
Nasabi & Fatima

Contents

Figures

Tables

Acknowledgments

We owe incalculable debts to many individuals and organizations for making this book happen. Our collaboration would not be possible without the Program on New Approaches to Research and Security in Eurasia (PONARS Eurasia) funded by the Carnegie Corporation of New York and the John D. and Catherine T. MacArthur Foundation and its founding director, Celeste Wallander, who brought the authors together at the PONARS workshop in Tbilisi, Georgia, in 2008. As we conducted our research, we benefited significantly from the PONARS conferences – notably the first extensive report on our focus group findings at the 2010 PONARS workshop in Odessa, Ukraine, and policy conferences in Washington, DC in 2009 and 2011. We thank the organizers and discussants at these conferences and the Tbilisi workshop – Georgi Derluguian, Henry Hale, Yoshiko Herrera, Mark Kramer, Olga Novikova, Scott Radnitz, Sasha Schmemann, Nona Shahnazarian, Vadim Volkov, Cory Welt, and Ayşe Zarakol.

Above all, we extend gratitude to all the wonderful people in the North Caucasus who made our fieldwork possible – Nazir-hajji Akhmatov and Atmir-hajji Khamurzov, the leader and the doctor of the 2009 pilgrimage group where we conducted participant observation, and pilgrims Zamir-hajji Khatsukov and Batyr-hajji Berov for helping set up most of our in-depth interviews; all the hajjis and hajjiahs in that group for being generous and cooperative; the late Nina-hajjiah Shibzukhova for sharing with us her pilgrimage diaries and photos; Zarina Goplacheva, Safudin-hajji Kazharov, Zeynab-hajjiah Pagova, and Chamal-hajji Zhemukhov for organizing our four focus groups in Nalchik; Marianna Kerimova for transcribing our focus group discussions and inspiring us with her faith;

Alim Eleev for filming and photographing our events, fieldwork, and side tours, including the ascent along the slopes of Europe's tallest mountain, the twin-peaked Mt. Elbrus; Fatima-hajjiah, Samirat-hajjiah, Bitsa, Nafisat-hajjiah, Mukhamed-hajji, Marina, Madina, Salikh-hajji, Nokh-hajji, Ismail-hajji, Khizir-hajji, Ruslan, Zaur-hajji, Bolya-hajji, Khasan-hajji; Al'bina, Madina, Zamira, Zarema, Marina, both Mukhameds, both Zalims, Said, Alim, Osman, Mukhtar, and Anzor for taking part in our focus groups; and Igor Kuznetsov for setting up exploratory interviews with local Muslims in Russia's Republic of Adygea. We also would like to thank Zhilyabi Kalmykov and Barasbi Karamurzov for providing us with an opportunity to make our presentation "The Impact of Hajj on Development of Tolerance in Contemporary Society in Kabardino-Balkaria" at the 2010 policy conference organized by Kabardino-Balkaria State University and the Civic Chamber of Kabardino-Balkaria, Russia, and for inviting us to a private dinner after the conference where important issues relevant to our research were discussed.

The College of Arts and Letters and the Department of Political Science at the San Diego State University deserve credit for maintaining travel funding that partly covered Mikhail Alexseev's expenses during fieldwork in the North Caucasus. The Institute of International Education's Scholar Rescue Fund and the George Washington University's Institute for European, Russian, and Eurasian Studies at the Elliott School of International Affairs provided financial and institutional support for Sufian Zhemukhov's research.

We thank Farid Abdel-Nour, Iurii Anchabadze, Marjorie and Harley Balzer, Alexei Bekshokov, Martha Bloem, Kate Brown, Henry Hale, Stephen Hanson, Hope Harrison, Michael Khodarkovsky, Charles King, Ahmet Kuru, Igor Kuznetsov, Ian Lanzillotti, Marlene Laruelle, Cindy Machen, James Meyer, Harris Mylonas, Ahmed Farid Moustafa, Andrew Nolan, Robert Orttung, Margaret Paxson, Jean-François Ratelle, Sasha Schmemann, Richard Sharp, Nart Shekim, Regina Smyth, Ronald Grigor Suny, Cory Welt, Sarah Willcox, Jonty Yamisha, and Sajjad Ali Zahir for helpful conversations, friendly support, and insightful feedback on our ideas and various drafts of what eventually became this manuscript, and particularly Amy Beth Kay for straightening out some of our rough writing and Cindy Dobler Davis for inspiring the analysis that culminated in Chapter 8. Our special thanks also go to the anonymous reviewers of the manuscript for the Cambridge University Press whose comments were crucial in helping us position our study with respect to broader comparative research on Islam, intergroup relations, and politics. Portions of Chapters 2 and 6 were derived, in part, from our article "From Mecca with Tolerance: Religion, Social Re-categorization, and Social Capital" published in *Religion, State and Society* online in January 2016 (www .tandfonline.com) – we are grateful to the editor and anonymous reviewers for suggestions and to the publisher for granting use without seeking permission.

Ultimately, this book would not happen without enthusiastic initial interest in our proposal as well as the invaluable intellectual and organizational stewardship on the part of Lewis Bateman of the Cambridge University Press who also steered the manuscript through a rigorous peer-review process and improving manuscript revisions. We deeply appreciate his contribution. We are also thankful to Sara Doskow, who seamlessly took over from Lewis after his retirement and expeditiously saw the manuscript through to publication. We also thank Shaun Vigil and Claudia Bona-Cohen who assisted Lewis and Sara, respectively, and Ami Naramor and Srilakshmi Gobidass, editors, and Thomas Haynes for managing the cover design.

Introduction

Please be warned. This is a counterintuitive book. This is a story of how religious fervor translates into social tolerance. We tell it by examining empirically how the Hajj – the annual mass pilgrimage of Muslims to their holiest sites in Mecca – affects the pilgrims as individuals and as members of their communities and societies. After all, not only is the Hajj one of the Five Pillars of Islamic faith, it is a particularly intense exercise of religious worship bringing together more than 2 million Muslims annually from all over the world. In the Muslim world, it is the most exalted expression of both religious doctrine and religious practice, with individual believers coming into contact with the center of the Islamic universe in space and its point of origin in time. We focused on this experience as a powerful magnifying lens through which to examine how religious rituals may affect social relations. Our findings gave rise to generalizations that took us analytically beyond the Hajj, beyond Islam, and beyond religion.

Through participant observation, diaries, interviews, and focus group discussions we start by taking you inside the life-world and the minds of pilgrims from Russia's turbulent North Caucasus. We let you trace with us the Hajj's impacts on them. From there, we tease out theoretical insights that apply to relations among human groups of any kind. In doing so, we synthesize Mircea Eliade's classic philosophical exploration of the sacred and profane with theories of social categorization in psychology and social capital in political science. The result is a book about religion, personality, society, and the state – yet not necessarily in a familiar sense, at least not to those who have immersed themselves in debates on Islam, society, and politics – particularly after 9/11.

Our principal concern is with the paradoxical side of our findings. We examine empirically and theoretically why, on the one hand, the Hajj strengthened the pilgrims' pride in being Muslim, and yet, on the other hand, our in-depth interviews and focus groups showed that the pilgrims were on the whole more prosocial and tolerant than the non-pilgrims who also strongly desired to perform the Hajj. We call it the Pilgrims' Paradox and develop a synthetic theoretical solution. Specifically, we trace the socially benign effects of the Hajj to socialization dynamics in high-identity-value, high-diversity common group settings – that is, when many different subgroups of a common group come into contact to positively affirm their common (superordinate) identity in a nondiscriminatory fashion. Drawing on social identity theory and social capital theory, we explain how inclusive views that arise inside a group in these settings extend to outgroups – including the religious and ethnic "others." This book is about the Hajj model of tolerance and its under-lying perceptual and behavioral causal mechanisms.

It is important, however, to warn you now what our work is *principally* not about.

It is not about what Islam is as a faith or how its rituals should be performed.

It is not about the pilgrimage rules or domestic Hajj politics.

It is not about whether Islamic faith is *by nature* tolerant or intolerant or capable of reformation or compatible with Marxism, or adaptable as a set of universal norms and values to different cultures.

It is not primarily about Islamic transnationalism or the pilgrimage as part of globalization or the effects of globalization on Islamic practices.[1]

It is not a descriptive historical-ethnographic narrative of the pilgrimage.[2]

Nor is it about whether Islamic law and social practices are compatible with democracy, as it is understood in the West.

It is not about the meaning of secularism or whether secularization can happen through religion, or whether the absence of a distinction between state and religion secularizes religion more than it makes politics religious.

It is not about whether the separation of church and state is the same as the separation of religion from politics, of the sacred from the profane.

And it is not about whether Muslims are more likely to engage in political violence or terrorism than non-Muslims.

And yet, our study is germane to all these questions and debates. In fact, we suspect it may well be more germane to them than we realize. Some of our insights arise directly from observation of the Hajj's effects in the part of the world that has been a relative newcomer to the global Islamic resurgence. But most come from broader theoretical arguments we develop about the nature of social interactions and the perceptual micro foundations of intergroup behavior. They come from our analysis of individual repositioning, recategorization, and repersonalization that we find in the pilgrimage experiences. We outline some of the implications of our theoretical arguments later in this volume. Many more, we hope, will become apparent when scholars in their respective research lacunae discuss this book.

Our study makes three fundamental contributions to scholarship. The first concerns the impacts of the Hajj as a religious *ritual* as well as a religious and social *experience* in the life of Muslims. It is surprising how cursorily at best the Hajj pilgrimage – Islam's doctrinally fundamental and spectacular mass ritual – has been treated in extensive academic debates on Islam, society, and politics. Going through book after book and article after article by key figures in these debates – Bernard Lewis, Samuel Huntington, John Esposito, Olivier Roy, Peter Mandaville, Tariq Ramadan, Juan Cole, Charles Kurzman, Steven Fish, Ahmet Kuru, Robert Hefner, Fawaz A. Gerges, and others – made us realize that our study would be filling a substantial knowledge gap. It may be understandable why none of these authors undertook a focused examination of the sociopolitical impacts of the Hajj empirically the way we did. Yet, it was nevertheless puzzling to note the absence of references to substantial literature that examines these effects, from mass opinion surveys in Pakistan to historical explorations into the lives of Muslim luminaries – studies that we bring in when we interpret our findings theoretically.

Only John Esposito among the prominent scholars of Islam and politics listed earlier, in *Islam: The Straight Path, Who Speaks for Islam,* and *Future of Islam,* dedicates a separate section to the significance of the Hajj spiritually and socially.[3] In all these books, however, the discussions are short (about two pages), they are almost identical, and they focus on the conceptual underpinnings of the pilgrimage. Specifically, Esposito presents the Hajj as a symbol of Muslim unity across nations, of gender nondiscrimination, of spiritual contact with God, and of joint overcoming of human struggles through life. These points illustrate Esposito's general argument that the potential to reform itself and to be more inclusive and tolerant of other religions and of secularism is within Islam's doctrinal core. We have no issue with these general arguments. However, as social scientists we looked for systematic evidence of causal linkages. We wanted to look beyond John Esposito's illustrative single-case evidence of the actual effects of the Hajj on Muslims. Esposito typically references a well-known story of Malcom X, a leading militant black American activist, and his "spiritual transformation" to a more inclusive and tolerant "understanding of human brotherhood" as a result of performing the Hajj. In fact, Esposito makes a well-argued case that Malcolm X's pilgrimage galvanized a transformation of the entire American black movement away from extremist ideology as other movement leaders followed Malcolm X's example and amplified his message through their public sharing of the Hajj effects they experienced.[4]

Esposito and others, however, do not systematically refute an obvious counterargument – i.e., that some of the most militant jihadist leaders including Osama Bin Laden also performed the Hajj. Adam Robinson, who wrote a biography of Bin Laden, argued that Bin Laden's pilgrimage to Mecca, in 1977, radicalized him.

It was an entirely different Osama Bin Laden who arrived home in Jeddah at the end of Hajj. He now prayed five times a day, something that he had not done since his early days in Lebanon. In the days following his return he made a fresh start and did everything within his power to effect an immediate change of direction. First, he rid himself of the symbol of his old life, his yellow Mercedes SL 450 convertible. His drinking friends were similarly dispatched from his life, with a sermon on their sins, and Osama visited the mosque to deliberate with God over his loss of faith. Within weeks Osama was growing his beard long as an indication of his piety; he threw himself into his studies at King Abdul Aziz University and immersed himself in the religious studies he had shunned for so long.[5]

Why wouldn't Bin Laden get spiritually transformed like Malcolm X? What kind of spiritual transformation – if it happens during the pilgrimage – is more typical? A broader point here is that one cannot merely extrapolate from symbolic meaning of a ritual in which a person participates to actual social behavior of that person after the ritual. If that behavior nevertheless changes – as many students of the pilgrimage, including us, have found – then something more must be in play than the meaning of faith and the religious content of the ritual.

Peter Mandaville, in *Global Political Islam*, devotes more than twice as much space to the Hajj than John Esposito does, but Mandaville frames the Hajj as a weathervane of larger political processes, not as a religious and social experience *sui generis*. In particular, we learn from Mandaville how the Hajj reflects domestic politics in key pilgrim-sending states (Pakistan, Malaysia, Indonesia, Nigeria, Turkey); relations between major states within the Muslim world; increasing transnational networking and social mobilization; and the emergence of regional economic subsystems. Mandaville also mentions the benign transformative effects of the Hajj not only on Malcolm X, but also on Iran's Muslim progressive, Ali Shariati. Yet, aside from briefly mentioning this, the impacts of the Hajj as a religious and social practice on participants' worldviews are left unexamined.[6]

We wondered if we would find a systematic analysis of the Hajj's sociopolitical effects in the work of prominent scholars in political science and sociology who used large quantitative and qualitative datasets to examine the relationship between Islam and political behavior. Our extensive searches of academic datasets yielded limited results. Notably, from Steven Fish, Francesca Jensenius, and Katherine Michel we learned that violent political strife is just about as likely in Muslim-majority countries as anywhere else.[7] And from Charles Kurzman, David Schanzer, and Ebrahim Moosa we learned why Muslim terrorists are relatively scarce despite post-9/11 fears and, by extension, even despite a spate of terrorist attacks throughout Europe in 2015 and 2016, as well as how generally unreceptive young Muslims are to incendiary radical Islamist indoctrination. On the other hand, we also revisited large quantitative studies that we discuss in detail in Chapter 3 showing that religious divides make intrastate violent conflicts deadlier and more protracted. These analyses go back to comprehensive seminal work on civil wars by scholars such as David Laitin and James Fearon. Yet, we found no study in this vast literature where participation in the Hajj or engagement in any similar rituals or protracted exposure to social contexts that resemble what happens during the Hajj was a causal or control variable – qualitatively or quantitatively.[8]

The exception was a mass opinion survey in Pakistan by a Harvard University research team in 2008. Its authors, David Clingingsmith, Asim Ijaz Khwaja, and Michael Kremer, focused specifically on how performing the Hajj affected religious beliefs and social attitudes of Muslims – yet it was framed outside the big debates on the political and social dimensions of Islam. For their own part, studies of Islam's relationships with politics, intergroup conflict, or violence have not considered the implications of its findings. In fact, the Pakistan survey did much to inspire us to proceed – and to extend the scope of investigation, from examining statistical associations to examining causalities through process tracing, with extensive reliance on cultural anthropological methods and content analysis of in-depth interviews with the pilgrims and non-pilgrims. It also inspired us to go beyond the empirical findings and to think of how to explain them systematically and how to advance social theory. Curiously, however, we noted how little traction the Pakistan survey findings have had in the discussions of Islam and politics, either in the work of social philosophers such as Esposito, Roy, and Ramadan or of social scientists, such as Robert Putnam, Charles Kurzman, and Steven Fish. And so we hoped that our study would also attract attention to other inside-out analyses of the Hajj and thus contribute to productive cross-pollination of ideas.

Our second contribution is to take the analysis of religion's social impacts out of the "culturalist trap." Olivier Roy in *Globalized Islam* used this term to describe a serious problem in research on Islam – the tendency of debates on Muslims turning around one question: What is Islam? "Most events involving Muslims," Roy lamented, "are related to Islam as such: what does Islam say about *jihad*, suicide bombers, violence, Judaism, Christianity, democracy, secularization, and so on?"[9] In doing so, according to Roy, scholars and pundits have been willingly or unwillingly perpetuating the misconception of Islam as "a discrete entity, a coherent and closed set of beliefs, values and anthropological patterns embodied in a common society, history and territory, which allows us to use the term as an explanatory concept for almost anything involving Muslims."[10] Critics and defenders of Islam alike have fallen into this culturalist trap – "traditional orientalists like Bernard Lewis ... social scientists (like Huntington), politicians, newspaper leader-writers, strongly pro-Israel right-wing academics (such as Daniel Pipes), and the person in the street."[11] The trap, as Roy showed, also closed in on fundamentalists and conservative Muslims, on opponents of Islamophobia and moderate Muslims, on claimants to the monopoly on interpretation of the Qur'an, and on the organizers of "apologetic and boring conferences" on Islam as a message of peace. The resulting "mirror effect," Roy pointed out, "ossifies the debate and misses what is happening under our own eyes but lies outside our mental framework."[12]

We did not want to miss that. And so, we explicitly don't ask: What is Islam? Rather, we do what Roy recommended as a remedy against the culturalist trap: "The issue here is not Islam as a theological corpus, but the discourses and practices of Muslims." Ours is precisely the study of such *discourses and practices* (yet in a way that Roy himself did not pursue). And it is about the discourses and practices of humans in general. We do not assume that being Muslim would somehow make their humanity different. At the heart of our project is the empirical process – tracing how the Hajj affects participating individuals. We examine specific practices of the pilgrims and non-pilgrims not only from media reports or memoirs, but also and primarily through our own targeted participant observation of the Hajj and of life in the Hajj-sending region of Kabardino-Balkaria in Russia's North Caucasus. We were able to do this because one of the authors, Sufian Zhemukhov, is a native of this region who lived there for more than forty years and who also performed the Hajj both as a Muslim and as a researcher for this project. We draw extensively on Sufian's diaries, notes, and interview transcripts during the pilgrimage. This in itself is a contribution. We have not found systematic participant observation analyses of the Hajj's effects on individuals.

We also analyze individual and group discourses in depth, examining thousands of statements qualitatively and quantitatively to compare the views of the hajjis and the non-hajjis. In addition to Sufian's interviews, we use the transcripts of several group interviews and four extensive, quasi-experimentally designed focus group sessions that both authors conducted in Kabardino-Balkaria.

Ours is not the only research project that takes studies of Islam out of the culturalist trap. We engage other studies extensively. Our project's contribution to these efforts is twofold. First, it differs substantially from analyses such as that of Charles Kurzman and his colleagues who studied how community-building and political engagement among American Muslims reduced their proclivity to engage in terrorism. In a sense, we reverse cause and effect here – rather than analyzing the effects of community life on Muslims' behavior, we examine the effects of Muslims' ritualistic behavior on their views of community life and preferences for community practices. In this sense, our project also differs from Juan Cole's masterful exploration of how demographic and socioeconomic forces have shaped political views and mass behavior of Muslims in the Middle East.[13] And with respect to the quantitative analyses of large surveys that tested for correlation between participation in religious rituals (including the Pakistan Hajj survey) and sociopolitical attitudes, we add a systematic investigation of perceptual and behavioral causal mechanisms. The latter are impossible to capture with event or survey data. This is where our ethnography of the Hajj and content analysis of interviews and focus group conversations add value.

Our third contribution is the most far-reaching. We generalize from the Hajj experiences to intergroup relations within and outside religion. This contribution is not about what else we can *learn about* Islam and Muslims, but about what else we can learn about human group interactions in general *from learning* about Islam and Muslims. At the heart of this contribution is what we identify as the Pilgrims' Paradox – the simultaneous increase of in-group pride and out-group tolerance among the pilgrims compared to the non-pilgrims who are also dedicated Muslims. We establish this paradox empirically with our qualitative data.

We also show how this paradox reflects major theoretical debates across social science disciplines. On the one hand, the swelling in-group pride is consistent with the divisive us/them logic posited by the social identity theory in psychology. On the other hand, the rise in tolerance is consistent with the social capital logic developed in sociology and political science. The paradox is two-sided. As far as the social identity theory is concerned, the challenge is to explain why more devout Muslim believers turn out to be more socially tolerant and more open to participation in civic life. As far as the social capital theory is concerned, the challenge is to explain why the hajjis came through as more tolerant toward non-Muslims, with whom they practically never engage in social contact while performing the Hajj.

We develop an explanation based on a synthesis of major theoretical perspectives. Our starting point is Mircea Eliade's (1987) philosophy of the sacred and profane, which highlights a crucial aspect of the Hajj as physical and symbolic repositioning of individuals into settings that combine the intrinsically high value of their common in-group identity and high social diversity. Second, by drawing on the social identity and on social capital theories, we explain how social recategorization into common groups could engender not only common in-group, but also out-group tolerance. Critically in this regard, we identify aspects of the Hajj experience that help systematically explain why benign socialization effects within a group could be transitive to outgroups – a process that we show remains undertheorized. Finally, we trace the impacts of repositioning and recategorization to the emergence of a renewed sense of individuality – repersonalization – that promotes social and political tolerance. Our predominant approach is multi-method process tracing that also distinguishes this analysis from existing correlational studies based on variously designed indices of religiosity (none of which, however, factors in mass ritual participation akin to the Hajj).[14]

As we generate and discuss these insights, we bring in important theoretical literature that has typically been left on the margins of debates about Islam, politics, and society in Islamic studies and political science. This includes seminal work on social identity theory, going back to the path-breaking experiments of Henry Tajfel and John Turner and their followers, as well as the classic research by Robert Putnam and David Campbell in laying down the theoretical and empirical foundations of the social capital – including religious social capital. It also includes our reinterpretation of Mircea Eliade's philosophy and sociology of the sacred and profane to explain important puzzles that our Hajj investigation revealed in the social identity and social capital theories. As we hope to make students of Islam and politics aware of these theoretical perspectives, we also hope to make social psychologists, political scientists, and sociologists more aware of how ritualistic behavior in Islam may challenge and help advance their theoretical explanations of intergroup relations. We hope to spark more stimulating and productive dialog among these literatures. If this were the only thing we achieved with this volume, we will feel its publication would be justified.

As we present the repositioning-recategorization-repersonalization (3 R's) model explaining the Pilgrims' Paradox, we illustrate it with the findings of quantitative content analysis of focus groups we held among Muslims in Russia's Republic of Kabardino-Balkaria designed to systematically compare the views of the Hajj pilgrims to those of the non-pilgrims.[15]

Our principal insight is the identification of what we term the *Axis Mundi* effect: In high-identity-value, high-diversity common group settings, social inclusive views within an ingroup extend to outgroups. This means that intergroup conflict could be reduced by not only maximizing contact across conflicting groups, but also by bringing together as many subgroups as possible within each conflicting group in settings where their common identity is affirmed in a positive and nondiscriminatory fashion. We call it the Hajj model of tolerance.

In the final part of this book, we explore the Hajj model's significance by first taking it outside the Hajj context and then by taking it outside Islam and religion in general. We start with a mini case study on Muslim integration in predominantly secular societies. We compare the evolution of Muslim associations, mosque design debates, and Muslim public views in the United States and Europe. We then apply the Hajj tolerance model outside Islam and outside religion. We show how the *Axis Mundi* effect explains why Hispanic immigrants to the United States failed to live up to the dark forebodings of the clash of civilization theorists through promoting intra-Hispanic/Latino diversity within their leading public association.

We feel that our Hajj model of tolerance has serious, far-reaching implications for interactions among any human collectivities and thus for resolving intergroup conflicts of any kind. To distill the three principal contributions we outlined here into one sentence – ultimately, our work shows not only what studying society can tell us about religion or what studying religion can tell us about society, but what studying the social in the religious can tell us about both.

* * *

Looking back, we realize that our own collaboration on this project has important elements of the Hajj model of social interaction. We represent different ethnocultural backgrounds (Circassian and Russian-Ukrainian); different religious orientations (Muslim and broadly Christian agnostic); and different academic backgrounds (historical ethnography and political science). As part of this project, we combined different research methods – qualitative cultural anthropology of the pilgrimage and quantitative analysis of focus group discussions.

We do not claim to have delivered conclusive proof of the Hajj model, but we believe the paradox of social tolerance emerging out of intensely passionate mass rituals exhibiting devotion to religious unity – of which the Hajj pilgrimage is an instance – is worth presenting and analyzing in depth. As we do so, we hope to inspire new pilgrimages and new discoveries along this path of inquiry.

PART I

THE PILGRIMS' PARADOX

I

Russia's North Caucasus: The State, the Hajj, and the Revival of the Sacred

Russia's North Caucasus and the Kabardino-Balkaria Republic in its geographic center offered us an excellent setting for exploring the impact of the Hajj pilgrimage on individual Muslims and on their sociopolitical views and behavior. Our study took place in the midst of Islamic resurgence – local residents were turning to Islam as a source of identity, power, meaning, and hope. We also found ourselves in the midst of social tensions, conflict, and violent antigovernment insurgency that Russia's national and local leaders implicitly linked to the Islamic resurgence.

On Friday, April 30, 2010, we were having breakfast in Sufian's apartment on the second floor of a typical Soviet five-story cube of a building – a ubiquitous design one finds from Kaliningrad to Vladivostok with a living room, a bedroom, a kitchen, and a bathroom squeezed into about 400 square feet of space. We were in the town of Nartkala, a suburb of Nalchik, the capital of Kabardino-Balkaria – the center of the North Caucasus region and home to Europe's tallest mountain, the twin-peaked Mt. Elbrus. From the window we could see the emerald green cone of the minaret towering over a monumental dome that capped a circular white building set on a lush green lawn. It was a mosque built in the late 1990s to replace a dreary Soviet-style strip mall once featuring a hair salon, a photo shop, and a dry-cleaning service. It was the sign of the times, the replacement of the vestiges of socialist planned economy with the spaces of resurgent Islamic identity. By the time we had that breakfast, the mosque had witnessed both the resurgence of Islam among Circassians after the fall of Communism, and the wholesale crackdown on that resurgence by the Russian government. Right there, from his window, Sufian had once observed masses of young people streaming to the mosque – which was something he recounted in a conference paper on why young people turn to Islam in the North Caucasus that he presented at a conference in Tbilisi, Georgia, in June 2008. It was the presentation that brought us together and sparked our creative partnership. And it was from the same window that Mikhail observed the desolate mosque entrance and an empty parking lot and, from time to time, perhaps an oddball human figure or two appearing after multiple calls for prayer beamed throughout the neighborhood from the mosque's powerful loudspeakers. When Mikhail first saw the emptiness, he felt strange, almost deceived. He came to visit Sufian primed by the latter's presentation in Tbilisi. He expected to observe and to analyze from his ringside seat at Sufian's living room window multitudes of local Muslims he believed would attend the mosque. Instead, during call after call to prayer, we looked outside only to observe the quiet empty space around the mosque. The well-maintained green lawn somehow made the area around the mosque look even emptier, stranger, and more desolate. When Mikhail asked why the mosque had so few visitors, Sufian explained it was the result of the Russian government crackdown on local believers in the previous couple of years. Alarmed by the crowds seeking to attend the mosque, the police and the government security services started checking personal identification documents of every aspiring entrant to the mosque's fenced and gated territory. According to Sufian, the government security personnel also recorded every entrant's individually identifying information. As he found out from socializing with local Muslims, the latter did not like this practice and they did not trust the local law enforcement agencies. It was easy to understand why. Two days earlier, we had participated in a conference at the Kabardino-Balkaria State University on religion, society, and security. One speaker, a prominent and fearless local human rights lawyer, presented case after case of local law enforcement agencies indiscriminately arresting and violently treating individuals who exhibited devotion to Islam in public. So, ordinary local Muslims stopped coming to the central Nartkala mosque and attended smaller, more circumspect houses of prayer. The latter, in fact, were crowded at Friday prayer times, as we witnessed the very day of our breakfast.

Sadly, our breakfast morning also illustrated how volatile the region was. Midway through the breakfast, Sufian's cell phone rang. One could discern a male voice speaking Circassian coming from the receiver. Circassian is distinct to someone who has heard it before – it has not one, but two "r" sounds, one similar to the Spanish or Russian rolling "r," and the other to the French guttural twirling "r." In some words, both "r" versions are used. As Sufian listened, his face darkened with alarm and concern. In a few minutes, Sufian hang up and gave Mikhail the bad news. A car bomb targeting local policemen had exploded in downtown Nalchik overnight. Two police officers were injured. The explosion – reported in the Russian media later – took place near the intersection of Tolstoy and Shogentsukov Streets.[1] We realized it was just a block or so away from the apartment building where we had arranged to hold our fourth focus group for this study. The news, sadly, was hardly a surprise. It was the fifth armed attack on local police and government security servicemen that month. Militant groups operating as a loose association of the radical Islamist Caucasus Emirate claimed responsibility for these acts.

The next day, having completed our focus groups, Sufian took Mikhail to the airport, located about sixty miles away in Mineral'nye Vody. On our way out of Nalchik, the traffic thickened. Through rows of slowly creeping cars we saw police officers blocking the intersection ahead. Luckily, Sufian knew the back roads well and we got out of the city in time for Mikhail to make his flight to Moscow. Once there, Mikhail turned on the TV at his hotel room and watched a BBC report on a massive explosion earlier that day at a racehorse track in Nalchik, not too far from where the police had blocked the road to the airport. On the news, Mikhail watched the flames with black smoke shooting up and engulfing a nearby city block. According to the report, the explosion likely targeted Kabardino-Balkaria's governor, Arsen Kanokov, and possibly the strongman leader of Chechnya and one of the key Putin protégés in the region, Ramzan Kadyrov, who, according to the news reports, had been expected to attend the race. Ramzan Kadyrov's father, Akhmat Kadyrov, who served as Chechnya's governor from 2000 to 2004, was assassinated in a similar explosion at a stadium in Chechnya's capital, Grozny, during a World War II victory day parade.

Was the violence around us an ominous outcome of Islam's resurgence – of which the object of our study, the Hajj pilgrimage, was part and parcel? One could not help asking oneself and discussing this issue while in Kabardino-Balkaria in those days. We were torn apart. On the one hand, we were well aware that we were not studying the relationship between Islam and violence. We knew of well-documented analyses showing that significant and persistent violence in internal wars is typically the work of small insurgent groups whose radical motivations are typically not those of societies at large. The more we looked at the situation in Kabardino-Balkaria and the neighboring North Caucasus provinces through the eyes of ordinary Muslims, the more the putative causal linkage from Islam to violent conflict appeared unreal, outlandish, a dangerously crude oversimplification. At the same time, the linkage appeared so intuitive to so many in Russia and elsewhere that we could not dismiss it. It was clear that while our study was not about violent behavior, it would probably have significant implications concerning the latter.

And so we start our examination by locating the Hajj in a broader historical context of both Islamic revival and violent conflict in the North Caucasus. This is not a history of the Hajj in the region, but a story of the turning points in the relationship between the state, religion, and society that paint a comprehensive picture of the Hajj as both a religious and social experience. This story has a central theme of utmost relevance today – the ebb and flow of tension between a society in which a given religion is embedded, and the state that seeks to rule over that society.

The upshot of our observations was disconcerting, if undeniable. The big picture was alarmingly convincing to someone watching the region. The revival of Islam, of which the Hajj pilgrimage was an important part, and of Circassian nationalism loomed all too plausible as the principal cause of tension and violent conflict with the Russian state.

THE HAJJ, THE STATE, AND SOCIETY IN KABARDINO-BALKARIA: TENSIONS AND REVIVALS

Pilgrimage to Mecca has strong roots in the North Caucasus, including Kabardino-Balkaria.[2] The ritual has a high intrinsic value in local Muslim societies. Circassians – a broader regional ethnic identification that comprises Kabardians, or 57 percent of present-day Kabardino-Balkaria's population – have more than 100 given names connected to the Hajj symbols. These roots are evident in the widespread naming of children with derivatives of the words *Hajj* and *Ka'aba* – such as Hajumar for males and Kaabakhan for females. Today, parents in the region typically want their children to become hajjis. Most local residents are aware that in the nineteenth century, many North Caucasus Muslims in their old age went to Mecca to die and to be buried in what they saw as sacred land. Those who had the money for the journey but were not able to go to Mecca themselves sent other people on their behalf. It was customary in the North Caucasus, particularly prior to the Soviet period, to make wills deeding one's entire property to be sold and the proceeds to be taken to Mecca and given there as alms. Thinking about the Hajj also evokes pride among Circassians in their history as a nation and as an emerging state before Russia's forceful and violent military conquest of Circassian lands that started in the second half of the 1700s and ended with the incorporation of the North Caucasus into the Soviet Union in the early 1920s. One proud memory Sufian shared is of a prominent Kabardian politician, Jabagi Kazanoko. Kazanoko served as an ambassador of Kabarda to the Crimean Khan about 300 years ago. After completing his diplomatic mission, Kazanoko made a pilgrimage to Mecca. It is a memory of one's ethnic homeland having a state established well enough to send its own ambassadors abroad.

Looking back over the tumultuous history of the North Caucasus since Kazanoko's pilgrimage, one realizes that the post-Soviet revival of the Hajj tradition, in which we participated by dint of circumstance, was not necessarily a given. The tradition survived two long and challenging periods – the defeat in battle and mass exodus of Circassians from their homeland in the nineteenth century, as well as the wholesale suppression and manipulation of religion by the Soviet government in the twentieth. And yet, as we shall see, association with the exodus turned into hopes for return of Circassians from around the world to their homeland while association with oppression turned into hopes for the revival of the faith. With these hopes, Islam embeds itself as one of the pillars of Circassian national identity.

Our fieldwork illustrated this multifaceted relationship between Islam and nationalism in Kabardino-Balkaria. While discussing how Islam relates to Circassian ethnic traditions, one participant in our focus group conversations stated with passion: "They are inseparable, of course! Just look at the Circassian flag. Did you notice how our twelve stars[3] are arranged? Yes, they form a crescent, like a symbol of Islam. And the flag color is green, the Prophet's favorite color." A few days later, we drove to see the beautiful waterfalls in the mountains. At one point, an unabashedly speeding sedan overtook us, the green-starred Circassian flag sticking out of the back window and fluttering savagely in the wind. This flag, incidentally, is officially recognized as a flag in Adygea, one of the North Caucasus provinces with a sizeable ethnic Circassian population. However, people who flagrantly display it in Kabardino-Balkaria and Karachaevo-Cherkessia (the two other provinces with large Circassian populations) usually want to demonstrate the strength of nationalist aspirations and, to a degree, deep-seated dissatisfaction with the current configuration of the Russian Federation, in which ethnic Circassian populations are broken apart into different administrative-territorial units.

Later, we came across the people who overtook us on the road while waving the flag. They were all young men and they were having a rambunctious lunch party at a roadside café in the mountains. As we passed by their table, they pointed to Mikhail and invited him to drink a toast with them. Once he told them he was from California, they immediately filled a shot glass with local brandy. Sufian stepped up to Mikhail and urgently whispered in his ear that the filled glass in local customs meant a very serious intent to honor a guest. That kind of invitation could not be refused at the risk of gravely offending the hosts. And so we came up to their table. The young men insisted Mikhail should drink "to President Bush's health." Mikhail countered – over Sufian's vehement protests that the host's toast cannot be challenged – that everyone should raise a toast instead to the health of the then current U.S. president, Barak Obama. The young men agreed, some of them saying they would drink to both. A moment later, the edgy, palate-scraping local brandy flew down Mikhail's throat. Everyone cheered and clapped. V-signs were flashed and high-fives slapped. We gave a big cheer to Kabardino-Balkaria and moved outside at a fast clip. Some of the young men were clearly not sober, and we did not want to experience too heavy a share of local nationalist hospitality. They clearly did not see celebrating their Circassian identity with hard liquor as contradicting the behavioral norms represented by the crescent and the color that others associate with Islam. This episode sheds light on why later in our focus groups the compatibility of Islam with Circassian ethnic customs would be an important conversation topic and the one that illustrated systematic differences between the pilgrims and the non-pilgrims.

UNDER THE RUSSIAN EMPIRE: A PATH TO EXODUS

In the North Caucasus during the nineteenth century, the Hajj played a part in the heroic – but ultimately doomed – local resistance to Russia's sweeping territorial expansion.[4] The pilgrimage's principal role by far was not in mobilizing armed resistance to that expansion, but in helping the locals escape Russia's imperial rule. One notable case involved Imam Shamil, known as the "Lion of Dagestan,"[5] who for almost a quarter century fought an unequal war against Russia's imperial government and led an Islamic state in the North Caucasus. To this day, Imam Shamil is probably the most revered figure across that whole region. After he surrendered to the Russian forces in 1859, Shamil was allowed by the Russian emperor to perform the Hajj. Having done so, Shamil never came back to Russia. In Mecca, Shamil was treated as a celebrity – according to historians, "the police had to assign special hours for his prayer to prevent public disturbance."[6] The cultural reference to Islam was strong in the Caucasus. Parts of the Circassian community that fled from Russian rule to the still unoccupied part of western Circassia in the 1820s started calling themselves *Hajret* (from Hijra), comparing their flight to the escape of the Muslim community from Mecca to Medina in 622. When in 1840, Imam Shamil had taken refuge in Chechnya in the face of the Russian forces advancing into his native Dagestan, his followers would also compare his journey to the Prophet Mohammad's flight from Mecca to Medina.[7]

For the overwhelming majority of the Circassian pilgrims in the nineteenth century, the Hajj was a one-way journey. When the Russian military advanced on the traditional Circassian lands in 1861–1862, an estimated 10,343 Kabardians from eighty-one villages, including the entire population of some settlements – approximately 20 percent of the total population of Kabarda at the time – immigrated to the Ottoman Empire under the pretext of the Hajj. The situation repeated itself in 1865 and 1871 when 3,000 and 2,000 Kabardians, respectively, left for the Hajj and never came back. The residents of mountain *aul* villages expressed a desire to make the pilgrimage with their whole *aul*. In addition to entire families making the pilgrimage – which had happened before – this time, the pilgrims sold off all their property and residences. Among those who left was the whole *aul* of hajji Kaisyn Shogenov, the former chief *qadi* of Kabarda. A rumor went around at the time that those who died under non-Muslim Russian rule would never go to heaven. Pursuing the Hajj meant a chance to safeguard one's Islamic and Circassian identities. All in all, by 1865, about one-third of Kabardians fled from their North Caucasus homelands to the Ottoman Empire.[8] The Russian imperial government restricted and periodically banned the Hajj, although it never imposed a wholesale ban on it for more than a few years.

The Hajj pilgrimage, through these experiences, came to be associated with the formative Circassian identity narratives. Members of the Circassian diaspora worldwide since the late nineteenth century coordinated their activities and formed a common ideology based on the shared memories of what they regarded as genocide that the tsarist state committed during Russia's conquest of the North Caucasus in the nineteenth century. The Circassians maintained three goals – recognition of the genocide by Moscow, unification of Circassian territories in the homeland, and repatriation of the expelled population. These strategic goals formed the ideological foundation of the Circassian nationalist movement.

History and memory have persistently informed the debates about modern Circassian identity. Many Circassian organizations opposed the celebration of the 450th anniversary of Russian–Kabardian relations by the Russian state in 2007. The organizers of the celebration in Moscow announced the festivities as the anniversary of Kabarda's voluntarily joining the Muscovite principality in 1557. That was a return to the Soviet-era view, largely discredited by responsible scholars after the Soviet Union collapsed. Circassian history experts and activists pointed out that the Kabardian principality had equal status with the principality of Moscow (Muscovy or Moskovia) in the middle of the sixteenth century. It was therefore impossible for Kabarda to be absorbed into it. In fact, Kabarda remained for all intents and purposes an independent state until the expanding Russian Empire conquered it in the nineteenth century.

These memories stirred public debates in the run-up to the 2014 Winter Olympic Games that Russia hosted in Sochi. The Circassian nongovernmental organizations (NGOs) stepped up their activities of raising the Circassian genocide question and expressing historical grievances going back to Russia's conquest of the North Caucasus in the nineteenth century. In a sadly ironic turn of history, the 2014 Olympic Games in Sochi coincided with the 150th anniversary of the Circassian defeat in 1864, when, after more than a century of fighting, Tsar Alexander II established Russian sovereign power over the formerly independent Circassian territories. Every year on that day (May 21) – marking the final defeat in their 101-year-long war against Russia and the mass killings of their co-ethnics – Circassians around the world gather in groups and light 101 candles to commemorate the victims of that defeat with a minute of silence. Not only the time, but also the location of the games animated symbols of defeat and humiliation. Sochi was the site of the war's last battles, and its port was the place from which the Circassians were expelled to the Ottoman Empire. Krasnaya Polyana (Kbaada in Circassian), where major competitions of the 2014 Olympic Games unfolded, was exactly the place where, on May 21, 1864, a parade of Russian troops celebrated the end of the war. Sochi, as it happens, was named after the Circassian Shache ethnic group, who lived there until 1864. In fact, from 1861 to 1864, Sochi served as the last capital of independent Circassia. In the 2000s, from their base in New Jersey, Circassian activists launched the international "No Sochi 2014" campaign, with a message to the world: "If you let the 2014 games go on as planned in Russia, you'll be skiing on the graves of our oppressed ancestors."[9]

The government of imperial Russia took the diametrically opposite view, regarding the pilgrimage to Mecca as a political act and implementing periodic restrictions on the Hajj. When, in 1822, eastern Circassia (Kabarda) – located in the central part of the North Caucasus – joined Russia, the first decree of Russia's envoy in the Caucasus, General Aleksey Yermolov, was to ban the Hajj for five years. Though the pilgrimage was reluctantly allowed after the ban, the negative attitude toward the Hajj did not change over decades. One Russian official explained the sources of this threat perception back in 1872: "The pilgrimage of the Caucasian Muslims for prayers [in Mecca] develops in them fanaticism, which sustains among them constant hostility towards the [Russian] Government and serves as the only obstacle for them to reconcile with the current state of affairs."[10]

Eileen Kane's research about the Hajj in the Russian Empire revealed that while the Russian government tolerated the Hajj from Central Asia,[11] it developed a different policy toward the Hajj from the North Caucasus. The prevailing view among Russian government officials was that the Hajj had a negative effect on Caucasus Muslims and that adherence to Islamic norms in personal life threatened the security, if not existence of the Russian state. In 1898, the Russian imperial government sponsored the Hajj pilgrimage of Abdul-Aziz Davletshin (subsequently put in charge of the Asia section of the Russian army's chiefs of staff) – specifically to assess the pilgrimage's impacts. His conclusion illustrates the pervasive official alarmism about "fanaticism" and "radicalism" allegedly resulting from the Hajj. It reflected impressionistic interpretations of everyday behavior of the pilgrims without any systematic examination of the reasons why such behavior posed a security threat to Russia. Specifically cited in the report was the pilgrims' allegedly "greater abstinence from alcohol and from 'innocuous pleasures like [the] theater or circus.'" In essence, this was a primordialist – and in this manner internally unsustainable, yet outwardly tenacious and persuasive – logic.

THE SOVIET PERIOD: SUPPRESSION AND MANIPULATION

After arriving in power in 1917, the Bolsheviks co-opted the North Caucasus Muslims to fight the anti-Bolshevik coalition in a civil war that lasted through the 1920s. The alliance with the local Muslims was instrumental in the Bolshevik victories and the institutionalization of the

Soviet power in the North Caucasus after the civil war. In 1918, the so-called First Shariah Column took Nal'chik with the slogan "Long live Soviet power and Shariah!" Authority in Nal'chik okrug was turned over to the Military-Shariah Revolutionary Council. Subsequently, the leader of the "Red Shariahtist" movement, Nazyr Katkhanov, became a member of the executive committee of the Kabardian Autonomous Oblast. He held a number of government posts until 1928, when Stalin consolidated power and turned to suppress religion. Katkhanov was arrested and executed by a firing squad. Moscow gradually restricted the Hajj until banning it completely in 1930, with the onset of Stalin's totalitarian rule. The Kingdom of Saudi Arabia's (KSA) Emir Feisal ibn Abdel-Aziz, upon visiting the Soviet Union in 1932, offered Moscow a quota of 10,000 to 15,000 Hajj pilgrims. But the Kremlin had no interest. In 1944, when the necessity of mobilizing public support for fighting the Nazis prompted Stalin to relax suppression of religion, the Kremlin allowed a limited number of heavily vetted pilgrims to go to Mecca. It was truly a strictly controlled, state-serving endeavor.

The Soviet government created the Council of Religious Cults Affairs (Sovet Po Delam Religioznykh Kul'tov) (SDRK), which controlled the Hajj. In 1944 and 1945, the SDRK organized pilgrimages for two groups, recruiting candidates mainly among intelligentsia, including scholars and university instructors, as well as a few imams. The groups also included KGB officers to monitor and control the pilgrims. After World War II, the pilgrimage was again banned until Stalin's death in March 1953. On July 4, 1953, the SDRK's agenda included an item on preparation and the budget for the Hajj. A group of eighteen Soviet pilgrims departed for the Hajj that August. After returning a month later, all pilgrims submitted obligatory reports about their pilgrimage to the Soviet government.

Yet, despite suppression and control, the Hajj continued to be a valued tradition, and religious practices adapted to atheistic Soviet rule. The latter, in fact, had the unintended consequence of fueling the more flexible and harder-to-control Sufi practices. Historians Chen Bram and Moshe Gammer concluded as much:

Soviet policies, formulated under Stalin and changed only slightly by his successors, were designed from the very beginning to destroy the hold of Islam and the Sufi brotherhoods over society and to suppress all vestiges of resistance. Thus, the aggressive persecution of religion; the creation during the Second World War of an official Islamic administration to control the believers; and the massive involvement of the secret police – in its successive acronyms from

ChK to KGB – in every aspect of the above two. Far from eliminating the role and influence of the Sufi brotherhoods in the life of society, however, all these only served to enhance it.[12]

Whereas the Soviet government learned to manipulate the believers and use the Hajj as a cover for propaganda and espionage, the values embedded in the Hajj tradition persisted and revealed themselves in counterintuitive ways. The Soviet Hajj groups from 1953 through 1989 typically numbered about twenty pilgrims each. One of the characteristics of the Soviet Hajj was that some pilgrims publicly admitted they were atheists. The archival materials show that at least three pilgrims in 1963 were members of the Communist Party. One of the most famous pilgrims, Bobojan Gafurov, during his career occupied such positions as editor in chief of the government newspaper *The Tajikistan Unbeliever* and First Secretary of the Central Committee (CC) of Tajikistan's Communist Party (CP). A Russian scholar of the Orient, Igor Dyakonov, recorded in his memoirs Gafurov's words after he performed Hajj. "It was not a big deal that I occupied the position of first secretary of the CC of Tajikistan's CP. It was not a big deal that I was elected into the CC of CP of Soviet Union. It is the fact that I became a *hajji* that my co-villagers will appreciate the most."[13]

In other words, whereas the Soviet government thought it made the Hajj a tool of its policies, the hajjis viewed the Soviet government's domination as a tool to achieve deeply held religious aspirations. In limited, passive-aggressive by necessity, but symbolically important ways, local Muslim societies struck back at the Soviet empire. They preserved their religious beliefs as much as they could, often mixing them with folklore and traditions. North Caucasus experts Marat Shterin and Akhmet Yarlykapov describe the Islamic views at the end of the Soviet era. "For the latter Soviet generations, the 'folk Islam' was the only Islam they knew; for them, it was 'proper' and 'traditional.' . . . They had very little knowledge of the institutionally validated forms of prayer, worship and charity (*zakyat*), and they could not even conceive of performing the Hajj. Instead, hybrid folk rituals emerged built out of whatever remained of the discarded debris of pre-revolutionary Islam, taking into consideration whatever was permitted by the Soviet status quo."[14]

Yet, the Soviet state penetration of the Muslim establishment was thorough. Not a single case, in fact, was recorded when any hajji defected from the Soviet Union while on a pilgrimage from 1944 through 1989.

At first glance, this may seem quite unusual given that many Soviet athletes, scholars, writers, and artists preferred not to return once they traveled abroad in the Soviet era. It also confounds the nineteenth-century pattern when thousands of Muslims emigrated from the North Caucasus under the pretext of the Hajj. A Russian scholar of Islam, Vyacheslav Akhmadullin, who examined this phenomenon, argued that the absence of defection among the Soviet hajjis was due to the special attention the KGB paid to the issue – which resulted in a stringent selection process winnowing out everyone who could not credibly demonstrate loyalty to the Soviet state.[15]

And yet, while Communist officials staged public presentations denouncing "The Pillars of Islam and Their Reactionary Essence," they could not eradicate the intrinsic value of the Hajj in traditionally Muslim societies within Russia, particularly in the North Caucasus. It is unclear, however, if this value would be retained if the Communist rule continued for another generation or two. From 1944 to 1989, only 900 Soviets completed the Hajj – many of whom traveled several times. Moscow allowed the pilgrimage not in the spirit of religious openness, but as a public relations and intelligence exercise on specific assignments set by the Communist leaders. The government required that the pilgrims stay away from religious activities in their home regions, yet have a good command of Arabic or other Middle Eastern languages, be adept in Islamic behavioral norms, be intelligent, and have good looks. The idea, according to the official documents, was to "promote a correct impression about life in the Soviet Union among the Muslims of the world."[16]

POST-SOVIET REVIVAL

The fall of the Soviet Union brought dramatic changes in all spheres of Russian society, including religious revival in the North Caucasus.[17] And so, after nearly a century of serving as a conduit to exodus and after seven decades of suppression under atheistic Soviet rule, the Hajj reemerged across the North Caucasus as part of the return to the sacred. On the one hand, enough memories of the tradition stayed alive to sustain aspirations to undertake the pilgrimage, to honor one of the Five Pillars of Islamic faith. On the other hand, suppression of religious practice created the forbidden fruit effect and a spiritual vacuum – activating latent interest in performing the Hajj. However, economic shocks, uncertainty about government regulation, the daunting travel logistics, and the interruption of the Hajj tradition under Communism slowed down the resumption of the mass Hajj travel during the first post-Soviet decade.

Saudi Arabia's government began issuing quotas to perform the Hajj to Russia's Muslims in response to Mikhail Gorbachev's *glasnost* reforms that initiated political and social liberalization of the Soviet Union in the late 1980s. The enactment of the 1990 "On Freedom of Conscience and Religious Organizations" law of the Soviet Union and of the 1997 "On Freedom of Religion" law of the Russian Federation under President Boris Yeltsin gave rise to an unprecedented growth of Islamic belief and worship across Russia. Among Russia's predominantly Muslim-populated areas, the pilgrimage tradition revived most rapidly in the North Caucasus – starting with the Republic of Dagestan, where Islamic traditions had the deepest roots in the region. In 1990, about 1,500 Soviet Union Muslims performed the Hajj; among them approximately 450 were from Dagestan. In 1991, the total number of Soviet hajjis was about 2,500, and nearly 1,000 of them came from Dagestan. The KSA leaders welcomed the rebirth of the pilgrimage from the former Soviet Union. From 1989 to 1991, pilgrims from the Soviet Union were hosted as personal guests of King Fahd Bin Abdulaziz, who also paid the cost of their pilgrimage.

However, it took more than a decade for the Hajj tradition to resurge, even in the North Caucasus, in many parts of which Muslims historically accounted for the majority of the population. Out of nearly half a million residents of the Republic of Kabardino-Balkaria representing traditionally Muslim ethnic populations (according to the 1989 census), just about 100 made the pilgrimage to Mecca from 1987 and 2000. That was fewer than ten pilgrims per year. Part of the explanation was the enduring legacies of the Soviet rule that suppressed religious practice. Another part was lack of access to information about the pilgrimage. The local bureaucrats who obtained and distributed quota-based invitations to the Hajj kept the process opaque and restricted participation mostly to fellow officials. During the 1990s, when basic consumer goods were in short supply in Russia following the collapse of the Soviet planned economy, some pilgrims combined trade with Hajj and brought goods from the KSA for resale in Russia. Local religious leaders, including a famous Sufi, Said-Affandi Chirkavi, criticized mixing profitmaking with the Hajj. That said, such a practice is not necessarily prohibited in Islam, regarding that the Prophet himself was a merchant. In the early 2000s, the political and socioeconomic context in the region saw profound changes driving up the number of common citizens who were able to afford and pursue the

Hajj pilgrimage. In the new millennium's first decade, just as before the consolidation of the Soviet rule in the region in the 1920s, most pilgrims went to Mecca with only one goal in mind – to participate in a holy ritual that constituted one of the Five Pillars of Islamic faith. At the time of writing in 2013–2015, the North Caucasus hajjis bringing goods to sell in Mecca for profit was a rarity. Coming home from Mecca, some pilgrims brought with them the sanctified ZamZam water from the source, which was also probably the most common such item. In all cases, as far as the authors learned through interviews and socializing with local Muslims, none of the pilgrims brought back ZamZam for resale, but rather as gifts or for use in religious rituals.

Though some scholars, notably Olivier Roy, estimate the number of Muslims in Russia at 25 million (almost certainly an overestimate by as many as 10 million), the majority of Russia's Muslims do not exercise the Five Pillars of Islam. Post-Soviet Muslims developed their religious identity through the revival of their ethnic identity. Roy refers to this process as *ethnicization* of religious identity. Muslim minorities may not see religion as a faith, but as a set of cultural patterns that are inherited and not related to a person's spiritual life. Olivier Roy argues, "This ethnicisation may also take the form of subgroups, often defined through the prism of colonial history."[18]

Paradoxically, Muslim leaders also may openly recognize the absence of religious practices in the process of ethnicization. In the context of post-atheist society, religious leaders may broaden the definition of who could be regarded as Muslim. In 2006, the chief of the Spiritual Directorate in Kabardino-Balkaria, Anas Pshikhachev, defined Muslim identity as follows: "A person who recognizes Allah, the Qur'an, the Sunnah and the Prophet is a Muslim, even if s/he does not perform any religious practices."[19] Notably, the Hajj – one of Islam's Five Pillars – was not mentioned. This reflects the perception of associated hardships and the long shadow of the Soviet atheistic legacies that made the pilgrimage in particular appear as something unreal, something out of this world, when viewed from the post-Soviet North Caucasus. This explains, in part, a rather slow takeoff of the Hajj revival compared to other Islamic practices – particularly those with a longer history of ethnicization.

The following excerpt from Sufian's participant observer diaries personalizes these effects of the social context in the North Caucasus – highlighting in particular the legacy of the 1917–1991 Soviet rule, which banned public religious expression, imposed stiff social costs (such as denial of higher education) to those who openly professed religion, and practically forbade foreign travel. And so, by the time Sufian was to undertake his 2009 pilgrimage – eighteen years after the Soviet Union collapsed – some hajjis still perceived their journey as a personal break-away from the atheistic ("profane") Soviet legacies. Their parents served as a natural proxy for those legacies. Socialized in Soviet atheistic society, most of the under-forty hajjis' parents did not observe Islam's rituals. Collectivist and atheistic social norms they internalized constrained their capacity to visualize their children as Muslims. And so, as a pilgrim and a participant observer, Sufian recorded an illustrative confession of a fellow hajji from Kabardino-Balkaria in 2009 illustrating this. Here's his diary excerpt:

"My father passed away seven years ago, my mother five years ago. And I have never had a dream about them," complained Zamir about two weeks before the pilgrimage to Mecca. He had never observed Islamic rituals regularly in his life when he decided to perform the Hajj. He completed his first Islamic prayer (*namaz*) in the morning at the airport in Jeddah shortly after arriving in Saudi Arabia. In Medina, Zamir went to the Mosque of Prophet Mohammad where they say that every prayer equals a thousand prayers in an ordinary mosque, and he performed a prayer for [both] of his late parents who never saw in their son any inclination toward religion during their lives. Somebody told Zamir that his prayers would make the burden of his parents' sins easier for them in the other world. "Will they really learn that I performed a prayer for [both] of them in the very Mosque of the Prophet?" asked Zamir. When assured they would, he added dreamily, "I can only imagine how they are going to be shocked!" Later, in Mecca, he paid two Islamic students a thousand dollars each so they would perform the Hajj on behalf of his deceased parents. It would be not appropriate to ask Zamir why he was feeling guilty about his parents' lives, but one could see he found peace with them on his journey to Mecca.

And in this way, Zamir told us how the revival of Islam came out of letting go of the restrictive Soviet legacies epitomized in the shock and wonder-ment he anticipated his parents would feel if they could ever learn he was performing the pilgrimage to Mecca, so incredible and inconceivable it seemed in their times.

A CONCURRENT DANGEROUS REVIVAL: VIOLENCE IN THE POST-SOVIET NORTH CAUCASUS

A decade after the Soviet Union's 1991 collapse someone living in the North Caucasus could well feel they were traveling in time back to the nineteenth century. Then, the spread of Islamic and ethnic nationalism in the region clashed with – and was thus incalculably amplified by – Russia's imperial expansionism and Russian nationalist assertiveness. The clash resulted in decades of intense and deadly armed conflict. For most of the nineteenth century, Russia concentrated more of its military power in the North Caucasus than it did anywhere else. It projected this power to defeat – in a quarter-century war – Imam Shamil's *Imamate* quasi-state in the region's east, as well as to exterminate or expel ethnic Circassians from their native lands in the region's center and west. The Soviet domination solidified those victories. The precipitous collapse of the Soviet Union reversed this long historical pattern. The 1990s saw the Russian state retreat economically, politically, and militarily. And yet, as Islam and nationalism – including Circassian nationalism – were undergoing a revival, Russia's political elites who were hurt and disgruntled by the Soviet collapse (whose views Putin singularly represented and represents to this day) started calling for Russia "gathering back its lands" they considered "lost" due to the collapse of Communism. Already in the early 1990s, prominent Russian political leaders were reclaiming territories that used to be under Soviet or imperial Russian rule – from Crimea in Ukraine to Alaska in the United States. Toward the late 1990s, the neo-imperial resurgence was in full swing, as these views became predominant across Russia's key political parties and especially within Russia's foreign policy and national security establishment.[20] It was intuitively conceivable, if not obvious, that the revival of Russia's imperial aspirations and authoritarianism – epitomized and enhanced by Putin's arrival in power – clashed with the revival of religious and cultural identities across the North Caucasus societies (to a great extent enabled by the Soviet collapse, which Putin abhorred). Mass violence, of the kind that local residence could not deem possible under the Soviet rule, became reality.[21]

Mass violent conflicts erupted in the North Caucasus in the early 1990s. They peaked with two wars over the independence claims of Chechnya. According to official Russian statistics, 5,042 Russian soldiers and officers were killed and 16,098 wounded during the First Chechen War (1994–1996) and 4,852 were killed and 16,536 wounded during the Second Chechen War (1999–2000).[22]

In both wars, more than 160,000 Chechens were estimated to have died, while about 200,000 – 20 percent of Chechnya's total population – fled.[23] The end of the Second Chechen War saw the rise of radical Islamist militants who vowed revenge for the mass killings of Chechens by the Russian military. The militants, supported by their loss-suffering families, clans, and communities, struck back at the Kremlin with atrocious terrorist acts – most notably taking hundreds of hostages in a Moscow theater in

2002 and in an elementary school in Beslan, North Ossetia (which borders Chechnya and Kabardino-Balkaria) in 2004. Just these two attacks (dozens of others were staged) and the Russian government responses resulted in hundreds of deaths.

By 2003, instability and violence arrived in Kabardino-Balkaria. To preempt the spread of Islamist radicalism from Chechnya, local authorities started persecuting Muslims by closing all local Mosques (more than 100), arresting and forcing Muslim men to shave their beards, and even shaving crosses on their heads. Chechen Islamist terrorists exploited the surging backlash among local Muslims against these brutal police crackdowns. On October 13 and 14, 2005, a group of about 100 local Muslims attacked the police headquarters and government security checkpoints in the Kabardino-Balkaria capital city of Nalchik. One hundred and forty-two people were killed, including at least twelve civilians and thirty-five law enforcement officers (*siloviki*). More than 100 people were injured, eighty-five of them *siloviki*. Controversies arose around the killed and persecuted terrorists. According to the Russian officials, eighty-nine insurgents were killed and thirty-six captured. However, according to local media, some of the dead listed as "terrorists" were actually civilians accidentally killed in the crossfire. Fifty-nine people were accused of involvement in terrorism and persecuted. After the raid, Arsen Kanokov, the newly appointed governor of Kabardino-Balkaria, admitted publicly that the violence could have been triggered at least in part by brutal crackdowns by local police. "The law enforcement agencies didn't know how to fight against radical Islam; they decided to close mosques and restrict the believers. Of course, such actions were based not only on incompetence, but [some officials] wanted to provoke disturbances in the republic very much."[24]

About two years after these events, most Islamist militants across the North Caucasus united as Imarat Kavkaz (Caucasus Emirate) and renewed attacks on government security forces with vigor, ending a relative lull in hostilities following the capture or killing of key Chechen separatist and Islamist radical leaders. The government security forces, in turn, stepped up counterinsurgency operations. Thousands of civilians, government personnel, and Islamist insurgents perished in the ensuing hostilities that continue at the time of writing, albeit it their intensity subsided significantly after 2012. Overlaying this violence in Kabardino-Balkaria, tensions mounted among the Kabardians (Circassians), the Turkic Balkars, and the Russians, on some occasions resulting in violent conflicts.[25]

The increase in the Hajj pilgrimage from the region raised security concerns. Being associated with the religious and cultural revival across the North Caucasus, the pilgrimage to Mecca could well be seen as an enabler of militant antigovernment resistance in the region. In fact, Russian and local government officials, for the most part, indeed believed the Hajj pilgrimage radicalized local Muslims and thus contributed to violence. At the time of our fieldwork in 2009 and 2010, the security situation in Kabardino-Balkaria worsened significantly. The number of casualties in insurgent attacks – by then targeting almost exclusively government security forces and law enforcement officials – as well as the government's counterinsurgency operations increased from about fifty in 2008 to 173 in 2010. The ideological leader of the Imarat Kavkaz (Caucasus Emirate) North Caucasus militant Islamist movement, Anzor Astemirov, was, according to regional sources, based in Kabardino-Balkaria. From mid-2008 through mid-2010, insurgency-related violence in the central-eastern North Caucasus – Chechnya, Dagestan, Ingushetia, and Kabardino-Balkaria – claimed the lives of approximately 1,500 people.[26] This casualty rate is consistent with the conventional classification of internal violent conflicts as civil wars.

Government officials in Russia publicly drew parallels between the Hajj and antigovernment insurgency (termed "terrorism"). Vladimir Markin, a spokesman for the powerful Investigative Committee of Russia, said his committee suspected that the sales of the Hajj tours could generate funding for terrorists.[27] Putin's envoy to the Volga Federal District, in which most of Russia's Muslims reside, Mikhail Babich, stated on his office's website that proceeds from the sale of the Hajj tours in the republic of Tatarstan could have been used, "among other things, to fund radical Islamist cells responsible for terrorist acts."[28] Neither the Investigative Committee's nor Putin's envoy subsequently confirmed that their warnings had been substantiated – but the deeply alarmist view of the Hajj behind those warnings remained widespread in Russia's law enforcement agencies and the national security establishment.

Substantiated or not, association of the Hajj with militant Islamist radicalism among Russia's public and policymakers increased and hardened over a protracted violent conflict in the North Caucasus since the early 1990s.[29] These perceptions fueled tensions between Muslims and non-Muslims throughout Russia, some of which turned violent. The most notorious case of such violence in Russia – directly related to the Hajj – concerned an ethnic Ossetian poet, Shamil Dzhigkayev, who also served as a dean at North Ossetian State University. North Ossetia is a constituent republic of the Russian Federation in the North Caucasus. Whereas most of its residents are Christians, a significant minority (16%) of Ossetians is Muslim. In 2008, Dzhigkayev published a poem in the Ossetian language, titled *Wolf Cubs Doing the Hajj.*[30] It was a response to a story about ethnic Chechen pilgrims who were returning home from the Hajj through North Ossetia. Allegedly, the Chechens made a stop by a medical center that happened to be located less than half a mile from the "City of Angels" in Beslan–a memorial cemetery to the victims of the terrorist mass hostage-taking at a local school in September 2004. More than 300 people, most of them children, perished in that gruesome incident. According to the local police reports and the testimony of the Chechen pilgrims, they made a stop at that location to do *namaz* – one of five daily prayers mandated in Islam. Local Ossetian teenagers saw the Chechen pilgrims and pelted them with stones – apparently out of lingering animosity toward Muslims blamed for the terror attack on the Beslan school four years earlier. The pilgrims boarded their buses and left under a police escort. Later, a rumor spread among local residents that the Chechen pilgrims stopped not at the medical center, but in the "City of Angels" and that they relieved themselves at the children's burial site. The rumors were most likely false. According to Russia's reputable business daily *Kommersant*, the highway along which the pilgrims were bused across Ossetia passed far away from the Beslan cemetery.[31]

However, the rumors stirred indignation among Ossetians, including Dzhigkayev. A month after the incident, he published his poem in an Ossetian literary journal, *Makh Dug*. The reference to "wolf cubs" made clear the poem was about young Chechens – the wolf is an old, epic symbol of Chechnya, and antigovernment Chechen insurgents have been branded by the Russian official propaganda as "the wolves of Islam."[32]

The poem's very title links the Hajj with radical antigovernment militancy in the North Caucasus. The first verse builds up this disparaging image, calling the "the Hajj-going wolf cubs" unredeemable criminals and "blood-thirsty predators who pounce on the sun itself." Branding the Islamic faith as inherently inhumane, Dzhigkayev waxed poetic: "The holy book of these wolves is their claws. Even their prayers have criminal intent. Like pigs at our cemetery, these green beasts are committing an atrocity under God." The poem ended with mocking and cursing the pilgrims, calling on the poet's dog to relieve itself at the "black prayer stone" – a reference to the black stone built into one of the corners of the

Ka'aba in Mecca, one of Islam's most sacred symbols that the Hajj pilgrims travel to see.

The poem provoked a passionate negative backlash among the North Ossetian Muslims. The Spiritual Directorate of Muslims of North Ossetia – an association of local Muslim clerics approved and monitored by the Russian government – asked the public prosecutor's office to investigate. Following up on this request, the Institute of Criminology of the Special Technologies Center of Russia's FSB (former KGB) conducted "an expert evaluation" of the poem. The evaluation concluded that the poem had no manifestations of extremism – and therefore, under Russia's law, was not subject to a government ban. Three years after the poem was published, Shamil Dzhigkayev, then seventy-one, was brutally murdered. The prime suspect, the poet's distant relative David Murashev, thirty-four, was killed when security forces, using armored vehicles, attempted to detain him. Three years before that – at about the time the poem came out – Murashev had converted to Islam. In the raid targeting Murashev, the security forces arrested eighteen Muslims and charged them with illegal possession of narcotics and firearms. The arrest sparked further tension. While condemning Dzhigkayev's murder, North Ossetia's Spiritual Directorate asked for protection for the arrested Muslims, whose rights, it believed, were violated. The Directorate claimed they had been tortured while in detention and that law enforcement agents planted the narcotics and weapons on them prior to the arrest. Russia's Public Chamber – a token forum of the Kremlin-approved public figures to lend Putin's regime a vestige of legitimacy – expressed concern about persecution of Muslims in North Ossetia. The clerics reminded the Russian government of violent clashes between aggrieved Muslims and government security in the neighboring Kabardino-Balkaria Republic in 2005 that resulted in dozens of deaths.[33] These admonitions notwith-standing, the executive branch–controlled courts sentenced the arrested Muslims to jail terms ranging from one and a half to three years. Among them was the imam of the Vladikavkaz mosque, Kuvat Ismailov, arrested on charges of illegal possession of weapons.[34]

* * *

The concurrent resurgence of Islam, nationalism, and violent conflict in the North Caucasus after the Soviet collapse made arguments that the three were related appear popular and persuasive. In fact, at one point, we considered doing a quantitative analysis of whether more armed conflict took place in locations throughout the region to which more people returned from the pilgrimage to Mecca. Yet, as we shall see in the next chapter, once we began systematically comparing the perceptions of the pilgrims and non-pilgrims on key aspects of Islamic faith and social tolerance, we realized that the linkage between the Hajj and violence was more likely than not to be spurious. And the more we revisited the history of the Hajj and Islam in the region, the more it became clear that association of the pilgrimage with violence in public, scholarly, and official discourses reflected more the state of relations between the Russian state and local societies than any actual effects of the pilgrimage itself. Those remained unexplored systematically. And so, we delved into ethnographic observations, interviews, and focus group content analysis to tease out those impacts. As you will see, they contradict the alarmist perceptions. Juxtaposed to the historic stereotypes and conventional wisdoms, our explorations of the Hajj establish the Pilgrims' Paradox – with Muslims who were exposed to intense, passionate celebration of Islamic global unity through the Hajj exhibiting greater appreciation of religious and social diversity than non-pilgrims. The Muslims who – to repeat the alarmist assessments of the imperial Russian government in the nineteenth century – were exposed to the alleged "fanaticism" of the Hajj somehow converted that exposure into tolerance. We explain how we arrived at our findings and present the Paradox in granular empirical detail in the next chapter.

2

The Paths of the Paradox: From Passion to Tolerance

INITIAL DILEMMAS

Our journey toward the Pilgrims' Paradox began with conversations at an academic conference in post-Soviet Georgia in June 2008. We followed up in the summer of 2009 with exploratory interviews in Russia's North Caucasus, in the republics (ethnically designated provinces) of Adygea and Kabardino-Balkaria. In both, traditionally Muslim-ethnic Circassian (Adyge) residents comprised a significant share of the population. Mikhail's interview with Murat in the latter's medical doctor's office in the town of Adygeysk on June 16 that year gave us a preview of the puzzles we would later examine systematically. The interview was serendipitous. Mikhail was holding a focus group in the region for a project on migration attitudes. His colleague at the Kuban State University in the nearest regional metropolis of Krasnodar had told him earlier about "this remarkable young person who performed the Hajj." Through this colleague Mikhail was able to arrange an exploratory interview with Murat. Mikhail was interested to hear Murat's impressions of the Hajj and to probe how he felt the pilgrimage might have affected him at a personal level. Murat was about thirty, soft spoken, with a thoughtful, serious, and engaging demeanor. As Murat spoke about his first impressions of the holy land, Mikhail grew deeply impressed with the intensity of emotion that Murat conveyed in his unassuming, almost matter-of-fact tone:

A lot of things I saw were not particularly interesting. The airport, the deserts. . . . But then I saw the Mosque of the Prophet. That was the first time I felt something. All emotions overflowed me like a breaking wave. I was suddenly imagining history. And the most striking thing was anticipation of more emotions to overwhelm me, to sweep me in [the] moment, to tear me apart. I felt like a gladiator awaiting to enter the arena of battle.

Murat opened the folder on his office computer where he stored the photos he took during the pilgrimage. As Murat shared the images of Mecca, of the holy sites, and of the pilgrims, his face lit up, as if the emotions refilled him, as if his sense of amazement and awe was recharged. He talked about how he was drawn to lectures that local luminaries gave on the fundamentals of the Islamic faith, how much more intimately he believed in the singularity of God, of divinity, of the truth under Islam. And yet, Murat conveyed emotional restraint, a certain emotional wisdom. He displayed his deep feelings calmly, almost cautiously. Was it in the juxtaposition of the emotional depth of religious devotion and emotional restraint that Mikhail sensed something puzzling, something paradoxical – at the visceral, intuitive level? It was hard to tell then. When Mikhail reviewed the notes he took during the interview, a few other things amplified the initial sense of the puzzle. On the one hand, for example, Murat strongly emphasized the importance of healthy lifestyles that he associated with Islam, particularly abstinence from alcohol and drugs. He also talked about younger men he knew increasingly sharing this view. And yet, he expressed no insistence on turning abstinence into law and enforcing it zealously and indiscriminately. Instead, Murat talked about the importance of a dialog between society and the government, between believers and secular authorities. And in response to the question about the effects of the Hajj on him personally, Murat made two big points in one breath. The first thing he mentioned was realizing the importance of pleasing God more acutely, and to him personally that meant, first and foremost, changing his own character, striving to become "less volatile." The path to that for Murat was to observe more prayers, in particular, to perform the pre-dawn *namaz* prayers consistently. Was it possible then, Mikhail wondered, that stronger religious devotion, if not determined ardor, could be a path to greater tolerance of Muslims toward secular authorities, a path to resolving social tensions, to reducing social and political volatility in the turbulent region where he interviewed Murat?

It was about a year before that interview that the authors of this book first discussed doing research together on the social and political impacts of Islamic revival in the North Caucasus. That idea emerged during our conversations after we met for the first time at a policy workshop in Tbilisi, Georgia, in June 2008, organized by the Program on New Approaches to Research and Security in Eurasia, then based at Georgetown University and guided by its founder, Celeste Wallander. Sufian's presentation of his research on why young people in Kabardino-

Balkaria turned to Islam sparked our conversations, leading to the idea of focusing on the Hajj as a phenomenon representing the Islamic revival in the region.

Prior to our first brainstorming of this topic in Tbilisi, both of us had studied the impact of Islam on society and intergroup relations in Muslim-majority regions of the Russian Federation. Sufian approached these questions as a cultural anthropologist and historian; Mikhail approached them as a political scientist who engaged in theoretical work in comparative politics, social psychology, and sociology. We followed up on our Tbilisi conversations, with Mikhail interviewing Murat in Adygea and with an exchange of views over e-mail. The more we considered it, the more interesting and exciting the idea to examine the Hajj effects in the North Caucasus appeared. In one e-mail exchange, Mikhail shared his excitement by noting that it could lead to a counterintuitive and nontrivial research question. In particular, he proposed "setting up perhaps a study that would focus on how international interactions affect local populations in Kabardino-Balkaria – are they becoming, for example, more 'Islamicized' as a result of the exposure to these connections, or are they – perhaps paradoxically – becoming more globalized in a secular kind of way, or would they broaden their outlook?"[1]

With these broad themes in mind, we conducted two rounds of exploratory interviews, in Kabardino-Balkaria and Adygea. Sufian had seven in-depth interviews with young people he knew closely and who would trust him with intimate details about their religious beliefs and social attitudes. In the summer of 2009, Mikhail visited Kuban State University in Krasnodar and traveled to Adygea, where he conducted focus groups with Muslims and interviewed Murat. All the while, we continued via e-mail to develop and refine questions about the Hajj experiences, Islamic faith and rituals, and sociopolitical views that we felt were important if we conducted systematic interviews, an opinion survey, or focus groups. In late August 2009, we met in Nalchik and staged a focus group probe with four hajjis. The group interview took place at the Kabardino-Balkaria State Agricultural Academy with the help of Chamal, a hajji and an employee at the Academy. In retrospect, that group interview served as a pretest of our subsequent focus group study that compared the views of pilgrims and non-pilgrims.

Our preliminary findings suggested to us that performing the Hajj had significant, yet paradoxical effects on Muslims in the North Caucasus. In addition to Mikhail's impressions of the interview with Murat in Adygea, we compared the prevalent impressions that emerged from

Sufian's private interviews with young devout Muslims versus those that emerged from our focus group pretest. Our sense of the paradox strengthened. On the one hand, the in-depth interviews indicated that as young local Muslims started to observe mandated religious practices, they became more devout in their faith and, to some extent, more intolerant of other religious perspectives and secular habits. They confessed to Sufian they felt they were becoming more isolated and possibly alienated from those who didn't practice Islam. On the other hand, the focus group pretest with the hajjis made us recognize that their pilgrimage to Mecca had a certain mind-broadening impact on their worldview, even though all the hajjis were advanced in years and had well-formed social views prior to the pilgrimage. The hajjis described how they felt they were becoming more tolerant toward other faiths and secular society, and less judgmental toward the state's domestic and foreign policies. They proudly told us how the Hajj experience stimulated them to become better persons in life in general.

We also found these contradictory impressions consistent with the findings of a group of Harvard scholars, David Clingingsmith, Asim Ijaz Khwaja, and Michael Kremer, who conducted quasi-experimental mass opinion surveys in Pakistan in 2008. The authors compared religious and social views of the Hajj pilgrims and the non-pilgrims, drawing their respondents randomly from among the participants in the national Hajj lottery who succeeded and those who did not succeed in making the quota.[2] The Pakistan study came up with the findings that presented a similar paradox that was emerging in our qualitative ethnographic work. As the pilgrims became more devout in mainstream concepts and rituals in Islam, they also came to view other religious and social groups more tolerantly. We will discuss these findings in greater detail in subsequent chapters. For us, at that point, our preliminary findings and the Pakistan survey made two questions particularly important: Why was the paradox observed? And how can we explore the causal linkages, if any, between the Hajj performance and putative tolerance?

At some level, as Sufian phrased it, we realized we were dealing with something so basic – with something that could be so embarrassingly simple – and yet also with something not immediately obvious. This drove our quest for more in-depth investigation. We needed to examine what people thought and how they felt as Muslims and citizens before the Hajj, after the Hajj, and during the Hajj. We needed to trace this process. We settled on a two-pronged strategy. First, we decided that Sufian would perform the Hajj as an ordinary local Muslim and also as a participant observer who would record his experiences and conversations. We followed the procedures of the delegated or split participant observation so as to minimize substantive biases between this study's authors in recording and interpreting the Hajj observations. These biases could plausibly result from differences in our religious and other cultural backgrounds, socioeconomic differences, or residence in different countries. In split participant observation, one scholar participates in the event of interest (the Hajj pilgrimage) while the other asks control questions from outside the event to reduce the "going native" effect and to boost recollection. (We would later extend this approach to evaluation of interviews and focus group analysis.) And so Sufian performed the pilgrimage to Mecca from November 13 to December 4, 2009. In the process he conducted twenty-four in-depth interviews with Hajj participants. He also kept a detailed daily record of his experiences and conversations. He regularly sent his notes to Mikhail, who read them and responded with follow-up queries.

Second, we decided to use focus groups to compare and contrast the religious and social views of the pilgrims and non-pilgrims in Kabardino-Balkaria. This proved a more challenging task in Kabardino-Balkaria than we initially envisioned, and its accomplishment is worth detailing as part of the ethnography of the Hajj effects in the region in its own right.

FOCUS GROUPS WITH KABARDINO-BALKARIA MUSLIMS: DESIGN AND PARTICIPANT SELECTION

We built on our 2008 and 2009 exploratory interviews and Sufian's personal ethnography of the pilgrimage with a series of focus groups in April 2010. We held four focus group sessions with a total of thirty-three participants (twelve of them hajjis and twenty-one non-hajjis), including twenty-eight participants who substantively contributed to the conversation (twelve of them hajjis and sixteen non-hajjis) and whose statements we analyzed. In the social context of Kabardino-Balkaria, Sufian's position as a native, his connections acquired during the pilgrimage, and his elevated status as a hajji were a significant help in assembling these focus groups. His connections helped recruit the focus groups among the hajjis. His hajji status was indispensable in recruiting the focus groups among the devout non-hajji Muslims – a cohort, as we found later, that was generally less sociable and therefore more difficult to recruit than the hajji Muslims. His sense of the local society and Muslim community helped to ascertain that the non-pilgrims we selected strongly desired to perform the Hajj. In sociological terms, we used a controlled snowball recruitment method. Sufian first established connections with authoritative members in local Muslim communities who then invited other participants from these communities. Sufian instructed his contacts not to recruit direct and immediate relatives (parents or children) and to minimize the number of other relatives or close friends. This was not as easy a task as it may appear, given the strong embeddedness of family and friendship networks in Kabardian society. We knew there would have to be trade-offs if we wanted to assemble these groups at all. We dealt with them as we recruited participants and conducted the focus groups. In many ways, we were fortunate that while these trade-offs somewhat complicated the assessment of results, they proved not to introduce systematic biases that could invalidate our comparison of the pilgrims and non-pilgrims.

The first group, held on April 26, 2010, was put together with the assistance of Zeynab, a local woman who completed the Hajj in 2009 along with Sufian. She invited three other women from her Hajj group (Nafisat, Samirat, and Fatima), as well as her brother, Mukhamed, who was also a hajji. Three women friends who were non-hajjis attended our meeting, mostly as helpers and observers. (We did not include the statements some of them occasionally made in our quantitative analysis of conversations presented in the next chapter.) The meeting took place at one of the participants' apartments – in a typical Soviet-era, five-storied, gray, concrete block of flats – located in the city of Baksan, about a forty-minute ride from Kabardino-Balkaria's capital, Nalchik. Baksan was one of the hottest locations in the then increasingly active radical Islamist insurgency. The city was the base of operations of the Kabardino-Balkaria branch of the Islamist Imarat Kavkaz (Caucasus Emirate) anti-government and separatist insurgency movement – whose leader, Anzor Astemirov, was the chief ideologist of the entire Imarat. In the first four months of 2010, local media reported thirty-one violent events in Baksan County involving operations by the militants and the government security forces. These events resulted in twenty-one casualties. Moreover, operations by the militants based in Baksan County also contributed to fifty-eight violent events and seventy-one casualties in nearby Nalchik.[3] As we found out, the insurgency-related violence, which was then on the rise in Kabardino-Balkaria, also made local Muslims apprehensive that government security agencies could be watching them and could interpret any of their group meetings as hostile. In fear of surveillance and reprisals for alleged "terrorist-supporting activities," local Muslims were reluctant to participate in focus groups unless assured by trusted community leaders that such a gathering would be acceptable.

To generate candid group discussions, we were also aware that participants needed to gather in familiar and nonthreatening settings – particularly in the light of concerns about government surveillance of Muslims. Thus, we held our first focus group at a private apartment, starting with a traditional sit-down welcome meal the hosts graciously served. We also followed the Circassian custom of having all those gathered around the table exchange elaborate and extensive greetings and introductions that took up more than an hour. The participants addressed their statements to everybody at the table. The authors sat next to each other so that Sufian could whisper translations of anything said in Circassian to Mikhail and keep both of us engaged in conversation. In this setting, the participants did not feel compelled to speak Russian and spoke in whichever language they felt more comfortable with to make any particular statement. This pattern continued as we later moved on from the welcoming remarks to substantive group conversations.

One of the authors' uncle and a hajji, Chamal – interviews with whom in 2009 in his basement chemistry lab at the Kabardino-Balkaria State Agricultural Academy in Nalchik motivated us to proceed with the whole project – was pivotal in assembling the second focus group on April 27, 2010. Through the former hajji networks, Chamal gathered together six other pilgrims (Salikh, Nokh, Khizir, Zaur, Bolya, and Hasan). He recruited participants by phone, inviting friends and acquaintances who performed the Hajj with him to join him. He also asked them, in turn, to call their friends and acquaintances and invite them. Two non-hajji friends of the participants (Ruslan and Ismail) also attended the focus group session, mostly as observers.[4] The discussions took place in a classroom at the Academy where we talked to Chamal in 2009. Sufian delegated the choice of venue to Chamal – who played the institutional host and considered the setting appropriate for a senior male group. An informal setting within a respected college, Chamal believed, would put his invitees at ease while making them feel also dignified and respected. This strategy worked. After the customary round of long greetings and introductions – with some participants reading prepared statements – the conversation became increasingly relaxed. After about forty minutes, the discussions flowed naturally and, sometimes, turned emotional. It was clear the participants felt comfortable. They rarely if ever turned their heads toward the video camera that was filming the session – as someone would if they were cognizant of being taped and modified their behavior accordingly. Nor did they pay attention during our discussions to a government official who sat unobtrusively about forty feet away in the corner of the classroom, invited by the Academy's president to ensure that the focus group meeting was officially approved. (We believe the president – who was at the time head of the regional branch and member of the governing council of Putin's ruling party, United Russia – felt such approval was necessary given the tense security situation in Kabardino-Balkaria related to the militant antigovernment Islamist insurgency.) The official in question privately introduced himself to us as an employee of the local branch of Russia's Federal Security Service (FSB) and explained the purpose of his presence when we arrived. We did not see him introduce himself to focus group participants.

The third focus group took place on April 30, 2010 in a small neighborhood mosque in Nalchik. Taking part were nine non-pilgrim men, with an age spread from twenty to sixty. The imam of the mosque, Safudin, whom one of the authors met while on the pilgrimage in Mecca in 2009, provided the venue and helped with recruitment. Prior to that, the authors attempted twice – and unsuccessfully – to assemble devout non-hajji Muslims for a focus group. We certainly came to appreciate the general issue that focus groups are not a well-known practice in Kabardino-Balkaria among common folks. The Muslim males, particularly younger ones, found the idea of gathering for a conversation moderated by strangers suspicious. Dozens of prospective participants declined invitations. (And they were not even told that one of the discussion moderators would be a U.S. citizen and political science professor.) We felt that security-related tensions in Kabardino-Balkaria at the time – feeding to a great extent on widely circulating stories of surveillance, harassment, abuse, unlawful detention, abduction, and killing of local Muslims on mere suspicion of aiding the insurgency – explained the wariness of prospective participants and their refusals. After all, they sensed keenly that, in viciously circular logic, their being Muslim made them disproportionately likely suspects in the eyes of local law enforcement agencies of supporting the antigovernment insurgency. The imam made the focus group possible by assuaging these fears of local Muslims.

The authors arrived at the mosque for the Friday prayer, in which Sufian participated and which Mikhail observed as a guest. After the prayer ended, the imam came out into the hallway near the exit and announced our call for volunteers to have a discussion about the Hajj in a separate room inside the mosque. Out of approximately 100 men, 8 agreed to take part. It was important to us that these men were not relatives or friends of the imam and that they came from different locations and represented diverse socioeconomic backgrounds. As our analysis of the socioeconomic status of respondents will show later in this chapter, these participants were not likely to have homogenous and/or unusual views due to any sort of putative special relationship with the imam. They were not related to the imam in any special way, or in any way that would be different from most other Muslims attending that mosque.

This selection method – important to us – was consistent with our research design requirement that the non-hajjis we interviewed were motivated to perform the Hajj – otherwise any differences between the views of the hajjis and the non-hajjis could well be attributed to differences in their prior (and most likely overall) sense of commitment to observing all Five Pillars of Islam. We felt that the worshippers who would stay on at the mosque after completing the prayer (and probably having initially other plans for the day) would be more likely to be those who had a strong interest in performing the Hajj. As it turned out, in subsequent discussions our participants expressed this interest strongly.

The atmosphere at the start of the discussion was tense. As Sufian wrote in his notes, the participants at first appeared cautious, as if they were trying to figure out whether the moderators were indeed who they said they were. Among other things, Sufian wondered if these men might suspect that the moderators could report their statements to – or be forced to share them with – the Russian government security services. An unexpected incident helped us break the ice. After explaining the purpose of our meeting, we asked if any of the participants objected to the conversation being audio recorded. Otherwise, we explained, we would not be able to analyze the discussion content for our research. The participants sat in a semicircle, some on the couch, others on the ornate wool carpet on the floor. Sufian placed the voice recorder in the middle of the semicircle. No one objected. It was as if the position of the voice recorder facing the semicircle of men was deliberately symbolic. It resembled a star facing the crescent on some flags of predominantly Muslim countries or a small, tight bundle of arrows facing the crescent of twelve small, gold stars on the green Circassian national flag one could often see waved from car windows across Kabardino-Balkaria.

After a brief silence, the conversation took off. We realized that our request to record the discussion probably made the participants feel we were playing openly. Had we truly had the intent to report their statements to anyone against their wishes, we could claim the conversation was to be off the record, but then secretly record it on a device we could easily conceal in our clothes or bags. By not claiming confidentiality, we increased the participants' trust. And they started opening up in return. The conversations started slowly and cautiously. The traditional introductions were succinct. It helped, however, that early in the discussion, Sufian started switching from time to time to the Circassian language. Gradually, the participants warmed up, they expressed the desire to talk more, and they started having dialogs among themselves rather than waiting for the moderators' guidance. They also began talking more in Russian, so as to convey their views more directly to Mikhail, who did not understand Circassian and relied on Sufian's summary translations as the conversation unfolded. After that the participants had an extensive, substantively rich discussion on topics related to our research questions. After we thanked the participants and said our good-byes, we felt a strong sense of accomplishment – that group was the hardest to put together and to engage in a meaningful, open-minded conversation.

We convened our fourth focus group later the same day, April 30, 2010. Zarina, a former student of Sufian when he was a high school teacher in the 1990s, hosted the group. She made possible the recruitment of the participants, all women from nineteen to forty-three years of age. Among them were Zarina's sisters (Albina, Madina, Zamira, and Zarema) and two other women (Marianna and Marina) who were not their relatives. Recruiting the sisters was an opportunity, because devout younger Muslim women abiding by local traditions were unwilling to agree to participate in a discussion with unknown men without the oversight of close and typically senior male relatives or husbands – and the latter would have certainly led to restraint on the part of the women regarding certain discussion topics, such as Islam and family. The presence of such male chaperons would have also meant they could have interrupted the discussion if they did not like something that might have been said and taken the chaperoned woman back home. In our case, the focus group organizer, Zarina, was Sufian's former student and did not need any chaperon.

We hesitated whether to convene this group, given that most participants were related. However, we determined the trade-off was sustainable on methodological grounds. We overrode our initial concern that the sisters may hold non-randomly homogenous views due to kinship, potentially introducing a substantive bias in the focus group content. We made this decision on the basis of the best available empirical research. Behavioral scientists generally concur that siblings growing up in the same family – while alike in appearance and intelligence – develop very different personalities. In 2011, the authoritative *International Journal of Epidemiology* reprinted a 1987 paper that pulled together considerable empirical evidence in support of that argument. The journal invited comments and published thirty-two of them along with the original paper. The comments showed the original conclusions withstood the test of time and other studies well. None of the comments disagreed with the initial finding. One popular website thus summarized this and other research in behavioral sciences on sibling worldviews: "even though we share similar genetic material and upbringing, brothers and sisters often can't be more different. Tests done on siblings to measure personality demonstrated that siblings might as well be strangers."[5]

THE HAJJ VERSUS OTHER DIFFERENCES ACROSS FOCUS GROUPS

Intent and Time Passage

Admittedly, our focus group selection was not ideal. We had to resort to trade-offs. Could the resulting composition of focus groups make some differences among them more important than the fact that some participants performed the Hajj and others did not? To give you the bottom line up front, examining key characteristics of focus group participants and the recruitment process in detail gave us confidence that the pilgrimage factor would most likely account for any major differences in discussion content across all groups.

First, our selection process enabled us to rule out self-selection bias. We went a long way to ensure that the non-pilgrims had about the same degree of commitment to Islam's fundamentals and a similarly strong desire to perform the Hajj. For our non-hajji focus groups, we selected only those Muslims who expressed a strong wish to perform the pilgrimage, yet who have not had the opportunity to do so (mostly due to lack of funds, passport issues, employment conditions, family problems, or other forbidding circumstances).

Second, we controlled for the duration of the Hajj effects, assuming that immediate versus long-term recollections of the Hajj impressions could be systematically different. The hajjis in our focus groups performed the pilgrimage between 1998 and 2009. As it happened, the hajji groups ended up being about equally mixed on how recently participants made their pilgrimages.

With these first two design features, we thus minimized the likelihood that differences in prevalent positions recorded in the pilgrims versus non-pilgrims focus groups could stem from the differences in the initial desire to perform the Hajj or from prior levels of religiosity or be an artifact of how much time passed since their pilgrimage.

In addition, we could confidently rule out doctrinal differences within Islam. All focus group participants – the pilgrims and the non-pilgrims – were Sunni Muslims of the Hanafi school of Islamic law (Madhhab), which is predominant in Kabardino-Balkaria.[6]

AGE, GENDER, AND ETHNICITY

Systematic disproportions among the typical Hajj pilgrim populations by age and gender posed a methodological challenge in the design and analysis of focus groups. Typically among the hajjis, men outnumber women by two to one, since a Kingdom of Saudi Arabia (KSA) law bars women younger than forty-five from making the pilgrimage except in the company of close male relatives. This imbalance was sustained in the Kabardino-Balkaria pilgrim groups at the time we did our fieldwork – even though among pilgrims over sixty women outnumbered men. In groups from Nalchik, women accounted for 62 percent of pilgrims in this age cohort in 2008 and for 69 percent in 2009. However, men comprised 77 percent of the Nalchik pilgrims under fifty in 2008 and 82 percent in 2009. These age-gender proportions were similar to groups from elsewhere in the North Caucasus.

Reflecting the regional Hajj demographics, in our pilgrim focus groups, all women participants were over fifty, whereas in the non-pilgrims groups all women were under fifty. Male participants in both Hajj and non-Hajj groups were of mixed age. Compounding these demographic distributions were the informal speaking-order hierarchies embedded in local customs that would have made an open and uninhibited dialog difficult in mixed male-female focus groups. The best way we found to get around these problems – given our four-group research design commensurate with funding – was to segregate all focus groups by gender. With this split by gender and age differentiation across the male groups we could quasi-experimentally control partially for the effects of age and gender – by comparing views across different pairs of groups while holding some key factors (pilgrimage participation, age, and gender) constant and allowing others to vary. For example, with this we controlled for age effects by estimating how much discussion content in a group of non-pilgrim men differed from that in a group of non-pilgrim women and how both differed from that in a group of pilgrim men. As our analysis revealed, it is unlikely that age and gender could have accounted for the key differences in views we observed across the pilgrim and non-pilgrim groups.

Our selection also enabled us to rule out ethnic composition as a putative key factor across the focus groups. Of the twenty-eight focus group participants, twenty-five (about 90 percent) were ethnic Kabardians (Circassians). The remaining three participants were ethnic Balkars. All three of them participated in the hajji group that had a total of seven pilgrim participants. If ethnicity were the principal explanation of cross-group content differences, a relatively large proportion of Balkars in that group should have been a major factor. In that case, we should have found the views of that hajji group standing out from the remaining three groups. That did not happen. On issues of interest in this study, the more ethnically mixed hajji group resembled the ethnically homogenous first hajji group the most (while differing significantly from the ethnically homogenous non-hajji groups).

INCOME, OCCUPATION, AND EDUCATION

Our focus group selection generated satisfactory controls for socioeconomic differences among the participants – despite the trade-offs, to which we resorted to make recruitment possible in the first place. With the participants stating their occupation and with Sufian's extensive knowledge of incomes associated with specific occupations in Kabardino-Balkaria, as well as with his understanding of the participants' socioeconomic background, we estimated the likely income levels among our focus group participants. Comparing these estimates reveals two principal reasons why income differences across focus groups were unlikely to matter more than performing or not performing the pilgrimage. First, income variation across groups was not significant. The median income of the first Hajj group was around USD $200 per month; of the second Hajj group – $500/month; of the first non-Hajj group it was $500/month and the second non-Hajj group it was $200 month. If these income characteristics were decisive, we should have found more commonality in the views of the first Hajj group and the second non-Hajj group and in the views of the second Hajj group and the first non-Hajj group than in the views of either both Hajj groups or both non-Hajj groups. Yet, this is not what we observed, as we show later in this chapter. Income variation within groups was not significant enough either to systematically skew the findings. The average monthly income of all focus group participants was approximately $405 with the standard deviation of $231. The average monthly income of the pilgrims was $338 with the standard variation of $156. The average monthly income of the non-pilgrims was $488 with the standard variation of $263. Thus, the difference in average income between the pilgrims and the non-pilgrims was within just about a third of one standard deviation from the mean income of all participants. Based on the normal distribution, the likelihood of average income dispersal between the pilgrims and the non-pilgrims was within just about plus or minus 10 percent from the mean.

Second, even assuming this difference could have substantive significance, the average income of the non-pilgrims was higher than that of the pilgrims. This difference, if anything, made it more likely that the non-pilgrims might have more socially tolerant views. Prominent scholars of Islam John Esposito and Olivier Roy, among others, make a point that Muslim immigrants tend to be generally more tolerant of and adaptable to their host society in the United States than in Europe due to their higher wealth and income.[7]

We also rule out occupation as something that might have explained our principal findings. This is because the differences in social attitudes we found between the occupationally homogenous hajjis (pensioners) and the non-hajji students and teachers (Hajj and non-Hajj in Figure 2.1) were about the same as the difference we found between the mixed-occupation hajji and non-hajji groups. This indicated to us that the views of the pilgrims and the non-pilgrims were unlikely to differ because some groups might have been more occupationally homogenous than others, or because some groups might have systematically differed from others based on their participants' occupation. Overall, the participants were diverse enough by occupational background within and across groups to rule out systematic substantive biases. The first Hajj group participants were all retirees, yet they came from diverse pre-retirement backgrounds – two nurses, a teacher, a farmer, and an administrative assistant. The second Hajj group was made up of a physician, a long-term unemployed person, a chemical laboratory researcher, a retired merchant fleet sailor who became a city imam, a night watchman, a village imam, and a former teacher who served as a village imam in retirement. The first non-Hajj group comprised two business entrepreneurs, a manager of a sports complex, a carpenter, a student, two drivers, and an electrician. The second non-Hajj group featured two teachers, three college students, a librarian, and a housewife. If occupational differences were crucial in shaping group perspectives, one would expect us to find more differences between the first and the second Hajj groups and between the first and the second non-Hajj groups than between the Hajj and non-Hajj groups. But that, as we report later, turned out not to be the case.

Finally, we found it implausible that education-level differences across groups could have decisively affected our findings. Of the twelve pilgrims, four had full secondary education, three had incomplete college (no less than two years of coursework, but no earned degree), and five had complete college education. Of the sixteen non-pilgrims, four had full secondary education, five had incomplete college, and seven had complete college education. This hardly amounts to significant cross-group difference. If anything, the non-pilgrims had on average higher education levels than the non-pilgrims. The conventional wisdom in sociology is that education – particularly college education – makes individuals more cognitively sophisticated and therefore more tolerant. By that token, we should have found more tolerant views expressed among the non-pilgrims than among the pilgrims. Yet, that turned out not to be the case.

Finally, we checked for plausible cumulative cleavages with these factors considering all possible factor pairs. We found no plausible combination that could systematically override the Hajj-versus-non-Hajj difference.

IN THEIR OWN WORDS: SEMANTIC WATERSHEDS

We held four focus group sessions in Nalchik, in April 2010 with the participants we selected – one with both of the two groups of pilgrims and one with both of the two groups of non-pilgrims. We structured our focus groups' conversations and interviews around three core themes. First, we explored what the Hajj meant to individual participants and how they viewed its significance for and the likely impacts on Muslims in general. This approach, among other things, allowed us to differentiate between the Hajj impressions that may come from the anticipation of performing the ritual as opposed to those that took shape during and after performing the Hajj. Second, we focused on how the participants viewed other (religious, ethnic, and gender) groups as well as the state, including the state's interaction with religion. One way we found productive to initiate discussions on these topics was to ask participants how they imagined an ideal family and an ideal society. Third, we examined the participants' views on public life and their role in it. In particular, we asked what they thought about the mass media, civic engagement, and travel. We used an open-ended discussion format – i.e., on any core topic, we did not impose requirements that the participants should address every subtheme that was discussed in other focus groups. We let the conversations ebb and flow spontaneously within a theme. We took into consideration that this approach resulted in less time available to discuss the third theme. However, we also weighed that each group had the opportunity to develop this theme and the total discussion time was flexible, with no preset end time. Critically, this problem was constant across all groups, which means it was unlikely it could have caused systematically different outcomes specifically between the groups of pilgrims compared to the non-pilgrims. In our analysis, we concentrated on simple and unambiguous measures of topic salience – recording the duration of subtheme discussion within the big three topics and the number of people taking part in the discussion by subtheme. Having transcribed the discussions verbatim, we estimated the percentage of time by theme and subtheme relative to the total discussion duration, using word counts as a proxy for discussion duration.

Our findings clashed with the prevalent stereotypical perceptions of the Hajj impacts in Kabardino-Balkaria and Russia that we described in Chapter 1. Immersion in what Russian government analysts called religious "fanaticism" during the pilgrimage was more consistent in our open-ended focus group conversations with more tolerant and prosocial views. In this sense, our systematic conversations in focus groups reaffirm and empirically establish our Pilgrims' Paradox. We demonstrate this by comparing the discussion content on specific topics.

PASSION AND DEVOTION

When we asked focus group participants to comment on how important they considered the pilgrimage to Mecca, both the hajjis and the non-hajjis noted the ritual's significance as one of the Five Pillars of Islam. The pilgrims, as we shall see later (Figure 2.1), spent more time discussing this significance due to personally experiencing the Hajj. They talked about their emotions associated with the founding symbols of Islam – the comment of Murat from Adygea earlier in this chapter is a perfect illustration. The pilgrims, unsurprisingly, talked with more passion and personal involvement than the non-pilgrims. They gave us more details – perhaps we can call them emotional details – of their understanding of the religious significance of the Hajj. As we discuss more in Chapter 4, in many of their statements, the pilgrimage was a journey not only to the center of Islam, but also to the center of one's self. That focus on personal feelings enhanced the discussion of religious significance.

The following quotes from our discussions illustrate the difference. All the non-pilgrims told us they venerated the Hajj as one of the Five Pillars of Islamic faith, a divine commandment (*Fardh*) that each Muslim should fulfill in his or her lifetime.

There is no such Muslim who would not want to perform the Hajj, which Allah [recites a praise in Arabic] commands, since this is compulsory for every Muslim. ... All of us are trying to make it to Mecca. If a chance presents itself in the near future, and let there be Allah's grace to make it happen, all of us would make the journey and will perform [our] duty properly. ... When we watch on television how the pilgrims perform the Hajj, we rejoice to see that people make it there. They are able to fulfill one of the *Fardhs* prescribed by the Almighty Allah. Mukhammed, 58.

The Hajj is one of the Five Pillars of Islam. It is the duty of every Muslim – to perform the Hajj at least once in a lifetime, if possible. Faith in Allah as the only God, the prayer, the fasting, the almsgiving, and the Hajj are the *Fardhs*, you have to do them whether you want it or not. Zalim, 52.

As for the Hajj, it is everyone's dream to make it. If I could, I would go. If someone can afford it, they must perform the Hajj. I believe all Muslims have the same view – everyone wants to perform the Hajj at least once in a lifetime. Zalim, 42.

The non-hajjis spent some time discussing the sources of funding for the pilgrimage. Mukhammed made the point that the best way to perform the Hajj is to finance it oneself and – importantly – that the money is made honestly. Others noted that if someone has sufficient honest money for the Hajj, he or she has an especially strong, unequivocal obligation to perform it. To express their personal commitment to fulfilling this obligation, some stated that they would perform the Hajj so well that the Almighty would accept it (the hajjis, in contrast, did not make such claims, discussing instead the importance of not knowing in one's lifetime if one's Hajj had been accepted). Many non-pilgrims expressed wishes that God make it possible for them to secure funding and discussed how strongly they believed in Allah's will. Some young non-pilgrim women stated their desire to live up to what they saw as the fundamental obligation of Muslims by saying that even if they had already performed the Hajj and had the time and money to explore the world, they would first travel to repeat the Hajj or to revisit Medina and Mecca.

* * *

The hajjis went beyond stating the religious significance of the Hajj and brought in their personal feelings. As they linked these feelings with the significance of their faith and with social relations, they talked longer. The quotes that follow illustrate this interaction effect – e.g., note the first speaker's bringing in feelings about his family and the second speaker's personal journeys:

"On my first Hajj, I was in a group that included Shauki Balagov who was performing the Hajj for his deceased father; with Aminat Mirzakanova who was performing the Hajj for her deceased grandmother; and with Ingham, who was performing the Hajj for her mother. I went there with them. Words cannot describe it. On everyone's lips, like an anthem, were the words [in Arabic] '*Labeyka lahuma labeyk!*' which is translated as 'Here, Allah, I am in front of You!' And if you are in front of Allah, you are a guest in His house. This experience is such a pleasure that you forget about your children, your house, and everything else. You feel you are in Heaven. You cannot hold back your tears, because He called you. When you drink the holy ZamZam water, when you go to the mosque and pray for your family – all this time you are doing your special work and nothing bothers you. As soon as you return to the hotel, you start feeling sick. This means you go through spiritual cleansing from your sins," said Fatima, 60.

"Having been there, I ask people, so how was your Hajj? And I see how the tears flow down their faces as they begin to reminisce. ... Once a person performed the Hajj, they are called *hajji*. Some people disagree with that and say that there is no such official title as *hajji*. And yet people respect it; people love the fact that someone accomplished it. A person has to spend money, a person has no idea how everything will end. A person makes a long journey, thousands and thousands of kilometers. And a journey is always an unknown. People cross the oceans, they fly, they come by bus or by private car. It is risky. Among them are people of advanced age, sick people, and yet they undertake the journey. When a person, for the sake of one's God, for the sake of performing that duty, makes the journey, and spends money or sacrifices personal property and keeps his hands, legs, eyes, ears, and thoughts away from sin, and when he arrives there and performs his duty – of course, this is worthy of praise in every way and of respect in every way. And that is why it is meaningful always when people add *hajji* to the pilgrims' first names," said Khizir, 50.

In our conversations, the hajjis came out as more deeply involved with their faith, more emotionally invested in the fundamentals of Islam. This was something we expected. Yet, we could not anticipate how much the hajjis and the non-hajjis diverged on the topics that follow.

RELIGIOUS AND SOCIAL TOLERANCE

We found that conversations on themes related to sociopolitical tolerance and civic engagement in our focus groups with the North Caucasus Muslims differed in duration and in substance. Semantically, we identified the following themes and their components in our group discussions.

- Inclusiveness of Islam as religious faith:
  - How different from or compatible with Islam are other religions, such as Christianity and Judaism?
  - Is Islamic legacy superior to other religious and cultural legacies among ethnic Circassians?
  - How acceptable is diversity of religious belief and practice within Islam (e.g., can one regard non-Sunnis or members of Madhhabs other than the Hanafi as true Muslims)?
- Diversity of ritual codes within Islam:
  - How acceptable are diverse forms of prayer such as number of daily prayers or the ways of keeping your hands and fingers during the prayer?
  - How acceptable are diverse forms of personal appearance (such as shaving or dressing)?
- Church–state relations:
  - How acceptable is it to discuss government policy with respect to religion?
- Civic life/Public engagement:
  - To what extent can Muslims vote, attend secular public events, or be exposed to secular media (such as television)?
  - How acceptable is it for Muslims to be photographed or videotaped in public or to take pictures or videos in public?
  - To what extent can Muslims draw on their personal experiences (compared to referencing canonical texts or sacred/authoritative persons)?
- Socioeconomic diversity:
  - How much tolerance or intolerance is expressed regarding disparities in income and status within society?
  - How important is money in one's life?

The substantive differences between the pilgrims and the non-pilgrims came out strongly in the discussion of these themes. The contrast was prominent and systematic. Overall, our content analysis showed that the hajjis had a more inclusive concept of common Muslim identity. They were more inclined to socialize. They expressed a stronger proclivity for public engagement than the non-hajjis. They also showed a more developed sense of their individuality than the non-hajjis. The following sections illustrate these differences.

The non-pilgrims emphasized Islam's exclusivity, monotheism, and the singularity of the Qur'an and the Sunnah as the source of Islamic faith. In the group of male non-pilgrims, everybody agreed with one participant's claim: "The world is divided in two parts – pure Muslims worshipping only the Almighty Allah and the rest – Shiites, Jews, and whatever. . . . Every belief must be checked against the Qur'an. If even one word someone believes in contradicts the Qur'an, they are not Muslims. Their views cannot be shared." Interestingly, he argued that the Shiites were non-Muslim. He dug in and defended his position even when the moderators provocatively asked him if his statement meant that he didn't believe that the founder of the Islamic Republic of Iran, Ayatolla Khomeini, was Muslim.

The non-hajjis also expressed their antagonism to other religions by bringing up the role of religion in the history of the Circassian ethnic group. One must digress here to explain why this matters. While nowadays, the majority of the Circassians is Muslim and the minority is Orthodox Christian, it is a well-established fact that prior to adopting Islam, most Circassians were Christians. Before that, they predominantly followed their Circassian ethnic religion, worshipping the Higher Mind, the Mighty Tha. The religious history of Circassian people is the history of long and complex interactions of Circassian mythology, Christianity, and Islam – with each of these major belief systems, in turn, representing diverse and interacting influences. Circassian mythology was influenced by Greek mythology when ancient Greece established satellite city-states along the Black Sea coast. In turn, it is likely that the Greeks also borrowed from Circassian lore – with the resulting fusions probably influencing the *Khabze* in return. After it was introduced in the fourth century, Christianity initially grew under the influence of Greek Byzantine traditions and in the tenth century through the thirteenth experienced a significant influence of the Georgian Christian church. Islam grew into the predominant religion among Circassians between the sixteenth and the nineteenth centuries through interactions with the Persians, the Crimean Tatars, and the Ottoman Turks.[8] In short, the history of religion in Circassian lands is the history of interactive intra- and interreligious *diversity* – legacies of which abound at present. For instance, the names of days of the week in Circassian language reflect the Christian influence. Popular customs, such as the conduct of weddings and reception of dignitaries, have significant elements of traditional *Khabze*.

It is symptomatic in this context that the non-hajjis in our focus groups denied that Christianity and paganism left any traces in Circassian culture. They insisted that Islam laid the foundation of Circassian ethnic customs – and that the Islamic foundation was their only redeeming value. The non-pilgrims admitted that in some respects Circassian customs diverged from Islam, but characterized them as manifestations of "backwardness." One participant, Zalim, expressed these views as follows:

Our culture, our obligations have always been close to Islam. The only thing we lacked was the knowledge of what we were not allowed to do – of *haram*, or what is forbidden – as well as the knowledge of what we must by all means do. We could not distinguish between those two sides of the coin. That's the main point. In all other respects, our Circassian culture has been very close to Islam. Some people say that prior to Islam we had Christianity and paganism – yet neither our fathers, nor our grandfathers and great grandfathers ever experienced Christianity or paganism. All our relatives say that we have always been Muslims.

A similar theme – the prevalence of Islamic identity over native ethnic identity – also emerged in the discussion among younger women non-pilgrims. They spent more time than other groups discussing relationships and marriage. All participants in that group were ethnic Kabardian (Circassian). Sufian and Mikhail provocatively asked them whom would they pick as a husband – all other things being equal – a Christian Kabardian or a Muslim Kumyk (a Turkic ethnic group of Dagestan, distinct from the Circassians). Three women participants actively responded, while others nodded in agreement. The conversation went as follows:

MIKHAIL: So, you say you would not pick [an Orthodox Christian as your husband even if he were] a Kabardian? But he would know your local customs.

ZARINA: So what [even if he is a Kabardian, like me]? But he is Orthodox Christian.

MIKHAIL: And the Kabardian would speak the same native language as you, but [a Muslim] Kumyk would not.

ZARINA: This is unimportant. To me it is not significant.

MIKHAIL: What if he couldn't even speak Russian [and you could not communicate, because he also does not speak Kabardian]? [Everyone laughs].

MADINA: As the Prophet (*sal'yallahu aleyhi au salam*) said, "There is no difference between an Arab and non-Arab except for piety."

MARINA: When people decide to share their fate, they probably first and foremost identify their aspirations and life goals. And if these goals coincide, they, of course, would consider their spiritual aspirations. The latter would primarily determine their goals. And that is what would primarily unite them.

Later in that focus group session, participants discussed whether one could reconcile traditional ethnic customs and Islamic rituals. In the North Caucasus, it had long been considered – and still is by many – that an individual could be a true Muslim, yet sometimes violate behavioral norms associated with Islam (for example, by drinking alcoholic beverages or eating pork). On this topic, again, the participants asserted the preeminence of religion – on some issues straightforwardly, on others obliquely. They clearly objected to social behavior such as drinking alcohol as un-Islamic. On more complex customs, they discussed those that were in essence Islamic, yet interpreted as ethnic as part of the Soviet period's atheistic secularism. One outstanding example concerned the celebration of a holiday directly associated with the Hajj pilgrimage:

Let us take the holiday of sacrifice, *Kurban Bayram*. I often hear people say they need to sacrifice an animal on that day to honor other family members – the first year, the husband, the second year, the wife. But in reality, this must be done to honor Allah. When I tried to explain to one family that this should be done for Allah, they responded: "Since ancient times our grandmothers and grandfathers did it like that – first for the grandmother, then for the grandfather, then for the son, then for the daughter, and so on." And yet, the sacrifice is meant for Allah, not for any particular person. Marianna.

Strictly speaking, Marianna was correct. *Kurban Bayram* is, in fact, one of the names of Eid al-Adha or the Festival of the Sacrifice or the Festival of the Feast to honor Ibrahim's (Abraham's) consent to have his son sacrificed as a symbol of submission to Allah (the son, Ishmael, remained alive through Allah's intervention while the willingness to sacrifice was honored). Later, on Allah's command, Ibrahim and Ishmael would build a stone-and-mortar Ka'aba, the symbolic center of faithfulness to the Almighty.[9] Sufian, in fact, like most pilgrims, experienced the Eid al-Adha. This took place after completing the principal rituals

comprising the Hajj – half a day in the plains by Mount Arafat, climbing
and praying on that mountain, a night on the ground in Muzdalifah, the
"stoning of the devil," and the pilgrims shaving their heads or clipping
their hair.

Another dimension of religious inclusiveness concerned the attitude
toward *Madhhabs* (schools of law) within Islam. This topic came up
among younger women, and they overwhelmingly emphasized the need
to first and foremost maintain the uniformity of adherence to Allah and
the Sunnah regardless of pilgrims belonging to different *Madhhabs*.
The non-pilgrims did not know the nuances of the Hajj performance
based on *Madhhab* traditions. When Sufian mentioned that such differences exist, the participants did not ask for more detailed explanations.
Their comments were rather terse, once again emphasizing the importance
of what they saw as the putative uniformity of belief and practice that
transcended *Madhhab* differences. The most lenient comment was the one
asserting that all *Madhhabs* should still be based on the Qur'an and the
Sunnah and thus cannot be considered "new developments" (a term
influenced by Salafism and used by some devout Muslims to condemn
some aspects of faith or ritual that do not, in their view, conform to the
prescription of the Qur'an and the Sunnah). Only one in the group,
Marina, spoke of *Madhhabs* in a positive way.

SUFIAN: How do you feel about the followers of other *Madhhabs* or
about the rituals of other *Madhhabs*?
ZARINA: If a person follows a certain *Madhhab*, it means he is no longer
striving to observe the Qur'an and the Sunnah.
ZAREMA: He sees only that particular path.
ZARINA: Yes, he sees only that *Madhhab* and nothing else. He is not
searching.
MARINA: Well, most likely a person who follows a certain *Madhhab*
knows, first and foremost, that his *Madhhab* comes from the Qur'an
and the Sunnah. This is one way of interpreting the Qur'an and the
Sunnah. And so, it would be incorrect to say that *Madhhabs* are a form
of [unsolicited] innovation.

* * *

The pilgrims, in contrast, emphasized commonalities between Islam and
other major world religions as well as the Hanafi and other schools of law
(*Madhhabs*) within Islam. One theme the hajjis raised several times during
group discussions was that tolerance toward other religions is a basic

element of Islam. Mukhamed, age seventy, made this argument as follows: "Our Prophet (*allakhu aleykum assalam*) never persecuted believers of other religions. For him all people were equal." Another hajji participant, Khasan, age sixty-five, pointed out that Judaism, Christianity, and Islam have the same roots and therefore intolerance toward other religions would sow discord within Islam and undermine it: "According to Islam, you are not a Muslim if you don't believe in Jesus Christ and Moses. They were also both prophets and messengers. Allah spoke with Moses. We need to learn tolerance to other faiths, that is how one learns religion."

Regarding the relationship between ethnic customs and religious rituals and their compatibility, the pilgrims discussed it at length. Interestingly, unlike the non-pilgrims, they did not bring up the issue of *Kurban Bayram* and the need to purify it as purely Islamic tradition. Yet, intuitively, if participation in the Hajj increased the pilgrims' religiosity, one would expect the pilgrim groups to develop the discussion of this custom and the need to reassert its Islamic origins in Kabardino-Balkaria and for this discussion to be more prominent than it was in the non-pilgrim groups.

The pilgrims also exhibited greater tolerance toward other schools within Islam. It was acceptable, the hajjis said, for the Muslims of the Shafi'i *Madhhab* to perform the Hajj using the easier Hanafi *Madhhab* rules. Members of these schools coexist in the North Caucasus and perform the Hajj differently. The Shafi'i school is represented in the east of the North Caucasus (Chechnya, Dagestan, and Ingushetia), while the Hanafi school is represented in the western part of the region (Kabardino-Balkaria, Adygea, Karachaevo-Cherkessia, and North Ossetia). Those of the Hanafi school perform *Hajj-Tamattu*, which, on the whole, has more relaxed procedural rules of the two. For example, the pilgrims may change out of their ritual clothes between performing the arrival-to-Mecca ceremonies (Umrah) and the beginning of the main rituals (Hajj). They may also change out of their ritual clothes immediately after the main rituals are over. Those of the Shafi'i school perform *Hajj-Ifrad*. According to that tradition, pilgrims must wear the white *Ihram* robes at all times during the Hajj. That means, for example, that males must not shave or clip their hair so as not to get out of *Ihram*. The observance of these rules under *Hajj-Ifrad* is strict. In practice, according to the record of our participant observation in the KSA, "the pilgrims not only see that members of all the *Madhhabs* perform the Hajj, but also that members of different *Madhhabs* perform the Hajj as part of one and the same group." In this group of pilgrims from the North Caucasus, eighty-six were Hanafi (mostly from Karachaevo-Cherkessia and Kabardino-Balkaria) and twenty-three were Shafi'i Muslims (mostly from Ingushetia, Chechnya, and Dagestan). Each of these subgroups had its own leader who belonged to the same *Madhhab*. And yet, the Shafi'i group leader advised members of his subgroup that they had an option to perform the Hajj according to the less stringent Hanafi *Madhhab* rules. The Shafi'i pilgrims could opt for it by making a standard statement: "I belong to the Shafi'i *Madhhab*, but I will be performing the Hajj according to the canons of the Hanafi *Madhhab*." Most of these cases involved pilgrims who were ailing or had health issues. On the whole, these observations and experiences made the Hanafi hajjis more open to non-Hanafi schools within Islam compared to the Hanafi non-hajjis.[10]

This openness was profoundly paradoxical. Sufian's Hajj diaries record a telling episode. It shows, first, how the pilgrims may learn firsthand – including through physical hardship during the rituals – about the *Madhhab* differences. It also shows how being in the sacred center of Islam induces them to stick to the chosen method of performing the Hajj. (Before entering Mecca, every pilgrim gives a verbal pledge to commit to the rules of a specific *Madhhab*, while performing the Hajj. After that, a pilgrim cannot switch to a different form of ritual performance, unless s/he goes out of Mecca, makes a new commitment, and reenters the city.)

One Shafi'i pilgrim from Dagestan wanted to perform all the rituals strictly according to the rules and asked his group leader, a Dagestani imam, to accompany him personally and instruct what to recite and how to complete *Tawaf*, seven circles around the holy Ka'aba. He also insisted on performing the walk based on the Shafi'i school rules. At least as they were interpreted in his native Dagestan, those rules meant that if he touched a woman while walking around the Ka'aba, he would have to exit the crowd, perform ritual ablution, and start the walk all over again. The rule reflected a prohibition on Muslims touching the opposite sex in the Shafi'i teachings while performing religious rituals. The group leader accompanied the Dagestani pilgrim and so they started their walk. They made every effort to avoid the pilgrim's physical contact with women. Yet, in the dense, flowing sea of tens of thousands of people (close to half of them women), this proved next to impossible. Before completing the second circle, the undesired contact occurred. The pilgrim was upset and angry. He begged the group leader to start over, and they valiantly fought the crowds exiting across the circling flow of people. In the process he undoubtedly touched other women. Yet, despite the ordeal and the group leader's repeated instruction that accidental physical contact with women on the walk around Ka'aba was acceptable since it was inevitable, the pilgrim remained determined. The pilgrim performed the ritual ablution, and they started again. The same thing happened. After the third failed attempt, the tired group leader refused to accompany the stubborn pilgrim anymore. The pilgrim exited the crowd alone to perform the ritual ablution. After that, they lost each other in the crowd and completed the ritual separately. The group leader arrived back to the hotel several hours earlier than the pilgrim, who appeared exhausted but happy that he completed his circles around the Ka'aba the way he pledged he would, the strict Shafi'i way.

We wondered if the persistent pilgrim wished he were more open-minded when making his pledge and opted for the more lenient Hanafi rules. We surmised also that he probably wished he did not have to leave and reenter Mecca to switch his pledge from one form of performing the Hajj to another. He certainly had a long time to think through and physically feel the consequences of his commitment to a more stringent – i.e., less tolerant – way of performing the ritual. Whether he verbalized these thoughts in his mind or not, the pilgrim experienced how intolerance could hurt. One way or another, this is a paradoxical perceptual process, through which a pilgrim could conceivably develop more openness socially. In the group where we conducted participant observation, Sufian observed at least one case when, in Mecca, a pilgrim approached the group leader and asked if he could change his Hajj method from Shafi'i to Hanafi. The group leader explained that, in order to change his Hajj method, the pilgrim would have to leave and reenter Mecca, starting his pilgrimage over again. The pilgrim, however, decided that it wasn't worth starting Hajj over again and proceeded in the Shafi'i way. And this, incidentally, does not necessarily mean that if they performed the Hajj again, they would opt for the Hanafi *Madhhab*. They could probably compartmentalize these feelings and experiences. But those that they would compartmentalize outside the pilgrimage would prompt them to be more open-minded.

Paradoxical as it was, this logic was consistent with what we learned in conversations with the Kabardino-Balkaria Muslims. In the focus group of male hajjis – who all belonged to the Hanafi *Madhhab* – no one spoke about other *Madhhabs* as incompatible with Islam. In one instance when the pilgrims raised the issue of different forms of the Hajj, they focused on sincerity of belief in general rather than on the divergence among the schools of Islam. They focused, in essence, on generic differences among humans – on something that could affect behavior in any settings, whether religious or not. Religious value was *de facto* expressed through human value. Khizir summarized this perspective: "There are three ways of performing the Hajj. The first one is through Allah. These are the pilgrims who know religion and know what they are doing. The second one is also through Allah. These are the pilgrims who may not know the religion, but they strive to do it the best way possible and learn from the pilgrims of the first kind. The third kind also exists. Those are the *shaytans* (devils). They go so as to spoil the Hajj for other pilgrims."

Participants in all four focus groups said it was important that Muslims pray five times a day and that the *namaz* prayer, like the Hajj, was one of the Five Pillars of Islam. However, only the non-hajjis took this point further and argued that those who do not pray regularly five times a day are not only imperfect Muslims, but cannot be considered Muslims at all. In other words, they were significantly less tolerant. Their concept of Muslim identity was less inclusive. Zalim, one of the male non-hajjis, adamantly expressed the generally shared sentiment within his group when this question came up in discussion: "If you have not been to outer space, how could you call yourself an astronaut? You cannot! And it's the same about the Pillars of Islam – if you do not observe them, you are not a Muslim. Otherwise, it's all baloney. It's self-deception." Female non-pilgrims also refused to consider as Muslims those who fail to pray five times a day. One participant, Zamira, explained it like this: "Allah said – enter Islam completely, not partially."

In both non-hajji groups, the participants noted that in an ideal family both spouses must perform all the daily prayers.

In both hajji groups, however, the topic of spouses performing all five daily *namaz* prayers was not mentioned as an important part of an ideal family.

Two of our focus groups – one with the hajjis and the other with the non-hajjis – overlapped with prayer times, so the participants took time off to pray, taking turns to retire in a separate room. However, one of the authors of this book who is a Muslim missed those designated prayers while assisting with moderating group discussions. Based on stories of other Muslims he heard, some of them during the Hajj, he took it as a given that it would be possible to make up for the missed *namaz* prayers during the next designated prayer time. However, when he told the story to the women non-pilgrims, they upbraided him. They insisted that missing any of the five daily prayers was a sin and Muslims could not redeem themselves by praying twice or more at the next prayer time. They argued the makeup prayers did not count. This contrasted with the said author's earlier experience of missing the *namaz* during the hajji focus group. The pilgrims then said that in certain circumstances, making up for missed prayers was acceptable. One of the hajjis, Mukhamed, condoned this practice by telling a story – an oblique way of voicing opinion common among observant, but more tolerant believers. Once, Mukhamed told us, he had a guest who was an old man in need of care and attention. Preoccupied with hosting, Mukhamed missed a middle-of-the-day prayer. To correct for this, he said: "After the old man left, I made the obligatory prayer and also the prayer I had missed, and then went to sleep."

PERSONAL APPEARANCE: SHAVING AND SCARVES

Muslims know that Prophet Mohammed had a beautiful beard, and thus it is in fashion in some parts of the Islamic world to have a beard, especially in Arabic countries. However, doing so is not compulsory for Muslim men, and, for example, in Turkey, most men are shaved. Yet, many young men in the North Caucasus believe that growing a beard is an Islamic duty, which they developed from books describing the Prophet's appearance. It is sometimes a way to build self-esteem and pride by challenging others, because in the North Caucasus societies, a full beard has been often viewed as a manifestation of religious extremism – and systematically so on the part of the government security forces deployed to fight the Islamist insurgency. Police in Nalchik, for example, have been known to force Muslim men to shave. In one case, local police cut out a cross in the hair of several young Muslims as a punishment, because they refused to shave their beards. Those Hajj pilgrims from the North Caucasus who did not shave observed in Mecca that many Muslims cleanly shaved their faces. They understood that a beard is not necessarily something that distinguishes Muslims from non-Muslims. The same difference was evident among the pilgrims and the non-pilgrims in the discussion of personal dress code. Whereas the non-pilgrim Muslim women mostly disapproved of other women dressing in the Western fashion (e.g., exposing their body outlines, hair, or face), the pilgrim Muslim women were more tolerant, even though they all covered their heads with scarves or kerchiefs.

Among the non-pilgrims, all the men wore beards, while all the women had on toned-down, single-color, tight-fitting headscarves that concealed their hair completely. One of the women non-pilgrims, Madina, insisted with passion that even if a woman happened to have luscious and exquisitely done hair, she had no excuse whatsoever to appear in public without a headscarf. She explained it with reference to what she believed was her religious canon: "One will have to answer to God and that is more important."

Among the hajji participants, most men were clean shaved. Those men explained this by saying they came to believe that beards were not a necessary attribute of Muslim men that separated them from non-Muslims. They also said having a beard was not something that necessarily made a man a better Muslim. Whereas some women in our Hajj groups also wore headscarves, others wore more relaxed kerchiefs with their hair partially exposed. According to one of the Hajj group participants, Fatima, one would expect older married women like them to be more conservative in their dress than the younger women. Yet, she acknowledged diversity of dress codes: "You will see married women in their sixties who do not wear headscarves, but also young unmarried women who wear them." An important observation here is that Fatima did not insist that this is a violation of the norm and she did not refer to divine retribution awaiting someone who might deviate from the strict dress code.

RELIGION AND THE STATE

In focus groups, the non-pilgrims mostly avoided discussing the role of the state or government in their lives, even when discussing how they saw the ideal society. The women only one time expressed a grievance that local police officers often rudely told them to quit wearing scarves. The men stated from the outset that they wanted to stay away from government or politics. In this manner, the non-pilgrims in the focus groups – as well as would-be pilgrims whom one of the authors interviewed at the beginning of their journey to Mecca – expressed distrust of the capacity of the Russian state to be friendly to Muslims. Such a conception, understandably, is based on the experience of being raised in the violent environment of south Russia, where the state constantly fought against rebels inspired and mobilized by Muslim leaders during the Russian Empire, as well as in the Soviet and post-Soviet eras, all the way to the present.

* * *

The pilgrims spent considerable time discussing issues related to the role of the government in society. After their experiences in the KSA, they reported two things that significantly affected their views on the nature of state–church relations. First, the pilgrims talked about the KSA government providing accommodations that make life easier for Muslim believers. They said the trip made them realize that the laws and the sociopolitical environment could be negotiated and adjusted to better facilitate Islamic practices. They were also impressed to find a whole religious industry in the KSA. The most commonly mentioned examples were directions to the nearest mosques on traffic signs and road signs or billboards displaying quotes from the Qur'an. According to them, the Hajj made them get a better and more nuanced understanding that while statehood and governance are the domain of the secular, they could also meaningfully accommodate religious expression. They believed the secular and sacred spaces could and should coexist in harmony. The pilgrims also said having seen the KSA made them realize that many accommodations for Muslims in the North Caucasus since the collapse of the atheistic Soviet state in 1991 had been borrowed from the Islamic states. Thus, they said they could understand how much can be done at home to develop an Islam-friendly environment without changing Russia's political system and without politicizing Islam. For example, they said they understood that a state could, in principle, allow the building of mosques on every major city block and that nothing bad would come out of it. They relished the idea of having conveniently located neighborhood mosques within walking distance from their homes – something that would make it easier for them, especially those advanced in years, to pray five times a day. They talked about more prayer rooms that can be opened at the airports and at train and bus stations, and they saw these demands as realistic, having actually seen them during the pilgrimage, including at Russia's international airports. One of the pilgrims, Zaur, in a flashback to what he lived through while in the KSA, could not hide his awe on that point: "There are prayer rooms even in prisons."

Our group discussions reflect important ongoing debates about Muslim minorities living among non-Muslim majorities or in secular states. In the chapter "How to Live as a Stateless Muslim Minority" of his book *Globalized Islam*, Olivier Roy notes, "It is often argued that because Islam is an all-encompassing religion that addresses all aspects of individual and social life – from law to politics, from diet to socialization – it is impossible for true believers to live permanently under non-Muslim rule. . . . Following the example of the Prophet, who left Mecca for Medina to avoid the rule of pagans, hijra means a religiously motivated migration to a Muslim land from a territory that is no longer Muslim."[11] As we discussed in Chapter 1, the idea spread in the Caucasus after the Russian conquest in the nineteenth century that those who died under the non-Muslim Russian rule would never go to heaven. Tens of thousands Muslims, including about one-third of Kabardians, left their North Caucasus homelands for the Ottoman Empire in the aftermath of the

Russian conquest. The very term and idea of *hijra* became popular even earlier when part of the Kabardian community escaped the Russian rule moving to western Circassia in the 1820s. The term they used to call themselves was *Hajret*, a derivation of *hijra*.

The debates about what it means to be a Muslim minority became for all intents and purposes irrelevant during the Soviet era. The Communist state not only suppressed religion, but also closed the borders and pulled down the Iron Certain – not only to distance itself from the capitalist West, but also to cut off Russian Muslims from the rest of the Muslim world, from mainstream Islam.

Our focus group discussions indicated the revival of the debates about stateless Muslims in Russia's North Caucasus. It was a natural part of the revival of religion and identity in the region. Our focus discussions showed that hajjis were more positive and optimistic about their prospects of living as a Muslim minority in Russia in general than the non-hajjis were. Drawing on their observations and experiences during their pilgrimage, the hajjis went as far as to express specific practical measures how to make the coexistence of religious practice and secular rule more effective. In *Globalized Islam*, Olivier Roy analyzed how Muslim scholars discuss the issue of stateless Muslim minorities. According to Bernard Lewis, most scholars and religious authorities consider it impossible and impermissible for Muslims to live as a non-governing minority. However, Abou El Fadl, who graduated from the Near East Studies Center at Princeton University, disagrees. He shows that, according to authoritative Islamic scholars, the issue is significantly more complex. In fact, it is possible to make a case that the conditions most Islamic scholars identify that make it possible for Muslims to stay under non-Muslim rule correspond to the basic principles of religious freedom as understood in the West.[12] Our research also showed that ordinary Muslims – and the pilgrims more so than the non-pilgrims – could interpret religious freedom in a secular state as a condition for the thriving of Islam as a religion. Most importantly, our findings indicate that with their pilgrimage experience and elevated social status, the hajjis could act as an important social force for validating the idea and promoting practical measures for equitable integration of Muslims in Muslim-minority states.

OPENNESS TO CIVIC ENGAGEMENT

In the non-hajji focus groups, the participants failed to raise topics that did not directly relate to Islam and political issues were mentioned fewer than three times. After each of these rare mentions, everybody abruptly became silent, the topic was dropped instantly and not discussed, and it was not mentioned again for a long time. The non-pilgrims appeared uncomfortable to talk about politics in front of a group. They also said they did not vote during elections. Again, they implied or explained that they were concerned that discussing political or civic issues in public ran against the behavioral norms typical of devout Muslims. Nor did the non-pilgrims raise participation in public events as an issue. They talked little about it when we posed guiding or suggestive questions.

In our focus groups, the devout Muslims in the North Caucasus who wanted to perform the Hajj but had not done so usually said they had not their pictures taken in public places. They said they believed these activities go against the spirit of Islam. In the two non-hajji focus groups, the participants did not let us take individual or group pictures and refused to be videotaped. The authors' admonition that this could be acceptable if they took a photo with one of the authors who traveled a long way to visit them did not make the non-hajjis change their mind.

* * *

The conversations with the hajjis went differently. While the pilgrims did not participate in the political life of the KSA, they talked about witnessing or learning from others that local Muslims engage in political and social activities in the Holy Land – just like they probably did a millennium and a half ago. These statements revealed understanding that participation in public life among Muslims goes back to Islam's sacred "time of origin" – a perception that made the pilgrims see these activities as acceptable to Muslims. In focus groups, for example, the pilgrims discussed political differences between anti- and pro-West parties in Islamic countries. These observations helped the pilgrims become more interested in political and social life in general, and in their own country in particular.

The pilgrims reported participating in social activities, in which the non-pilgrims did not report being involved. Only the hajjis told us they attended public courses on Qur'an recital and only they proposed engaging in negotiations with the Russian government to work out compromises on building enough mosques, so that most Muslims in their hometown, Nalchik, could have one within reasonable walking distance from their homes. They believed praying in a mosque, a public space, was important. In fact, a number of pilgrim women – but none of the non-pilgrim women – from our focus groups attended the conference on terrorism and extremism organized by Kabardino-Balkaria State University (in which the authors were participants). Notably, this happened in a society where people usually do not do such things without personal invitation (which were not extended in our case), and women usually do not go at all.

The pilgrims spent much time discussing mainstream Russian TV programs, with most participants contributing to the conversation. They drew analogies with the KSA, remembering how Muslims there watched and discussed mainstream secular television channels the state made available to them. Whereas, like the non-hajjis, the pilgrims expressed discontent with much of the Russian popular television content – objecting to what they saw as gratuitous violence and indecency – they did not advocate strict government restrictions on content. Instead, they advocated a broader public discussion of these issues, the kind of discussion that could plausibly result in broader socially acceptable compromises. In a conversation on the sidelines of one of the hajji focus groups, the participants said they understood that they were part of a larger Russian national TV space that could not be changed to accommodate the preferences of minority populations, such as Muslim non-Russian ethnics. However, they believed dialog was important and more diverse content would help accommodate their preferences.

The hajjis told us that their pilgrimages – when they witnessed Muslims from all over the world recording their experiences on photo and video – made them understand that whereas Islam may not expressly allow taking photos, it never prohibited taking them either. They also felt taking pictures would enable them to share their experiences in the sacred land. It transpired in our focus group conversations and interviews that most hajjis made photo albums – in hard copy or/and electronic format – about the Hajj. They often downloaded pictures of their Hajj experiences onto their cell phones.

When we asked the pilgrim participants if they would mind that we videotaped the discussions so we could analyze them, and when we asked to have their pictures taken with us, they agreed enthusiastically (see Photos 1a and 1b). They were also at ease with the fact that the videotaping of the focus groups was done by the crews of the secular public TV stations "NOTR" and "Edelweiss" (who showed a few excerpts in their local programs). The non-pilgrims rejected these requests.

PHOTOS 1A AND 1B Hajji and Hajjiah focus groups. Both non-pilgrim groups refused to be photographed. We honored their request not to take their pictures.

SELF-CONFIDENCE

A stronger propensity among the pilgrims to express or present themselves in public was also linked to reported gains in self-confidence after performing the Hajj. Thus, in interviews and focus groups, when referring to the sources of their faith, the non-pilgrims predominantly mentioned Islamic books or sermons. They significantly more frequently referred to the Qur'an and the Sunnah, the two most basic written sources of Islamic faith. At the same time, they appeared to be less confident in their views when they did not reference those primary sources, frequently seeking validation from other participants through words, eye contact, or gestures. On balance, this suggested the non-pilgrims had stronger confidence in canonical religious texts than in their personal experiences. They also more frequently backed up their positions with reference to the views of local Islamic leaders they considered authoritative. When we analyzed the focus group transcripts audio- and video-recordings, it made sense to us that by anchoring their positions in external authoritative texts or messages – or rather the internalized and idolized versions of them–the non-pilgrims turned out to be less acceptant of diverse and contradictory viewpoints on social issues and civic engagement during their conversations than the pilgrims were. The latter, in contrast, developed their positions with frequent references to personal, real-world experiences including the Hajj. They brought in little anecdotes and stories and came through as more flexible in assessing contemporary social implications of the canonical narratives of Islam. These observations illustrate defundamentalization – an integral part of repersonalization linked, in theory, to more sociopolitically tolerant views.

SOCIOECONOMIC DIVERSITY AND THE ROLE OF MONEY

Overall, compared to the non-pilgrims, the hajjis came through as more tolerant of status and income disparities in society. This was a separate and prominent theme almost all the pilgrims discussed among themselves during the Hajj, and that is why we highlighted it. "What is the significance of the pilgrimage now that you experience it?" this book's author who participated in the Hajj asked fellow pilgrims during his journey. One of the most common answers was that everybody was equal during the Hajj. We already showed how this sense of equality explained greater acceptance of religious diversity. The same applied to views of different social classes or groups. The pilgrimage, the hajjis told us, made people more tolerant toward those who are wealthier/poorer and have higher/ lower positions in society. Commenting in his participant observer diary, Sufian noted: "In today's Russia many people are not satisfied with the gap between the rich and the poor. Some advocate reforms and technological modernization. Others even call for changing the political system. But those who perform the Hajj can see a very unique situation on their journey. We registered an overwhelming sense of satisfaction with commonality between the wealthy and the poor that the pilgrims experienced during the pilgrimage."

At the time of our participant observation journey in 2009, the standard pilgrimage package from Kabardino-Balkaria cost $3,800. This was the package that Sufian and most others in his group purchased. Several people in our observation group, however, paid significantly more by Kabardino-Balkaria income standards – around $5,800, mostly for better accommodations. These accommodations were different from those of others in only one, yet significant aspect – a better hotel in Mecca, located closer to the holy sites. The daily interactions between the standard and the upgrade groups could have hypothetically engendered the sense of relative deprivation – imbued with envy, negativity, inferiority, animosity, and related emotions – among the less privileged hajjis. As the Hajj participant observer, Sufian wondered in his diaries if his fellow pilgrims' negative feelings would burst to the surface. He was, in the end, surprised that they did not. In his notes, he explained this with reference to the sense of the commonality of fate experienced during the pilgrimage. When he looked back at his experiences, Sufian wrote this:

But those who bought a more expensive travel package still shared all experiences other than the hotel accommodation with the standard package group. Like everybody else, the higher-paying pilgrims spent several nights on the ground in the tent town of Mina and a night under the sky in Muzdalifah. There were other differences among the pilgrims, but they did not negate the prevailing sense of social equality under the Hajj. For example, some pilgrims from the United States and Europe had mattresses or sleeping bags when they had to sleep on the ground in Mina, but they still could not use them in Muzdalifah. One cannot buy anything in Muzdalifah and one has to share a precious bottle of water with others. In the end, the hajjis concurred that the differences between pilgrims of different socioeconomic standing were too small even to discuss them. Some pilgrims noted that the extra luxuries that the richest among the pilgrims could allow themselves during the Hajj – such as a more comfortable bed or sleeping arrangement – would be available to all other pilgrims for free once they returned home. Besides, most pilgrims questioned whether it would be good for them to have extra luxury, from the standpoint of their Hajj getting eventually validated by the Almighty.

As the participant observer noted in the diary and as the pilgrims reported in interviews and focus groups, the night in Muzdalifah was the most emotionally striking in this regard. Some said watching and being immersed in the sea of millions of people, all men in the same simple dress consisting of two white sheets (women could dress as they preferred), resembled a rehearsal of the Doomsday – when nobody would have any possessions, only their good or bad deeds, regardless of the wealth or power they accumulated over their lifetime. Overall, the dominance of these views among the pilgrims suggests the emergence of the shared understandings of commonality at the superordinate group level – i.e., humanity. In our case, these understandings related to greater socioeconomic diversity acceptance among the hajjis compared to the non-hajjis.

THE PILGRIMS' PARADOX THROUGH THE PRISM OF CONTENT ANALYSIS

These discussions left us with a strong sense that we were on to something important and counterintuitive. But what if a few particularly memorable statements distorted the broader view? To check on our perceptions, we carried out the most basic – but often the most revealing – form of content analysis. We transcribed all focus group discussions verbatim in Russian. The transcripts include translation into Russian of discussions that took place in Circassian (about 10 percent of the total volume). We then estimated the approximate proportion of discussion time in each group devoted to distinct substantive themes. As a proxy measure of the discussion duration, we used word counts in MS Word. We identified the themes in a two-stage process. First we generated *ex ante* (deductively) the key terms that would represent our topics of interest. As we coded the texts we supplemented them with terms identified inductively.[13] Whenever we added any term to the list inductively during the coding process, we made sure we also searched for that term in all group transcripts where we initially did not search for it. This way all terms were searched in all group transcripts.

We adhered to the basic coding procedure emphasizing clarity. On the first pass through the transcripts, we marked the text around each key terms identified according to the procedure just described as pertaining to each key topic (themes and subthemes). We marked paragraphs and strings of dialog on each theme as our principal coding units. Each of us read the marked passages and compared coding. The inter-coder reliability was above 95 percent and we recoded about 3 percent of the text volume. We coded each focus group transcript in its entirety, ensuring we had no indeterminate or omitted portions of the text, the inclusion of which in the word counts with a different code could substantively change the findings.[14] To minimize ambiguity and substantive bias, we did not code theme "valence" – i.e., the putatively positive, negative, or neutral attitude of participants on any given discussion topic. We ran word counts for each coding unit. To systematically compare each theme's salience across focus groups that lasted a different amount of time, we calculated each theme's percentage of the total discussion volume in each focus group.

The results offer a striking illustration of the Pilgrims' Paradox. The central theme among the pilgrims was the importance of the holiest sites of Islam, of its sacred center, and its global significance. It consumed about 45 percent of focus group discussion time. We made this estimate by tallying the length of segments on the following subthemes: (i) terms referring to Islam's sacred places, acts, and entities ("Mecca," "Medina," "Ka'aba," "Hajj," "Allah," "Prophet," "sacred," "blessed"); (ii) words pertaining to diversity and to the global significance associated with the Hajj ("diversity," "nations," country names, "world," "global," "Earth," "significant"); and (iii) words describing the performance of sacred rituals ("*Tawaf*," "experience" related to the Hajj, and "walking around" the Ka'aba). We excluded from the count some short discussion segments on travel and related logistics associated with performing the Hajj, such as arranging transportation or visa procedures.

Among the non-hajjis, this sacred center theme accounted for 16 percent of discussion time – almost three times less than among the hajjis.

The central theme among the non-pilgrims (68 percent of total discussion time) was the importance of the uniformity of Islam – particularly with respect to individual behavior and canons of faith. This is based on the discussion duration of three key subthemes identified with: (i) terms referring to elements of visual appearance or clothing (seen as pertinent with respect to observing the behavioral norms appropriate in Islam) (e.g., "hair," "dress," "beard," "shave," "hat," "skirt," "headscarf," "jewelry," "amulet"); (ii) terms referring to other religions and different schools within Islam (including "Shariah," "Shi'a," "*Madhhab*," "monotheism," "Bible," "Christian," "Jew," etc.); and (iii) references to the importance of Islamic worship relative to ethnicity and secular customs ("God-abiding," "tradition," "mountain" [people], "ethnic," "nationality," "Adyge," "Kabardian," "Balkar," "Circassian," "Russian," "Dagestani," etc.).

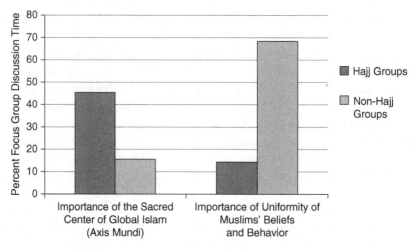

FIGURE 2.1   The Pilgrims' Paradox: Top Themes in Kabardino-Balkaria Focus
Groups (2010).

In sharp contrast, the hajjis devoted only 14 percent of their discussion
time to the importance of the uniformity of beliefs, appearance, and ritual
performance in Islam. Figure 2.1 illustrates the paradox – those Muslims
who experienced immediate proximity to the unifying sacred center of
Islam during the Hajj and who shared the pathos and deep feelings from
this experience, were significantly less likely than the non-pilgrims to talk
about the importance of maintaining the universal doctrinal and behavioral standards in Islam. And yet, one would expect that, having been
deeply impressed as they told us they were by the unifying symbols of
Islam, the hajjis could have conceivably spent *more* time on discussing
universal Islamic standards than the non-hajjis did. And thus our systematic observations and textual analyses flesh out what we call the Pilgrims'
Paradox, the central puzzle of our inquiry.

Of what, then, we asked ourselves, could this Paradox be an instance?
Just because our findings may confound popular stereotypes or fears of
government officials doesn't mean these findings are necessarily illogical.
Nor does it mean they simply confirm one or another established view.
And yet, the deeper we examined how they relate to broader theoretical
perspectives on intergroup perceptions and behavior and to earlier studies
of the Hajj's influence on individuals, the more confounding the Pilgrims'
Paradox appeared. In particular, we could not be satisfied with
a straightforward explanation of the Hajj effects implicit in the arguments

formulated by authors such as John Esposito – i.e., that by being benign and inclusive at its doctrinal core and by exposing individuals to diversity within Islam, the Hajj would contribute to more tolerance and prosocial views. After all, aside from the differences we identified here between the pilgrims and the non-pilgrims, we also recorded often passionate and long complaints that the pilgrims voiced about their experiences in the holy land. In particular, we were curious how these experiences and the result-ing hypothetical transformation of pilgrims may relate to broader beha-vioral theories – such as social identity, socialization, and instrumental motivation. Reevaluating our observations through the prism of these literatures revealed broader implications of the Muslim Pilgrims' Paradox in social theory that informs mainstream understandings and debates of intergroup relations and sociopolitical tolerance. We now examine how at the theoretical level the Pilgrims' Paradox highlights major controversies in interpreting the causes of intergroup conflict versus acceptance.

3

The Hajj as Social Identity and Social Capital

SOCIAL IDENTITY THREAT

Our principal findings confound popular views and prominent theories of identity that frequently expect intense religious experiences like the Hajj to promote in-group favoritism and out-group hostility. This perspective is rooted in closely related psychological theories of social identity and social categorization (SIT). Henri Tajfel and John C. Turner and their followers have found that identification with a common ingroup among individuals increases their in-group conformity – whereas it also increases their negative bias toward outgroups.[1] Other prominent psychologists and political scientists have established that the resulting intergroup bias tends to be particularly strong among higher-status group members and when mutual knowledge of common in-group membership increases.[2] Both of these conditions arguably reflect the essential elements of the Hajj experience – as we reported in Chapter 2, the sense of acquiring a higher social status of the hajji and the deeply emotional impressions of acquiring a deeper knowledge of common Islamic identity both increased considerably among the pilgrims. Psychological studies also cast doubt on optimistic and straightforward arguments – made by Islamic scholars such as John Esposito – that the Hajj would improve social tolerance through exposure of the pilgrims to sustained interactions with and to learning about other Muslims and about the heterogeneity within Islam. Yet, psychologists have shown that exposure to diversity in its own right may have negative effects, undermining tolerance. Juan M. Falomir-Pichastor and Natasha S. Frederic's research published in the *Journal of Experimental Social Psychology* found that learning about one's common group heterogeneity increases the sense of common group weakness and insecurity – and thus contributes to intergroup prejudices.[3]

In comparative politics and international relations, this logic has been used to explain how religion fuels violent intergroup and inter-state conflict. In a historical-interpretative analysis that continues to significantly influence academic and policy debates despite lethal conceptual flaws,[4] Samuel Huntington argued that global patterns of religious identities would make a "clash of civilizations" the principal driving force in world politics after the Cold War.[5] A detailed comparative analysis of mass violent conflict in Africa and Asia over most of the twentieth century led Donald Horowitz to conclude in his seminal book, *Ethnic Groups in Conflict*, that intergroup bias – the human tendency "to cleave and compare" – across ethnic and religious lines was an essential driver of mass violence dynamics.[6] Other scholars argued that religious markers were particularly strong drivers of us-versus-them bias. Religious norms, as Durkheim contended, produce stronger common identities than nonreligious norms because they offer individuals deliverance from evil and raise them above the mundane.[7] Group religious identity is also arguably stronger than individual religious identities. Harvard legal scholar Jeffrey Seul, in a detailed review of studies of religion, group identity, and conflict, offers a cogent explanation:

Each of the world's major religious traditions sacralizes group identity to an equal or even greater extent than individual identity. The ecclesia or Body of Christ (Christianity), the Ummah (Islam) and the Sangha (Buddhism) are notions central to their respective traditions. Whether many or few, liberally or narrowly construed, and strictly or minimally enforced, each tradition has some means by which it determines the boundaries of the group. Doctrines of salvation and chosenness, for example, provide ready in-group/out-group distinctions.[8]

This particular argument implies that the important aspect of a religious ritual such as the Hajj is not what it stands for from the viewpoint of Islamic doctrine and not its visual demonstration of the diversity of Islam, but that it *behaviorally* reinforces the *perceptual* intergroup boundaries. And that reinforcement, from the standpoint of SIT, is of crucial significance. Again, in this sense Seul confounds the notion that any religion or religious ritual – including Islam and the Hajj and notwithstanding the authority of scholars such as Esposito – could through *its content alone* significantly change social orientations of individual Muslims toward greater intergroup tolerance.

The same fundamental intergroup logic would apply in debates on Islam and democracy in political science and beyond. Summarizing the arguments implicit in research on fundamentalism as to why religious identity would undermine sociopolitical tolerance, a prominent specialist on religion and politics, political scientist Anthony Gill, noted: "Compromise and tolerance constitute essential values in functioning democracies. Religion, on the other hand, deals in absolute truths."[9] In other words, the harder any religious in-group identity of an individual, the less likely that individual would accept compromise and tolerance as important values in society and politics.

These arguments are borne out in a large body of quantitative analyses. In 2010, social psychologists Deborah Hall, David Matz, and Wendy Wood published a meta-analysis – a systematic statistical assessment of previous research – that comprised fifty-five independent studies with 22,075 participants in the prestigious *Personality and Social Psychology Review*. The results weighed on the side of earlier findings that strong religious in-group identity promotes racism and ethnocentrism.[10] Pippa Norris and Ronald Inglehart, in their book *Sacred and Secular: Religion and Politics Worldwide*, showed with comparative analysis of opinion survey data across most of the world religions in seventy-one countries that religiosity – associated with performing religious rituals – enhanced conservative values and ethnocentrism.[11] A multidisciplinary team of thirteen social scientists from Arizona State University and one from Albion College conducted a study of 194 ethnic, religious, national, and other groups in ninety-seven countries accounting for 79 percent of the world's population as part of their Global Group Relations Project. They found that "religious infusion" – i.e., the prominence of religious identity discourses in a society (indicative of intergroup religious divisions) – promoted prejudice and discrimination across social groups. The project's particularly notable finding was that in countries with high levels of religious infusion, socioeconomically disadvantaged groups were significantly more likely than in countries with low levels of religious infusion to act with aggression against resource-rich and powerful social groups – and to do so even when acting with aggression incurred significant and tangible costs to the disadvantaged groups.[12]

In comparative politics, empirical research – much of it drawing on event and opinion data – also indicates that religion erases an important behavioral barrier to organized intergroup conflict. Crucially, from the political science standpoint – as Matthias Basedau, Birte Pfeiffer, and Johannes Vüllers showed in a 2014 *Journal of Conflict Resolution* article – religious identity overcomes the collective action problem. By offering a stronger sense of in-group commonality, religion offers motivation to act for a common cause. This reinforces the sense of group divisions within a society and, hence, intergroup bias. Group mobilization for violent conflict is then more likely to occur.[13] Studies by scholars such as Jonathan Fox, Susanna Pearce, and Isak Svensson – mostly based on comparative statistical analysis of conflict data from around the world – have shown that fighting over religious ideas makes armed conflicts typically longer and deadlier.[14] Monica Duffy Toft, in a 2007 *International Security* journal article, developed this argument with specific reference to Islam. One of Toft's principal explanations as to why Islamists were more likely than representatives of other religions to get involved in religious civil wars between 1940 and 2000 *de facto* emphasizes the divisive effects of in-group commonality along the lines developed in psychology and political science – namely, the scarcity of religion-based wars *within* Islam analogous to the seventeenth century's Thirty Years' War in Europe.[15]

Uncertainty about the position of religious groups in politics also reinforces intergroup bias – particularly through intergroup conflict over power and resources, as Ann Bettencourt, Kelly Chapman, Nancy Dorr, and Deborah Hume showed with a meta-analysis of psychological research.[16] Other authors, notably John T. Sidel in his book *Riots, Pogroms, Jihad: Religious Violence in Indonesia*, showed that such bias-producing conflicts emerge through social networks within government institutions and through transnational religious networks affecting government distributional preferences.[17] Political scientists Sascha Helbardt, Dagmar Hellmann-Rajanayagam, and Rudiger Korff, in a case study of Sri Lanka, showed that "religionization of politics" – i.e., the hardening of political viewpoints around religious intergroup biases – engendered social intolerance and conflict.[18] And Jonathan Fox, in a 2006 article in *Comparative Political Studies*, found that one tangible measure of such religionization of politics – government involvement in religion – was on an upward global trend from 1990 to 2002. This, he showed, was particularly the case in countries with Muslim majorities.[19] Other studies found sociopolitical intolerance linked to "theocratic" values – a fusion of motivations ostensibly arising both from intergroup bias and privileged group position.[20] Motivation to avoid uncertainty and increase the sense of comfort about one's place in society – strongly associated with religion in many studies – could also add to intergroup bias.[21]

Several contributors to *The Oxford Handbook of Religion and Violence* argued that religious intergroup bias has deep roots in the evolution of human societies. Religious identity, from the evolutionary standpoint, is essential to the fitness and survival of individuals and societies. Historical and anthropological analyses show that certain rituals are costly signals of commitment to ingroup commonality or group unity. They are critical for human groups to stay cohesive and survive competition for power and resources in multi-group settings.[22] Religious identity would, in this sense, serve to overcome the collective action problem, as Basedau, Pfeiffer, and Vüllers and other political scientists have argued.

Thus, from the SIT perspective and related theoretical and empirical studies across social scientists, one would expect more devout Muslims to be less sociopolitically tolerant.

* * *

Empirical investigations in social sciences and humanities of the Hajj's impacts on individual believers have also been consistent with these arguments in important respects. The Hajj has been shown to significantly boost common in-group religious identity among the pilgrims. In a 2008 survey of 1,605 respondents in Pakistan, Clingingsmith, Khwaja, and Kremer found important systematic differences between the pilgrims and the non-pilgrims. The pilgrims came across as more openly religious, assertive of their Islamic identity and practices. They were more likely to identify themselves as "a religious person," to recite the Qur'an, to report performing all five daily prayers and the supererogatory night (*Tahajjud*) prayer, to participate in religious commemorations, and to fast not only during the obligatory month of Ramadan, but also at other times.[23] In his ethnographic analysis of second-generation Bengali immigrants in London, Daniel Nilsson DeHanas found a stronger commitment to Islam among those who had performed the Hajj.[24]

The Hajj has also been shown to raise a Muslim's social status. A 2007 Gallup survey of Muslims in Russia found very few performed the Hajj, yet most strongly desired to do so. Whereas only 5 percent of Russia's Muslims in that poll said they had performed the pilgrimage, more than 52 percent of those who had not ranked their desire to go on the Hajj at the maximum possible level – five on a five-point scale.[25]

Other studies – albeit outside Islam – illustrate how pilgrimages may help to overcome collective action problems. Anthropologists John Kantner and Kevin J. Vaughn showed through archeological analysis that in the pre-state Chaco Canyon region of the U.S. Southwest and in Cahuachi in Peru's Nasca region, sacral pilgrimages were valued as costly signals of commitment to religious systems and beliefs. In that manner they maintained common group unity.[26]

Historical record also contains SIT-consistent evidence that Hajj experiences could increase social alienation – or, at the very least, a withdrawal from civic engagement – among older pilgrims. The nineteenth-century Russian government observer Davletshin, tasked to record the impact of the Hajj on Muslims, reported:

Typically, old people appear retarded and indifferent to their surroundings. They pursue only the end goal of the journey and blindly perform all the Hajj rites down to the minutest details. Even in the Bedouin robberies they see some kind of impenetrable mystery and devil's curse designed only to thwart their performance of holy rites. They view all sanitary precautions as totally unnecessary, because, they feel, no one cannot escape their destiny. ... After they get back home, they turn into very pious *Sufis*, if they were not so before, and often they devote the rest of their lives exclusively to prayer and remove themselves from mundane chores.[27]

* * *

And yet, our empirical findings reported in Chapter 2 indicate that an increase in Muslim religiosity after the Hajj need not be automatically associated with support for uniformity of Islamic beliefs or behavior or with attitudes toward other religions or toward the secular state. Studies of socialization in religious practice have, in fact, established that participation in religious rituals may reduce out-group hostility.

SOCIAL CAPITAL HOPE

Social capital theory goes a long way to explaining why Muslims after the Hajj may be more tolerant toward outsiders. To be human is to socialize. In order to forge and secure identity, to overcome collective action problems, to defend and enhance one's group position, to send costly signals of commitment to common group identity, people need to socialize. From this perspective, religion would matter not so much on account of its beliefs or rites or symbols and their innate meaning, but on account of promoting sociability, social contact, civic skills, trust, and civic engagement.[28] Sociability – social skills, trust, and norms – stands to increase intergroup contact. The latter is likely to undermine intergroup anxieties and biases. In a 2006 meta-analysis of 515 independent studies across social science disciplines – using statistical techniques to assess the aggregate thrust of their findings – sociologists Thomas Pettigrew and Linda Tropp established that intergroup contact reduced intergroup prejudice across ethnic, racial, and religious divides.[29] Through a sweeping analysis of historical data on social interactions, political scientist Robert Putnam in *Bowling Alone* concluded that in the United States, church attendance was "arguably the most important repository of social capital."[30] While varying by denomination and racial/ethnic identification, religious participation has been found to be a consistent and robust predictor of nonreligious civic participation among North America's Christians. Individuals who had greater contact with other social groups within a church or a religious association appear more likely to socialize with other social groups in civic associations or other forums.[31] With mass surveys and in-depth ethnographic analysis, Robert Putnam and David Campbell demonstrated how familial and social networks simultaneously supported the growth of both religious commitment and religious pluralism in the United States from the 1960s to the early 2000s.[32] This concurrent rise of religiosity and pluralism would confound the SIT, but it suggests that the socialization and networking that are part of the Hajj experience would go a long way toward explaining the Muslim Pilgrims' Paradox. In particular, writing in *American Behavioral Scientist*, Andrew Greeley theorized religion as a source of social capital. Using World Values Survey data, Greeley found that respondents who attended religious services more frequently were also more likely than others to volunteer for religious and secular projects.[33] Political scientist Ani Sarkissian, using World Values Survey data from Albania (2002), Bangladesh (2002), Burkina Faso (2007), Egypt (2008), Indonesia (2006), Jordan (2007), Kyrgyzstan (2003), Mali (2007), and Turkey (2007), found that Muslims who reported being active in their religious organizations – mosques, charities, and Sufi brotherhoods – were more likely than other Muslims to join secular associations (such as sport or recreational groups; art, music, or educational organizations; labor unions; political parties; environmental organizations; professional associations; and humanitarian or charitable associations); to sign public petitions; and to attend demonstrations.[34]

Consonant with these findings are in-depth qualitative analyses by Robert W. Hefner and by Fawaz A. Gerges of the rise of "civil Islam" – showing how voluntary Islamic religious associations have been instrumental to strengthening a general public culture of tolerance in Indonesia and the Arab world.[35] Alfred Stepan, meanwhile, demonstrated how recurrent, public, and reciprocal "rituals of respect" – a form of socialization implying social capital building – contributed to improving relations between religious groups in Senegal, particularly among the Sufis and the Catholics.[36] In contemporary Europe, Agnieszka Halemba found that transnational Christian pilgrimages had promoted "cosmopolitan sociability."[37] In the United States, sociologists Charles Kurzman, David Schanzer, and Ebrahim Moosa carried out 120 in-depth interviews with Muslims in Seattle, Houston, Buffalo, and Raleigh/Durham. They found that community-building – understood as "protecting Muslim-Americans' rights, deepening community members' faith, and spreading the message of Islam to non-Muslims" – reduced radicalization among Muslim community members. It was one of the explanations as to why Islamist terrorism in the United States had been rare.[38]

Consistent with the social capital perspective, Clingingsmith, Khwaja, and Kremer, in their 2008 Pakistan survey that we mentioned earlier, found that through the Hajj Muslims generally improved their views of other schools of law within Islam. They downplayed the importance of uniformity in Islam, identified in-group strength with heterogeneity, and exhibited a stronger sense of individuality.[39] The pilgrims in that survey were statistically more likely than the non-pilgrims to express tolerant views toward non-Islamic religions, such as Judaism and Christianity. Male Muslim pilgrims also turned out to be more inclusive toward women than male Muslim non-pilgrims. Moreover, individual differences in the intensity of religious practices – such as prayer – during the Hajj did not explain increased tolerance toward other religions and social out-groups in general. This strongly suggested that socialization rather than religiosity accounted for the positive effects of the Hajj on tolerance. One finding was especially telling of the effects of social capital. Those Pakistanis who performed the pilgrimage in groups of smaller size – which increased opportunities and the incentives to socialize with people outside their group – came across in the survey as significantly more cognizant of religious diversity, gender inequality, and international developments than those who performed the pilgrimage in larger groups. (Typically, group size varied between two and twenty people).[40]

Similar findings emerged in Methal Mohammed-Marzouk's content analysis of narratives chronicling the experiences of the pilgrimage to Mecca of three medieval Muslim luminaries – Nasir Khasraw (1004–1077), Ibn Jubayr (1145–1217), and Ibn Battuta (1304–1378). The study was published in *Cross-Cultural Communication*, a well-regarded peer-reviewed journal. The three luminaries represented different times and social and cultural backgrounds, as well as Islamic religious schools and philosophies. After the Hajj, all three reported feeling greater pride in their religious identity as Muslims – just as the SIT would have predicted. Along with that, they all more strongly advocated peaceful relations among Muslims, Christians, and Jews – just as the social capital theory would have predicted.[41] Mohammed-Marzouk's findings suggest that the benign effects of the Hajj cannot be predominantly attributed to late twentieth-century globalization and cosmopolitanism.

Finally, our ethnographic and sociological research – based on focus groups and interviews in the North Caucasus in 2008–2010 and the participant observation of the pilgrimage in 2009 – indicated that the hajjis had more positive views of diverse groups within Islam and of other religions than the non-hajjis who strongly aspired to do the pilgrimage. At the same time, the participant observation of the Hajj showed that the pilgrims socialized extensively and with interest. When Mikhail asked Sufian what he felt was more important to the hajjis based on his participant observation of the pilgrimage and the interviews – socializing with other pilgrims or personal introspection – Sufian replied without hesitation: "Socializing." The response conveyed Sufian's impressions during participant observation of the Hajj as well as his general sense of his Hajj diaries and our in-depth interviews with the pilgrims.

SOCIAL CAPITAL AMBIGUITIES AND CONTROVERSIES

As a theoretical explanation of the Pilgrims' Paradox, however, social capital falls short. In particular, it is unclear *how* socialization during the Hajj may generate the benign impacts on social tolerance and civic engagement that we observed in our interviews and focus groups and that other scholars found with different research methods. This socialization has specific conditions. The pilgrims practically never contact and network with non-Muslims. Most social capital accumulates within relatively small ethno-regional hajji travel groups. Historically, the interaction of in-group cohesion and out-group hostility could be detected in one of the rituals of the Hajj. While performing *Tawaf* – the seven circles around the Ka'aba – the pilgrims walk faster on the eastern, northern, and southern sides of the Ka'aba and slow down on the western side. That was how the first Muslim pilgrims performed *Tawaf*. The reason for this was because, during the first Hajj led by the Prophet, a group of unfriendly Meccan citizens gathered across the eastern corner of the Ka'aba. While in the sight of non-Muslim Meccans, the Prophet encouraged his followers to walk faster and more energetically in order to intimidate the hostile spectators; while on the western side of the Ka'aba, concealed from the eyes of spectators, the Prophet allowed his followers a leisurely pace, in order to relax and prepare for the faster pace again as soon as they became exposed to the spectators on the eastern side of the Ka'ba. Social networks emerging from the Hajj do not engender almost everyday community socialization the way the familial and social networks did in the United States that Putnam and Campbell analyzed.[42] Socialization during the Hajj is not necessarily as cosmopolitan as it may appear. In fact, it may exacerbate hostility along the cumulative cleavages of ethnicity, nationality, and faith. An American ethnographer and hajji, Carol Delaney, made this point starkly: "The duality exists in the heart of Mecca. ... the various national contingents and their local constituents are housed and guided through the rituals and sacred territory separately. Such segregation erodes the theme of unity and brotherhood as it heightens national differences that exploded in Mecca in July 1987 when a group of Iranians (who are Shiites) began making inflammatory remarks and allegedly attacked Sunni Muslims. The resulting riot left more than 400 people dead."[43] Sufian observed and experienced much of this duality and ethno-regional limitations on socialization during his 2009 Hajj.

Social capital theory has a problem explaining how these dualities and limitations of socialization during the Hajj might still translate into benign prosocial impacts on the pilgrims. The principal ambiguities and controversies are reflected in two unresolved debates. The first one is whether religious social capital translates into secular social capital. On the one hand, Ani Sarkissian and Andrew Greeley's studies with World Values Surveys and some of the 2008 Pakistan survey findings that we discussed previously show that socialization in religious settings is conducive to social tolerance and secular civic engagement. On the other hand, Putnam, in his path-breaking 2000 book, *Bowling Alone*, concluded that people active in religious organizations were not more likely than others, on average, to participate in community projects. In other words, social capital is obtained differently in religious and secular settings. As Putnam reported, the former translated into "volunteering for ushering in church or visiting shut-in parishioners," the latter into volunteering "to work on cleaning up the local playground."[44] At issue here is the internal consistency of social capital theory. If socialization is the principal behavioral micro foundation of social capital, as Putnam appears to have argued at a more general level, its effects should be observed across social settings regardless of their content or context. But if social capital is split along the religious–secular divide, it means something other than socialization has a stronger impact.

Two issues compound the ambiguities arising from this debate. Sarkissian, for one, found that whether Muslims attend religious services (most notably, the Friday prayer at a local mosque) at least once a week or less than once a week had no significant impact on their likelihood to join secular associations, sign petitions, or participate in demonstrations.[45] This at the very least suggests that socialization during or around religious rituals may be inconsequential for social capital. Second, a survey of 1,695 individuals in Norway conducted by the Norwegian Centre of Research in Organization and Management in 1998 as part of the Johns Hopkins Comparative Nonprofit Sector Project found that the number of hours per week individuals participated or volunteered in public associations had no statistically significant impact on their proclivity for civic engagement (voting, reading the news, and expressing interest in politics).[46] At the same time, the number of associations an individual joined significantly improved civic engagement. But if passive membership is as good as active membership in predicting civic engagement, then social capital could obtain without its putative behavioral micro foundation – face-to-face socialization. If so, socialization during the Hajj would not explain the Pilgrims' Paradox.

The second debate is whether religious socialization content – as reflected in denominational differences – significantly affects social capital. Again, if socialization is all about building face-to-face social skills, denominational differences should not be significant. But many studies find that they are. However, the findings are hardly conclusive. On the one hand, some studies have found different levels of civic engagement associated with different denominations. In *Sacred and Secular*, Norris and Ingelhart show with cross-national analysis of survey data that religious participation is related to more secular public participation among Buddhists, Jews, Hindus, and Protestants, but not among Catholics, Orthodox Christians, and Muslims.[47] On the other hand, membership in the same denomination can be associated with different levels of civic engagement. Eric Patterson found evangelical Protestantism to be positively associated with civic and political engagement in Chile and Brazil.[48] David Campbell, however, found that in the United States, evangelical Protestants' participation in their churches reduced the time they socialized in a secular community.[49]

The knowledge gap in these debates is fundamentally about social capital transitivity. To what extent and what conditions are communication skills, interpersonal contact, trust, understanding, and other components of social capital obtained in one context transferrable to other contexts? This question needs to be addressed systematically in order to explain the Pilgrims' Paradox. We will do this in Chapter 5. For now, we need to take into account another major theoretical interpretation of the Hajj impacts that draws on different behavioral micro foundations than SIT or social capital theories.

INSTRUMENTALIST DILEMMAS

The third view is that identity is predominantly a product of interest. Therefore, religious identity is sociopolitically marginal or epiphenomenal. The putative effects of religious practice and beliefs could be an instance of something else, something outside religion. This view is deeply grounded in the secularist tradition in the social sciences hearkening back to Freud, Marx, Nietzsche, Voltaire, and Weber.[50] More recently, scholars using statistical analysis of the large number of cases observed over decades of multiyear data have marshaled considerable evidence showing that intergroup conflicts, such as civil wars, are most likely to arise due to material incentives, opportunity to act, and weak government regardless of ethnic or religious identity differences.[51] Surveys in Croatia after the Yugoslavia wars of the 1990s found that ethnic intolerance and religiosity were jointly determined by the sense of competition for scarce resources.[52] Data from the Middle East have indicated that avowedly religion-based suicide terrorism is embedded in the "strategic logic" where the key drivers are material gain, action-retaliation, and organized campaigning.[53] The religious economics school – though it recognizes the importance of religion in politics – focuses more on how institutions (rules of the game) in society shape individual religious identities.[54]

As one illustration of these arguments in the North Caucasus, one may consider the advisories the local religious leaders routinely issue to prospective pilgrims that the Hajj is not a form of tourism or entertainment and that it cannot be a conduit for commercial activity – or, in fact, any activity serving individual material gratification.[55] In ethnographic literature, one finds an exemplar of the instrumental logic in Susan O'Brien's research of the *bori* women from northern Nigeria. Being predominantly animist, a significant number of them had embarked on the Hajj to make money by selling sex and healing services in Saudi Arabia. Upon return, they also benefited by claiming the respect due their hajjiah status among Nigeria's Muslims. In other words, these women's motivations for pilgrimage were primarily economic gain and social status rather than religious identity.[56] Whereas the social capital resulting from the Hajj as a religious experience also played a role in promoting tolerance among

Muslims and the animist-Muslim (hybrid) believers, O'Brien's account suggests those could be no more than random side effects.

Views of the Hajj as epiphenomenal with respect to religious identity have been particularly common in the popular media and among policy-makers. This particularly concerns representations of the Hajj as an organizational platform for insurgency and terrorism. Security experts in the United States have argued that the Hajj provides radical Islamist groups with unparalleled opportunities to indoctrinate Muslims and recruit militants. Stratfor, a consulting firm with significant corporate and government clients around the world, speculated in a 2007 assessment that the Hajj gave Al Qaeda "an opportunity for representatives from all of its regional and affiliated groups to meet" without being monitored and also gave the Hamas radicals "a chance to meet with operatives and supporters from the United States and Europe." Militants, arguably, "may also use the Hajj as an excuse to relocate operatives for future operations." Finally, the Hajj "opens up the opportunity for militant groups to engage in fundraising." Stratfor referred to intelligence reports that "wealthy donors from Saudi Arabia and other countries literally provide bags of cash to representatives of militant groups." More importantly from the standpoint of this study, the Stratfor analysis suggested that socialization during the Hajj is a convenient cover for the indoctrination and recruitment of radicals – arranged as part of social mixing with "prominent Muslim politicians, jurists, theologians and militant leaders." The analysis pointed to the Bin Laden family as instrumental in organizing such socialization by hosting "hundreds of foreign pilgrims at their family homes during the Hajj season."[57] Echoing these security concerns, the official FBI webpage associated the Hajj with Osama Bin Laden by listing "the Hajj" as one of the latter's nicknames (most likely in error, instead of the hajji, or pilgrim).[58]

Throughout history, governments have feared – along the lines of the Stratfor report – that the Hajj was a channel of social support for insurgency, rebellions, and terrorism directed against non-Muslims and secular states. The British imperial government in the nineteenth century and the Dutch government along with Dutch-owned shipping conglomerates in the 1920s and 1930s put the pilgrims under control and surveillance in fear that religious networks would expose their subjects to anti-imperial and pan-Islamic ideas.[59] These apprehensions surged worldwide after 9/11. American television networks introduced discussions of new security threats with problematic representations of Islam, including footage of thousands of Muslims circling the sacred Ka'aba in Mecca interspersed with footage of Osama Bin Laden and armed jihadi fighters. Governments in England, India, and Russia suspected the hajjis (those who performed the Hajj) of spreading militant Islamist views and boosting social support for terrorism after 9/11.[60] A decade after the attacks on the World Trade Center – in which the majority of suicide bombers came from the Kingdom of Saudi Arabia (KSA) – security was a big issue during the Hajj. In 2011, the government of Saudi Arabia deployed approximately 63,000 security personnel, including 3,500 anti-riot police backed by 450 armored vehicles. The civil defense deployed 22,000 forces and 6,000 vehicles. Some 1,500 CCTV cameras have been installed in and around Mecca's Grand Mosque and twenty-nine police stations are open to serve the holy places. Some 20,000 health care workers were mobilized to cope with any emergency and five rescue helicopters also have been readied to serve the faithful.[61]

And, as we noted earlier, history abounds with illustrations of non-religious motivations driving the Hajj pilgrimage. During the Russian conquest of the North Caucasus in the nineteenth century, dozens of thousands of local residents fled and resettled in the Ottoman Empire under the pretext of performing the hajj. In some local villages, the entire population expressed the desire to undertake the pilgrimages. Not only did whole families make the pilgrimage together, as they had done in the past, but they also sold their homes and belongings, before leaving. One example of entire hometown doing the Hajj was the *aul* of hajji Kaisyn Shogenov, the former chief *qadi* of Kabarda – a prominent Circassian ethnic subgroup in the central part of the North Caucasus.[62] Even though most Hajj pilgrims at present are not refugees from violent conflict, cases such as this support the instrumentalist view in principle.

One strong – and not immediately obvious – reason we found to consider the epiphenomenal perspective came from within our own study. Sufian confronted a major personal dilemma when he performed the Hajj in 2009. If he totally devoted himself to the Hajj, he would commit the academic fallacy of "going native" during participant observation. This would be a lethal flaw in research methodology, jeopardizing the validity of inferences drawn from his experiences. However, if he stayed aloof, thinking and acting first and foremost as a scholar, could he then regard himself as a legitimate holy pilgrim? Would that make his Hajj invalid? And so he faithfully recorded in his Hajj diary how this dilemma made him feel – in fact, how it tormented and anguished him.

As we reread the diary, it became clear that the sincerity of intentions dilemma he emotionally described was not only a result of his dual role as a scholar and a pilgrim, but also something that every pilgrim experienced in different ways and with different intensity. One could think of the sincerity of intentions dilemma as a manifestation of the fear of epiphenomenality – i.e., fear that no matter how hard a pilgrim tries, one's efforts would never be enough to meet the high standards of the fundamental holy ritual such as the Hajj. Many hajjis we interviewed confessed that they performed (or wanted to perform) a second pilgrimage because they were not satisfied with how they did it the first time. It is, however, precisely this fear, angst, and self-tormenting that probably serve as the best cognitive and emotional evidence that the Hajj experiences are not epiphenomenal at the individual level. For this reason, we reproduce next the relevant excerpt from Sufian's Hajj diary. In the text, translated from the original Russian, he refers to himself as "Participant Observer" and to Mikhail as "Analytic Observer."

The problem of combining both religious and academic interests during the Hajj was a personal one for the Participant Observer and we had no intention at first to include it in our research. However, we discovered during our research that many other pilgrims questioned themselves regarding the sincerity of their intentions, as well.

The pilgrim usually attempts to separate the sacred from the profane in his/her worldview. There is a common vision among the pilgrims from the Caucasus of the Hajj as an event that is supposed to change their life dramatically. Many pilgrims regarded the Hajj as crossing some kind of Rubicon, after which they would give up sinning under the fear that every sin would be magnified seventy times. Such a myth has nothing to do with classic Islam, yet it is quite common among those Muslims who never performed the Hajj. However, during the pilgrimage, everybody discovers as self-evident that his/her worldview comprised one whole system that could not be separated into the sacred and profane without negatively affecting the person's mental health. Therefore, every pilgrim faces the problem of how to combine the "sacred" goal of the Hajj with the "profane" goals that arise inevitably as part of the pilgrimage. Since the beginning of Islam, merchants have brought with them goods for trade in Mecca while performing the Hajj and brought goods from Mecca to sell them back home; the leaders of pilgrim groups usually act as agents representing tourist companies that organize the Hajj the same way as any tourism abroad is organized; journalists have written articles and created documentaries while performing the pilgrimage; many pilgrims keep diaries in order later to write and publish their memoirs, etc. While those cases are the most obvious examples of "profane" motives during the "sacred" Hajj, they represent a broader pattern of rearrangement of values when the "sacred" includes the "profane," when the worldview changes from secular into religious colors.

In the Participant Observer's case, departing for the pilgrimage, he kept asking himself if his Hajj could be considered valid and ever be accepted by God if academic research was his initial primary goal; would he be able to focus on his own spiritual issues if instead of religious practice, prayers, and spiritual reflection he would spend most of his time observing and communicating with other pilgrims? At the time of departure, the Participant Observer felt so much guilt build up inside him that the problem of sincerity of intentions troubled him in earnest. He was to perform the Hajj for the first and maybe the last time in his life, which implied that his motivation issue would likely come up quite dramatically after his death. This troubled the Participant Observer to such a degree that he considered whether he should terminate his academic research and devote himself entirely to the Hajj.

Only one issue gave him pause – the Analytical Observer paid for his Hajj tour, worth 3,800 USD. The Participant Observer faced a moral problem that it would be dishonest to use his colleague's money for his personal goals and to later admit he did not do the job. This is not to mention also that such dishonesty would absolutely be incompatible with the religious meaning of the Hajj itself. The Participant Observer contemplated if he could resolve the problem by paying back the Analytical Observer after the Hajj. However, he dismissed that as well, on one hand, because such a unilateral termination of existing agreement was also dishonest, and on the other hand, because, knowing his colleague well, he could predict that the Analytical Observer would not agree to take his money back. Thus, the Participant Observer would have no other choice but to carry on with the project, which would suffer significantly if he would not do his share of work during the pilgrimage. The very fact that the Participant Observer was performing the pilgrimage paid by somebody else represented a problem of its own, though later he learned that it did not go against the rules of the Hajj and was an allowed and rather common practice. Yet, at first, he was absolutely sure that it would present problems.

The Participant Observer's inner struggle increased even more after he lost all communication with the Analytical Observer during the pilgrimage. As part of our plan, we intended to exchange emails regularly and started doing that before the Participant Observer's departure. He was writing to the Analytical Observer about his observations during the preparations to the Hajj who in his turn was commenting and raising questions helping to make the participant observation deeper. However, upon arrival in Medina, the Participant Observer failed to find an Internet connection as he had hoped and could not establish communication with the Analytical Observer. On top of that, the Participant Observer left his laptop's charger at home and could not use his laptop for a while until he bought a charger in Medina. In the pseudo-mystical environment of the pilgrimage, the Participant Observer kept wondering if all these problems might be some kind of a sign, indicating that he should stop his research and focus on the salvation of his soul. Only strong personal rejection of superstition prevented the Participant Observer from regarding these "signs" as worthy to take into consideration.

Also other people during and mostly after the pilgrimage kept challenging the Participant Observer with a direct and rather rude question: "Did you perform the Hajj or conduct research after all?" Remarkably enough, only those who never performed the Hajj raised that question, while the hajjis never saw a contradiction in conducting other activities alongside the pilgrimage. Such a different approach toward the problem of sacred and profane between those who did and did not perform pilgrimage could be one of the indications of how the Hajj affects people.

Rethinking Sufian's experiences made us realize that through resolving these dilemmas the pilgrims could arrive at a cognitive and emotional balance between the sacred and the secular within themselves. In fact, as Sufian found in an interview with Ahmed Farid Moustafa, an Islamic education activist and retired architect living in Medina, the appreciation of this balance hearkens back to the origins of the Hajj as a foundational ritual in Islam: "The Qur'an says firstly that the objective of the Hajj is that we have worldly benefit from it. Number two is to remember Allah Subhana Tahala and thank Him. Normally the Qur'an should have said first to remember Allah. But He means that the Hajj is a worldly affair. . . . We should feel the brotherhood of all mankind. We have people [of all races] coming from Africa, Europe, China, Latin America, and from everywhere. And you feel the brotherhood of mankind during the Hajj." Developing this idea of the balance between the sacred and the secular in the conceptualization of the Hajj, Ahmed Moustafa mentioned that a former minister of the Hajj of the Kingdom of Saudi Arabia, Ildus-sheikh Kutbi, proposed to establish social forums among professionals during the Hajj: "Muslim engineers could get together to exchange ideas; Muslim educationalists could get together to exchange ideas and to develop exchange programs; medical professionals could get together to promote knowledge and improve their tools. . . . These people have to come to exchange goods, knowledge, culture, and everything. That is the main thing according to the Qur'an."

*** ***

In summary, at the heart of the Pilgrims' Paradox as we defined it, is the concomitant rise of in-group pride (speaking to the logic of the social identity) and out-group tolerance (speaking to the logic of social capital). The paradox in theoretical terms is double-edged, drawing on but also challenging both of these underlying core perspectives. As far as the SIT is concerned, one wonders what could conceivably prompt more devout Muslims to become more sociopolitically tolerant as a result of the pilgrimage. How could fervor be a path to moderation? As far as theories of social capital and intergroup, one may wonder why the pilgrims would specifically develop tolerance toward non-Muslims, since during the Hajj the pilgrims rarely, if ever socially interact with them. Finally, both parts of the Pilgrims' Paradox defy the instrumentalist interpretation – if the rituals are epiphenomenal, it is hard to explain either the strengthening of religiosity *or* the increase in social tolerance following the pilgrimage.

PART II

THE HAJJ MODEL OF SOCIAL TOLERANCE

Preview: Keys to the Pilgrims' Paradox

One way to develop a solution for the Pilgrims' Paradox would be to argue that social capital and intergroup contact outweigh intergroup bias. At the theoretical level, however, such mechanistic argument would run into a major conceptual challenge of weighting *ex ante* the putative effects of social capital versus intergroup bias. It means, among other things, defining in abstract terms – qualitatively or quantitatively – how any given increment in the principal social capital measures would correspond to any given increment in the principal intergroup bias measures. It means, in turn, developing a generalizable theoretical basis for justifying this putative correspondence. For instance, it would mean justifying why, say, a one-unit increase on some X-point civic engagement scale is equivalent to a one-unit decrease on some Y-point religious group distance scale. We have not uncovered such theoretical justifications. Besides, the "outweighing" argument would face empirical challenges in interpreting the specific impacts of the Hajj experiences on pilgrims – e.g., how much and what kind of sociability would overcome the surge of common in-group pride and why would sociability matter in the context of ethnonational tour group segregation? And so it appeared unlikely to us that any mono-causal solution to the Pilgrims' Paradox could reconcile the conflicting theoretical claims and related empirical controversies.

Instead, we pursued a synthetic approach to explain why social capital effects obtain despite their seemingly transient nature and despite the allegedly strong intergroup bias counter-effects during the Hajj. Generalizing from our Hajj experiences and fieldwork in the North Caucasus, we developed a model of intergroup tolerance improvement. We present it in this part of the book. We start with Mircea Eliade's sociology of the sacred and profane to assess the identity implications of

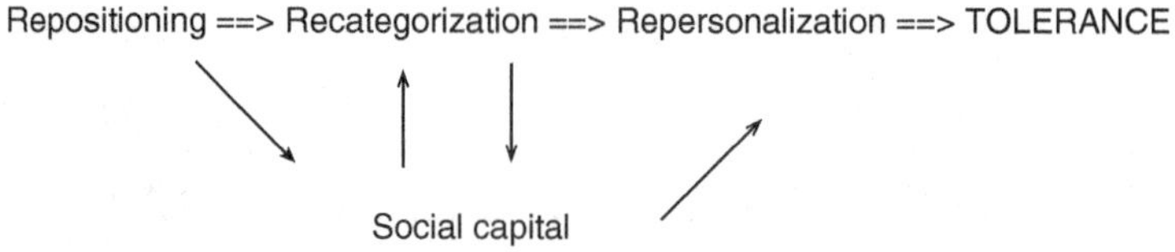

Repositioning ==> Recategorization ==> Repersonalization ==> TOLERANCE

Social capital

FIGURE 4.1 The Hajj Model of Tolerance Improvement.

the Hajj as physical and symbolic *repositioning*.[1] Second, we examine why the resulting *recategorization* and socialization enhance not only common Muslim identity, but also tolerance toward other religions. Third, we explain how a renewed sense of individuality – *repersonalization* – promotes sociopolitical tolerance and civic engagement.

Turning to our interviews, ethnographic observations, and focus groups in the North Caucasus and the Middle East, we develop a theoretical framework to explain the Pilgrims' Paradox. We theorize it as a three-step process of repositioning, recategorization, and repersonalization (the 3 R's model, Figure 4.1). We explore the model's internal consistency and probe its empirical plausibility. Our fieldwork and its theoretical assessment also led us to explore and propose a new way to improve intergroup relations – particularly religious and ethnic relations – based on our 3 R Hajj model of tolerance improvement. Our breakthrough insight is that ethnic and religious – or any intergroup – tolerance could be improved by promoting social contact not only *across* these groups, but also *within* these groups. This means that our study is about more than the Hajj and religion. It is about broader social implications of the Hajj model of tolerance-building. The model's key driver is socialization in high-common-identity-value, high-in-group-diversity settings.

4

Repositioning or the *Axis Mundi* Effect

The Hajj pilgrimage entails more than ordinary travel. The pilgrims journey from their homes all over the world to Saudi Arabia, perform physically demanding and emotionally engaging sacred rituals for approximately one month, and go back home contemplating the deep spiritual significance of their experiences. As they migrate from home to Mecca and back and from holy site to holy site, the pilgrims traverse not only physical boundaries dividing states, but also cultural boundaries dividing social groups and – crucially to us – the symbolic boundaries between the sacred and the profane. We define this process, or this bidirectional migration, as repositioning.[2] We particularly focus on two distinguishing features of repositioning that are quintessential for working out a theoretical explanation of the Pilgrims' Paradox generalizable to intergroup relations at large. The first one is the intrinsic value of common group identity. The second is social diversity within the common group. Based on these criteria, all common group repositioning could be imagined on a continuum between low-value, low-diversity and high-value, high-diversity settings, as shown in Figure 4.1. In it, the intensity of the big circle color and the solidity of its circumference line represent the common identity value, while the number and diversity of shapes and color of smaller objects inside the circle represent subgroup diversity. On this continuum, the Hajj would fall closer to Figure 4.2b.

INTRINSIC VALUE OF COMMON IDENTITY – THE "AXIS"

The most symbolically important destination of the Hajj journey is the Ka'aba in Mecca, also known as the House of God and the House of Allah, a granite cube structure at the center of the most sacred mosque in Islam, Al-Masjid al-Haram. It is also a point of global geographic

(a)   (b)

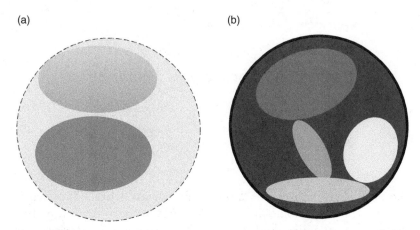

FIGURE 4.2 Common Group Repositioning Models: (a) low common group
value, low subgroup diversity; (b) high common group value, high
subgroup diversity.

orientation uniting all Muslims (the *Qibla*), being the point all Muslims
must face when praying wherever they are. In Eliade's conceptual framework, the Ka'aba is the Muslims' hub of the world, their axis of the
universe. Moreover, as Eliade pointed out, the symbolic significance of
this repositioning in space is magnified by repositioning in time – representing for each pilgrim "regeneration through the return to the times of
origins," a "festival time" entailing "reproduction of the paradigmatic
acts of the Gods."[3] It means immersion in "the sacred and indestructible
time," "the time that 'floweth not' because it does not participate in
profane temporal duration, because it is composed of eternal present
which is indefinitely recoverable."[4] It follows that repositioning with
respect to time would enhance the believers' repositioning with respect
to deeply symbolic religious values (*Axis Mundi*) and the overall intrinsic
significance of the pilgrimage.

A modern Iranian sociologist, Ali Shariati, describes the confluence of
sacred time and space in the Hajj ritual. According to Shariati, the Hajj
ritual symbolizes everything that God wished to say to people of the
Earth – transmitting through time and space the philosophy of humanity's
entire existence, the hope for its transformative progression from creation
to the peak of perfection, the flourishing of the global Muslim community,
the Ummah, the very model of humanity.[5] The monumentality of the
Hajj's value to Muslims is also expressed in the centuries-long richness
of material culture associated with the pilgrimage.[6]

The sense of proximity to the divine center of Islam among the pilgrims is embedded in the Hajj's theological meaning. According to the Qur'an, it was prescribed in God's revelation to Prophet Mohammad, "Allah made Hajj to the Ka'bah obligatory upon those who are able."[7] In 632 CE, the Prophet performed his first and only pilgrimage leading his followers. Since then, the Hajj became the fifth Pillar of Islam.[8] From the beginning of the sacred Islamic time the Hajj symbolized intense self-exploration, the acknowledgment of negative thoughts and behavior (sin), and the promise of purification and forgiveness. The Prophet's statement, according to a medieval Muslim luminary, Al-Bukhari, captures this meaning of the by asserting that whoever performs the Hajj and does not commit obscenity or transgression would return free from sin as the day his mother bore him.[9]

Yet, unlike the other Pillars of Islam – *shahada* (belief that there is only one God), *salat* (prayer five times a day), *zakyat* (charity), and *saum* (fasting) – the Hajj is not mandatory, because it typically involves long travel and is contingent on health, finances, border regimes, logistics, etc. Thus, many Muslims usually regard it as being less in men's power and more in God's will.

Eliade's particularly pertinent and nontrivial insight regarding repositioning is that by orienting individuals in the world, it helps them perceive their individual spaces in general as secure, orderly, and comprehensible. Repositioning takes the pilgrims to their entire faith's initial point of orientation. As such, it is likely to generate emotional and cognitive impressions they will most likely cherish and remember as long as they live. In this manner, repositioning will prime the pilgrims to explore their individual and group identities intensively and deeply while feeling more secure in their common identity as Muslims.

We showed in Chapter 2 how the Kabardino-Balkaria pilgrims discussed their impressions with deep emotional investment. In addition, having reread our interview transcripts through the prism of Eliade's conceptual frame, we paid attention to the pilgrims calling the Hajj the turning point – *de facto*, the Axis – of their lives. Most of them told us how they felt and what it meant to them:

"I do not feel my life before the Hajj had meaning. And starting the year after I made the Hajj, I consider myself to be one of the happiest people in the world," said Bolya.

"The Hajj is a great accomplishment. It totally changes a person. One has to withstand trials. One experiences there what one would never experience anywhere else," said Salikh.

"Compare the light of the day and the night – that is how I see my life. I lived in the dark and did not have anything. Then the light appeared and it became day. That is how big the difference is [before and after the Hajj]," said Zeinab.

"I believe that completing the Hajj was the best feat of my life. Nothing stands next to it. Three days in the Mosque of the Prophet [in Medina] were three days in Heaven," wrote Nina in her pilgrim diary that she shared with us.

One of the most striking examples of the profound intrinsic value of the Hajj were cases we encountered when Kabardino-Balkaria Muslims considered abandoning their scheduled pilgrimages on account of death or severe illness of close family members. All the individuals facing these heartbreaking dilemmas, whom Sufian interviewed as part of his participant observation in 2009, ultimately decided to proceed with the Hajj. In his diary, Sufian made the following entry:

The leader of the 2009 Nalchik pilgrimage group was Nazir-hajji, director of the Center for Research and Development of Traditional Confessions NGO and, previously, Rais-Imam [head] of the main mosque in Nalchik, Kabardino-Balkaria. Remarkably, even after grappling with his brother's sad death just a few days before the trip, Nazir-hajji decided to carry on with the pilgrimage. Another member of the group, Askhad, shared his own experience in a similar situation when the death of his close relative on the eve of his previous pilgrimage did not shake his determination to perform the Hajj, "Only my own death would cancel my pilgrimage." Another pilgrim, Atmir, recalled how his old and sick mother told him before his journey when he told her about his hesitation, "Do not cancel your Hajj even if I die."

* * *

The stories we recorded – through ethnographic research before, during, and after Sufian's 2009 pilgrimage – also illustrate how the Hajj experiences leveraged fundamental changes in the pilgrims' lives. Here are some of Sufian's Hajj diary entries and observation notes, fleshing out the *Axis Mundi* effects at a deeply personal level:

Mukhamedkhan, 48, felt that his standing in the community much improved after his first Hajj in 2008. He attributed it, to a large extent, to quitting smoking. Even though he quit drinking alcoholic beverages long before the Hajj, quitting smoking proved to be much harder. And so, he said, after coming back from the Holy Land, he noted his community elders showing him respect. They invited him to sit among them during religious ceremonies – these invitations are very important in Ingush society. Mukhamedkhan said, "Our elders know that I do not drink, do not womanize, do not smoke, and do not cheat."

Lidiya, 71, used to work as the head of the psychiatry department at the Nalchik hospital. She was a proverbial Communist leader type of woman – bossy, determined to make a career and a staunch atheist. She said her son kept telling her, "It would take a strong religion to turn somebody like you around 180 degrees." After performing the Hajj, Lidiya, in her 70s, entered the North Caucasian Islamic University and was making her next Hajj during a Muslim holiday break in 2009. Before departing for her second Hajj in 2009, Lidia renovated her house and gave away all her spare clothes, as if making space for a new life.

Khasan, 52, one of the pilgrims in the 2009 group from Nalchik, was probably the most dramatic example. He used to be an alcoholic, could never save any money, accidentally burned his house, and became homeless. His first Hajj in 2006 changed his attitude toward life; he got a steady job loading and unloading cargo trains at the Nalchik train depot. He was given board at the depot warehouse. He quit drinking and smoking. Khasan lived up to his ambition and earned the reputation of the strongest carrier at the station. He learned how to save money for Hajj – approximately four thousand U.S. dollars required for the journey was a hefty sum even for people who were well-off by Kabardino-Balkaria standards. In 2009, Khasan performed his third pilgrimage to Mecca. After the Hajj, Khasan felt much more secure. He said he felt as if earning the title of the *hajji* protected him even from law enforcement and secret services in the Northern Caucasus. The latter by then developed a reputation of unjustly persecuting local Muslims. Once a police officer stopped Khasan in the street and found out he did not have any identifying documents on him. [By Russian law, a person without ID could be detained and held at the police station until her or his identity is established.] The police officer delivered Khasan to the local FSB office and said he suspected that Khasan was a terrorist. Khasan told the FSB officer that they should have his name in the FSB database. "Why is that?" wondered the FSB man. "Because I performed the Hajj, and the FSB has to register foreign passports of all pilgrims going to Mecca," said Khasan. The officer apologized and released him. Some time later, when another police officer stopped him and asked for identification, Khasan told him to call to FSB right away, "They will tell you who I am." The police officer made a phone call, apologized, and let him go. "I reckon, FSB told him to look for other suspects rather than to investigate a twice-hajji," smiled Khasan.

* * *

In Islam, the intrinsic value of the Hajj to the pilgrims is also amplified through a deeply entrenched taboo on anthropomorphic concepts of God. Visual representations or their descriptions of Allah and the Prophet are forbidden. The violation of this taboo – as one cartoonist for a major Danish newspaper tragically found out in the early 2000s – could result in deadly reprisals. Even verbal imagining of God is problematic. In one of our focus groups with young women, the moderator asked the participants "to imagine a situation that you could be in the role of Allah one day." Several participants instantly protested with a scared "No, no." When the moderator continued, "so that you would be able to organize an ideal date for yourself," everybody remained silent and dropped the subject of dating and marriage that they had discussed with much interest prior to that.[10] This means the closer the pilgrims get to the *Axis Mundi* of Islam, to the core symbols of their common religious identity – and the more they use imagination and introspection visualizing their supreme deity, the more intimately wedded they become to their divine imaginations.[11] This intimacy of imagination enhances the intrinsic value of common identity experiences to individual participants.

SUBGROUP DIVERSITY – THE "MUNDI"

The second critical aspect of repositioning is exposure to high subgroup diversity within a common group. The Hajj illustrates how this happens – with Muslims of diverse backgrounds from all over the world spending time together to celebrate their common Islamic identity. The number of countries from which the pilgrims arrive in Mecca fluctuates every year – e.g., 188 countries in 2013, 163 in 2014, and 164 in 2015. The government of the Kingdom of Saudi Arabia (KSA) has established quotas for every country – allowing 1,000 pilgrims per million Muslims, or 0.1 percent of the Muslim population. As the world's Muslim population has increased, the government of Saudi Arabia has raised the quotas accordingly, except in years when construction work affecting the holy sites required temporary quota reductions. Muslims in Saudi Arabia have no restrictive quotas and the number of pilgrims among them fluctuates more from year to year. However, on the whole, significantly more pilgrims come from outside than from within the KSA. For example, in 2009, the KSA hosted 154,000 domestic and 1,613,000 foreign pilgrims. In 2010, those numbers were 989,798 and 1,799,601; in 2011, 1,099,522 and 1,828,195; in 2012, 1,408,641 and 1,752,932; in 2013, 700,000 and 1,379,531; in 2014, 700,000 and 1,389,053; and in 2015, 615,059 and 1,384,941, respectively. To accommodate the historical increases, the government of Saudi Arabia has spent more than $100 billion on the Hajj in the past five decades.[12] Male pilgrims somewhat outnumber the female pilgrims, largely because the rules of the Hajj forbid female pilgrims younger than forty-five to perform it unaccompanied by male relatives. From 2006 to 2010, women comprised approximately

45 percent of international Hajj pilgrims, including 45.7 percent in 2008, 35.7 percent in 2012, and 45 percent in 2013 and 2014.[13]

The KSA government does not provide statistics breaking down the pilgrims by race, ethnicity, or branches and schools of Islam. However, because quotas are representative of demographics in Muslim-populated states, the available data give one an approximate sense of intra-Islamic and ethnonational diversity among the pilgrims. In 2012, from 87 percent to 90 percent of the pilgrims were probably Sunnis and from 10 percent to 13 percent were Shi'a. Most pilgrims came from the countries of the Asia-Pacific region, where about 62 percent of all Muslims lived at the time. Other large groups of pilgrims arrived from the Middle East and North Africa (20 percent) and sub-Saharan Africa (16 percent). The remainder represented Europe including Russia (3 percent), North America (less than 1 percent), and Latin America and the Caribbean (also less than 1 percent). The top ten pilgrim-sending countries, besides the KSA, were Indonesia (13 percent), India (11 percent), Pakistan (11 percent), Bangladesh (8 percent), Nigeria (5 percent), Egypt (5 percent), Iran (5 percent), Turkey (5 percent), Algeria (2 percent), and Morocco (2 percent).[14]

The pilgrims typically have to traverse numerous interreligious and sacred–profane boundaries to reach their *Axis Mundi*. They may have to pass through countries and global regions with predominantly non-Muslim populations. At a minimum, they would be relying on the international transportation infrastructure operated by predominantly secular institutions. In the process, as Eliade emphasized, the pilgrims would start out like all the believers with the proclivity to categorize the followers of their own religion (in this case, Islam) as "our world" and everyone else as the "other world." The important point is, as Eliade noted, that "our world" is familiar, orderly, secure, and comprehensible. The "other world" is strange, chaotic, insecure, and incomprehensible. The pilgrims have to break through from one to another and back, most likely many times – not necessarily an easy experience or an experience one would anticipate would be easy. Crucially, the thing about the Hajj is not that the pilgrims have no choice but to go through with this our-to-other world crossing, but that doing so is endowed with a supremely symbolic, sacred meaning. Eliade identified these experiences as intergroup "break-throughs" and pointed out that they have truly profound effects on individuals when they become "possible and repeatable."[15] This is exactly what the pilgrims across diverse social backgrounds do, and it becomes an important shared experience.

These breakthroughs are one of the most memorable and striking experiences the pilgrims report. With the spread of Islam all over the world, the Hajj became a form of religious congregation explicitly designed to promote the unity of religion through a diversity of cultures – which millions of Muslims experience. Malcolm X perhaps most eloquently verbalized what living through the breakthrough to diversity felt like during his pilgrimage to Mecca in 1964:

> They asked me what about the Pilgrimage had impressed me the most. . . . I said, The brotherhood! The people of all races, colors, from all over the world coming together as one! . . . There were tens of thousands of pilgrims . . . of all colors, from blue-eyed blondes to black-skinned Africans. But we were all participating in the same ritual, displaying a spirit of unity and brotherhood that my experiences in America had led me to believe never could exist between the white and the non-white. America needs to understand Islam, because this is the one religion that erases from its society the race problem. You may be shocked by these words coming from me. But on this pilgrimage, what I have seen, and experienced, has forced me to rearrange much of my thought patterns previously held.[16]

When Sufian embarked on his Hajj pilgrimage in 2009, he had not heard about Malcolm X's Hajj impressions. After returning home from Mecca, he marveled the same way as Malcolm X did about Islam's global diversity. In our interviews and focus group discussions, the pilgrims from Russia's North Caucasus revealed that experiencing social diversity in the Holy Land firsthand was a powerful memory. Here are some typical statements:

> There are more than 2,000 different nationalities in the world and each of them has its own etiquette, customs, and pride for their ancestors. . . . It is impossible to stay the same after the pilgrimage. We experienced the magnificent event. We came close to God. Khasan, 65 (Focus group, April 27, 2010)
>
> Most importantly, the Hajj brings people together. Different people gather there, there is no place [in the world], from which people are not represented. Even people from small countries in Scandinavia perform the Hajj. Most importantly, those are peaceful people. And those very people pray to God to bring peace upon the Earth. The Hajj brings those people together and they get to know each other during the pilgrimage. The biggest happiness is when different people become close to each other so that they all can live in peace and agreement. Nokh, 70 (Focus group, April 27, 2010)

These direct experiences in repositioning during the Hajj translated into a striking difference in the dynamics of focus group discussions among Kabardino-Balkaria pilgrims compared to the non-pilgrim Muslims. As we showed in Chapter 2 (Figure 2.1), the pilgrims devoted almost three times as much time discussing the importance of the sacred center of global Islam – exactly the themes one would associate with Eliade's notion of *Axis Mundi*. This was in response to our invitation in all focus groups to discuss the significance of the Hajj. Some non-pilgrims talked exaltedly about the Hajj's significance in Islam and how much they wanted to perform it, yet these statements failed to translate into more sustained group discussions – the way they did among the pilgrims.

Another important insight from our content analysis of focus group conversations highlights the difference between repositioning in the Hajj model of tolerance compared to other forms of repositioning into situations where individuals experience social diversity. They show the importance of not merely being placed in a diverse intergroup setting, but in a diverse intergroup setting where these diverse groups get together to recognize their *common superordinate* identity. It means that exposure to diversity has stronger effects if groups A and B are brought together not only (and not even principally) to comprehend and bridge the differences between them, but if they are brought together to celebrate some common identity that transcends their identity as members of groups A and B. In other words, the *Axis Mundi* effects obtain as a synergy between the *Axis* (common identity) and the *Mundi* (in-group diversity) effects as we identified and illustrated them. In this synergy, the *Axis* effects make the realization of the *Mundi* effects significantly stronger. At the same time, the exposure to the *Mundi* effects animates the realization of the transformative power of the *Axis* effects – hence, the power of repositioning close to the symbolic center of common group identity.

We estimated how much time focus group participants spent on discussing the *Axis* themes compared to the *Mundi* themes (the sum of which comprises the "importance of the sacred center of global Islam" topic in Figure 2.1, Chapter 2). We counted as *Axis* themes discussions of the sacred entities and locations in Islam ("Allah," "Mecca," "Medina," "Prophet," "Ka'aba," "Hajj," "sacred," "blessed") and words pertaining to participation in the sacred activities ("*Tawaf*," "experience" related to the Hajj, and "going around" the Ka'aba). We coded as the *Mundi* themes conversations related to the global significance and diversity of the Hajj – with key words being "nations," "world," "global," "diversity," "Earth," "significant," and country names.[17]

We tallied the results by group. Across age and gender (including the associated socioeconomic status differences based on our focus groups selection), the hajjis devoted significantly more time to discussing both the *Axis* and the *Mundi* themes. When conversations centered on the importance of the Hajj, the pilgrims went back and forth between talking about

TABLE 4.1 *Pilgrims in Kabardino-Balkaria Focus Groups Devoted Significantly More Time than Non-Pilgrims to the Importance of the Hajj Pilgrimage (as percent of total discussion time within each group).*

	Hajj-1 (older men)	Hajj-2 (older women)	Non-Hajj-1 (younger women)	Non-Hajj-2 (men mixed age)
"*Axis*" (sacred center)	34	46	15	14
"*Mundi*" (global diversity)	6	4	0.0	1.3

the symbolic significance of the ritual for Muslims in general and talking about their impressions of experiencing firsthand the global diversity of Islam. This back-and-forth dynamic translated into more time they devoted to the *Axis Mundi* theme as a whole compared to the non-pilgrims who lacked the shared sense of repositioning (Table 4.1).

SPECIAL CASES OF AXIS MUNDI SYNERGY: THE MOSQUE OF THE TWO QIBLAS AND MT. ARAFAT

Mecca is not only the revered location of Islam's holiest sites, but also a physical reference point for daily religious rituals – as all Muslims are obligated to face it during every prayer. The direction of the Ka'aba in Mecca from one's position anywhere in the world is known as the *Qibla* – the existential *Axis Mundi* of Islamic faith. In Muslim countries, hotel rooms typically have signs, sometimes inside chests of drawers, indicating the *Qibla*. Muslims are usually buried with their heads facing toward the *Qibla*. When they butcher animals for food, Muslims point the animal's head toward the *Qibla* as a symbol that it is sacrificed to God – thus sanctifying the food's preparation as *halal* (proper to eat).

The hajjis learn firsthand about the origins of the *Qibla*. Though regarded by some as controversial, these origins *de facto* manifest the embeddedness of diversity in one of the foundational symbols of Islam. One may think of it as the embeddedness of the religious *Mundi* in Islam's existential *Axis*.

First established in 610 CE, the *Qibla* faced the Noble Sanctuary in Jerusalem, and later the location of the Al-Aqsa Mosque and the Dome of the Rock. The practice of facing Jerusalem is not mentioned in the Qur'an.

However, it is described in several sources, mostly the books of *Sirat Rasul Allah* (*Life and Career of the Prophet Mohammad*) and the Hadith collections.[18] Some scholars believe that the first *Qibla* was chosen under the influence of the Jewish religious custom of facing Jerusalem.[19] After using Jerusalem as the *Qibla* for thirteen years, Muslims changed it for the Ka'aba in Mecca on February 11, 624 CE. The change took place during a noon prayer in a mosque in Medina seven months after Prophet Mohammad moved there from Mecca. According to the sacred texts, Mohammad received a divine revelation instructing him to turn toward the Ka'aba: "So turn your face toward al-Masjid al-Haram. And wherever you [believers] are, turn your faces toward it [in prayer]."[20] Mohammad immediately turned himself toward Mecca and so did his followers. The mosque where the event happened was the third mosque ever built (after the Mosque of the Ka'aba in Mecca and the Mosque of the Prophet in Medina). To mark its role as the turning point in the orientation of the center of the Islamic world while paying respect to its origins – which included recognition of the role of Jerusalem with the implicit recognition of the common roots of the Judaic and the Muslim faiths – that mosque became known as Masjid al-Qiblatin or the Mosque of the Two Qiblas.[21]

The hajjis appreciate more than others that changing the whole *Axis Mundi* of Islam was a risky undertaking even for the Prophet. The abrupt changing of the *Qibla* caused a controversy among Muslims and non-Muslims at the time. A revelation in the Qur'an illuminates the seriousness of the issue and the grave doubts about the change when it talks about those who were confused with the change of the *Qibla* or questioned it: "The foolish among the people will say, 'What has turned them away from their Qibla, which they used to face?'"[22] In order to clarify the issue, the Qur'an included a detailed statement that the first *Qibla* (in Jerusalem) was not sanctioned by a divine revelation, but was rather chosen in order to distinguish Mohammad's followers from his enemies: "And We did not make the Qibla which you used to face except that We might make evident who would follow the Messenger from who would turn back on his heels."[23]

The Mosque of the Two Qiblas is still functioning and the group of pilgrims from Nalchik, which included Sufian, visited it. These visits are common, even though the formal rituals of the Hajj do not require them. In his notes, Sufian mentions that another group making the pilgrimage by car from Chechnya also visited the Mosque of Two Qiblas and after that drove to Jerusalem to pray there.

By changing its location from Jerusalem to Mecca, the *Qibla* stands out as a symbol that the *Axis Mundi* of Islam embodies a rich history of religious diversity, a symbol of Islam as a developing, living faith, open to change through divine revelation. And visiting the Mosque of the Two Qiblas is an important experience for the pilgrims that broadens their vision and helps them to understand that even such important things as the *Qibla* underwent change during the rise of Islam. The fact that even for the founder of the religion, the Prophet, changing the *Qibla* was a daunting endeavor – but that he took the risk nevertheless and succeeded – symbolizes the deeply embedded *Mundi* within the Islamic faith's *Axis*.

Another major experience of diversity in centrality during the Hajj is the time pilgrims spend in and around Mt. Arafat, located about twelve miles to Mecca's southeast. In fact, it is Mt. Arafat – a granite hill rising about 230 feet from the Arafat Valley – that is the center of the Hajj as a ritual. During his journey, Sufian learned a common saying among the pilgrims: "The Hajj is Arafat." The pilgrims treasure the notion that this saying originated with Prophet Mohammad repeating it three times, and it subsequently became a common phrase in Arabic (عَرَفَاتُ الْحَجُّ).[24] It is part of a shared understanding of the sacred among the Muslims that it was in the Arafat Valley, during the first Hajj in the history of Islam, that Prophet Mohammad delivered his deeply significant Farewell Sermon. All pilgrims proceed to Mt. Arafat on the ninth day of the twelfth and final month of the Islamic calendar, known as Dhu'l-Hijjah or "the Month of Pilgrimage." They spend about a day in prayers close to Mt. Arafat. Failure to go to Mt. Arafat as required on the second day of the Hajj invalidates the pilgrimage. Akhmat-Hajji, the leader of the pilgrim group that included Sufian, explained the significance of Mt. Arafat as an ultimate symbol of goodness, divine forgiveness, and absolution – a symbolic path to life for the multitudes united in their faith who braved the challenges of travel there from so many distant lands.

In the afternoon when pilgrims gather at Arafat, God descends down all the way to the First Heaven. And He says to His angels, pointing at the pilgrims, 'Look at My servants. They all are untidy. They are covered with dust. They are tired. They came to Me today. They ask for My mercy. They ask for My forgiveness. They ask Me to put them in the Paradise and not to put them into the Fire.' God likes His servants in such a state. He likes that His servants abandoned all their worldly needs and their worldly cares. He likes that they came there just for Him, remembering the Last Day when they will be standing in front of God. And He tells to His angels, 'Today, Angels, you will witness that I prepared the Paradise for these servants of Mine.'

The gathering of the pilgrims at Arafat is also a rare occasion when the Ka'aba looks forlorn. Mt. Arafat becomes the *Axis Mundi* of the Hajj at that moment instead of the Ka'aba. Mistakenly, popular culture regards the Ka'aba as the main site associated with the Hajj; photos and videos of pilgrims circling around the Ka'aba are mostly used for the visual presentation of the Hajj. The Ka'aba, though one of the most important and powerful elements of the Hajj, is not the experiential center – or perhaps to put it more precisely, not the unique experiential pinnacle – of the Hajj as a multiday ritual. At least twice during the Hajj, the arrival to and departure from Mecca, the pilgrims are required to perform *Tawaf*, or circling seven times around the Ka'aba in a counterclockwise direction. *Tawaf*, however, is not designated exclusively as part of the Hajj ritual. It may be performed separately as *Umrah*, which is known as a "lesser Hajj." Whereas *Umrah* is a mandatory part of the Hajj, pilgrims also identify *Umrah* as a separate ritual and sometimes refer to their pilgrimage as the Hajj and *Umrah* to emphasize the completeness of their experience, the combining of the Ka'aba and Mt. Arafat (as well as other) rituals. To make this point, to emphasize the synergetic diversity of central symbols of the Hajj, we picked a photo of Mt. Arafat for the front page of this book.

CONTRASTING EXAMPLES

In all respects we have discussed so far, the Hajj is an outstanding exemplar of a high-identity-value, high-diversity common group setting. Our discussion also implies that the Hajj should be uniquely suited for demonstrating the *Axis Mundi* effects not only in the specific context of Islam, but as a special form of common group repositioning in any context. The Hajj model, like a searchlight, points to other settings where some of the same effects could obtain and enables one to distinguish them from settings that may appear to be similar, but that are, in fact, different. It highlights the value of the Hajj as a proxy, as a conceptual lever for understanding a wide range of social phenomena. At the same time, considering these phenomena refines our explanation of how the *Axis Mundi* effects obtain in the real world. One may consider three contrasting settings – two in which either the intrinsic identity value or subgroup diversity is high while the other is low, and one in which both value and diversity are low. For example, two middle-class, middle-age, same-ethnic, male parliamentarians visiting the

British Parliament – the mother of all parliaments – from a country where the polity is modeled on Britain's would place themselves in a common identity setting with high intrinsic value, but with low subgroup diversity. Conversely, 100 tourists from ten countries representing a wide mix of ethnicities and social classes of both genders on a Tanzanian safari would be in a high-diversity, but low-value common group identity setting. Whereas a safari is probably valued highly as an *experience*, as a marker of common tourist identity it is not globally unique and outstanding – i.e., it is not necessarily more or less valuable intrinsically to individual tourists than climbing Mt. Kilimanjaro, descending into the Mayan caves of Belize, or walking through the serenity of Angkor Wat. A homogenous group of tourists that does not visit sites alongside different groups would be an example of a low-value, low-diversity context.

These contrasting contexts also explain why the *Axis Mundi* effects would be unlikely to come about strongly in local religious pilgrimages where local holy sites are visited by significantly less diverse groups of worshippers as those who congregate in Mecca and Medina. At best, these effects would be weaker as suggested by detailed historical examination of *ziyarat* pilgrimages in Islam, such as "Second Meccas" or local imitations of the holy shrines in Central Asia and Xinxiang, as well as the Mari and Udmurt pilgrimages to local pagan shrines. In particular, the history of these local shrines comes through as the history of common group value contestation rather than affirmation. Local stakeholders and worshippers tend to get consumed in controversies about the sacredness and historical legitimacy or significance of the shrines, as well as about the authenticity of claims to natural descent from the Prophet or, in the Mari-Udmurt case, of the Bulghar deities.[25]

At worst, absent authentic common identity symbols of high value, the secondary pilgrimages may have the reverse effect – i.e., they may enhance more exclusive, restrictive views of common group identity.

In one interview during Sufian's pilgrimage, he learned a story – narrated by Nazir-hajji, a former imam of Nalchik, and one of the Hajj group leaders – illuminating the problem with secondary pilgrimages (*ziyarat*), grounded in poor understanding of the importance and the meaning of *Axis Mundi* effects. The story concerned a 2005 conference at the Institute of Humanity Studies in Nalchik, a branch of the Russian Academy of Sciences, in which Nazir-hajji participated. The conference brought together leaders of the Muslim community and local scholars. According to our source, one high-placed local scholar, well known for research and teaching on atheism in the Soviet period, claimed that Muslims worshiped idols by facing toward the Black Stone built into the wall of the Ka'aba Mosque in Mecca during their prayers. The scholar proceeded by arguing that the Hajj is a superstitious custom developed from pre-Islamic traditions in Arab Peninsula. He also claimed that the *Qibla* and the Hajj emerged as purely historical artifacts. However, criticizing the pilgrimage as a superfluous custom – which he never performed himself – the scholar in question more than anything else revealed ignorance of the sacred meaning of the Hajj as an identity-affirming ritual. Our source said the scholar exhausted the patience of the audience when he arrived to practical recommendations grounded in his denial of the sacred meaning of the Hajj, and suggested opening a branch of the Ka'aba in the North Caucasus. He recommended building a local Black Stone so that local Muslims could perform the surrogate "Hajj" and save time and money by not traveling as far as Mecca. In his interview, Nazir-hajji said, "We could tolerate it when the scholar accused us of idolatry. However, his practical recommendations sounded so absurd that I could not help but telling him, 'Nobody argues that you must be a distinguished scholar in your own field of study, whatever it is. However, here you are talking on a subject about which you do not know even the basics.'"[26] This sense of disbelief, if not bewilderment, at the lack of understanding on the part of the atheist scholar of the high intrinsic value of the Hajj to Islamic identity, of its significance as the *Axis Mundi* of Islam, illustrates why pilgrimages to the "secondary Meccas" are unlikely to have the same prosocial effects as the Hajj.

* * *

High common identity value and high subgroup diversity within a common group are two crucial and synergetic aspects of repositioning, of which the Hajj is an exemplar. As the structural foundations of the *Axis Mundi* effect, they lay down the tracks for two perceptual processes that enhance intergroup tolerance and thus explain the Pilgrims' Paradox substantively – *recategorization* and *repersonalization*. The chapters that follow detail how these processes convert high common identity value and subgroup diversity into more tolerant, prosocial views of the Hajj pilgrims as compared to the non-pilgrims. This focus on the interaction effects of in-group identity and in-group diversity is something that differentiates our argument from that of scholars like John Esposito, who instead emphasizes the synergy between diversity acceptance in Islamic teachings and in the pilgrimage experience. In Eliade's terms, Esposito's model emphasizes *Mundi*, ours the *Axis Mundi*.

5

Recategorization

With repositioning, one can see how both SIT and social capital theory may explain why the Hajj would enhance acceptance among Muslims of religious and social diversity *within* Islam, while raising hostility to religious groups *outside* Islam. In other words, these theories can explain a part of the Pilgrims' Paradox, but not the most interesting part. Thus, in social psychology, this partial explanation would be consistent with Samuel Gaertner and John Dovidio's Common Ingroup Identity Model. In our model, we refer to these effects as *recategorization*. It applies to individuals who – when multiple identities are available – come to identify themselves first and foremost with a larger, more inclusive, higher-order (superordinate) social group. For instance, representatives of different ethnic groups at a stadium may identify themselves primarily as fans of the same soccer team. This is a common occurrence at college football games in the United States. Empirical research indicates that recategorization of this kind boosts prosocial behavior within a common group.[1] However, as tolerance toward subgroups within the common group increases, the common group becomes more united and prospectively more hostile toward other common outgroups (e.g., fans of rival football teams). Figure 4.1 (Chapter 4) can be used to illustrate this dynamic. As the number and diversity of shapes and colors of smaller objects within the big circle increase, the outer boundary of the big circle gets solid and thickens.

Transposed to the Hajj experiences, the Muslim pilgrim identity could be viewed as a common identity broadly inclusive of Islamic subgroup and social identities – i.e., pilgrims representing different schools of law within Islam and diverse ethnic, social, age, and gender groups. The common pilgrim identity is not only intrinsically valuable, but also socially prestigious. As we recall, those who completed the pilgrimage are typically viewed with special respect among Muslims and have the right to add the title *hajji* (men) or *hajjiah* (women) to their first name. After returning home from the Hajj, Sufian appreciated the fact that he could now be officially introduced in social situations with the title of *hajji* added to his first name. Mikhail remembers well the warm and happy smile lighting up Sufian's face when, upon arriving in Nalchik in April 2010 to conduct focus groups, he said: "Hello, Sufian-hajji." The more the pilgrims value this special status, the more one would expect them to accept intra-Islamic religious and social differences. From the social capital standpoint, the same effects would obtain from the pilgrims' interactions with diverse Islamic and social groups. In these settings, common in-group identity and social capital are likely to have mutually reinforcing prosocial effects.

However, non-Islamic religions could then be increasingly viewed as new common outgroups to pilgrims. The SIT would then predict the hajjis would view non-Muslims more negatively – or, at the very least, would retain any prior prejudices and animosities.

Moreover, it is unclear how social capital would contribute to inter-religious tolerance as a result of the Hajj. As we explained in Chapter 3, unresolved debates in the social capital literature – particularly concerning religious versus secular and denominational differences – raise the critical question: Is social capital transitive? In other words, do socially benign effects of face-to-face interpersonal contact experienced in one situation transpose to other situations – and, if so, to what extent, and under what conditions? This is crucial with regard to the Pilgrims' Paradox, since during the Hajj we found most pilgrims have interpersonal interactions almost exclusively with other Muslims. Why, then, would social capital make them more tolerant than the Muslim non-pilgrims toward Jews or Christians?

We believe that the logic of both SIT and social capital can be extended to explain why, on average, the Hajj experience is more likely to engender tolerance among Muslims to outgroups both within and outside Islam. This is to say, more generally, that these perspectives may tell us why exposure to and socialization with a more diverse mix of subgroups united by common identity would promote one's tolerance not only toward these subgroups, but also toward common outgroups. As for SIT, we unpack and critically reexamine the notion of *social projection* – a key mechanism putatively accounting for why diversity within a group may engender unified hostility toward outgroups. Regarding social capital, we take a more detailed look at studies suggesting socialization is *transitive* – i.e., the benign effects of socialization within a common group would

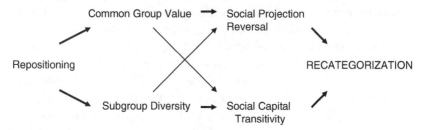

FIGURE 5.1 The Hajj Model of Common Group Recategorization.
Note: It is assumed that each arrow has a "+" sign (the stronger the source condition, the stronger the target impact and the more inclusive the resulting recategorization into a common group).

promote positive socialization outside the common group. The flow diagram in Figure 5.1 maps out these processes.

SOCIAL PROJECTION REVERSAL

To better understand the notion of social projection, it is important to go back to the fundamental premise of SIT – accepted as axiomatic in social sciences – that individuals have multiple identities. They may simultaneously identify with multiple categories and they may change identification with any given category relative to how they compare themselves to other groups.[2] Some forms of identification could be more fluid than others. Three variables are critical. One is the level of abstraction.[3] A Los Angeles resident in California becomes a Californian in the United States, an American in France, and an Earthling on Mars. Another is the comparative fit, or the ratio of the perceived similarities of the individual to out-group members versus in-group members (Haslam, Reicher, and Platow 2011). Mohammad and Ivan may view themselves as two distinct individuals, but they may view themselves as part of the same ingroup (men) if they find themselves among a group of ethnically and/or religiously diverse women – assuming that the gender difference is viewed as more salient to each one of them than ethnic difference. Combined, the level of abstraction and comparative fit logic suggests not only that social categorization is fluid, but that the more groups people compare, the more likely they are to recategorize themselves into more abstract (or superordinate) social groups. The more they do so, as the Common Ingroup Identity Model explains, the more they would be likely to view each other positively and to act prosocially.

The third variable, however, entails a less optimistic view. Recategorization into more common groups may also promote intolerance both within the common group and with respect to larger common outgroups. At issue is social projection. It rests on the perceived prototypicality of individual identities with respect to a group. From this perspective, recategorization is hardly an immutable and benign force. Social projection – the degree to which individuals perceive the standards and values of their subgroup as representative of the common in-group identity – would have a crucial impact on whether relations among subgroups (e.g., country of citizenship) sharing a more inclusive common identity (e.g., Hajj pilgrims) would get better or worse. As Amélie Mummendey and Michael Wenzel showed in an article in one of the leading psychology journals, *Personality and Social Psychology*, the more individuals believe they are prototypical of their common ingroup, the more they are likely to view other subgroups as deviant and inferior.[4] We thought of this as *matryoshka* discrimination – in reference to the Russian nested dolls: in the absence of outsiders to despise, individuals would find insiders to despise. This form of recategorization would understandably translate into social intolerance.

Our theoretical contribution is that social projection could also work *in reverse*. Mummendey and Wenzel's study that identified the negative effects of social projection represented settings where one subgroup within a common group is in a majority relative to other subgroups and the total number of subgroups is small. In these settings, individuals belonging to majority subgroups – by dint of their majority status – view themselves as more prototypical of common group identity and therefore superior to other subgroups. But what if no subgroup is in a majority and common in-group identity is held deeply important to one's core concept of self-identity, such as the common Muslim identity felt – and experienced – during the Hajj? One may then expect social projection to work in reverse. Individuals in this context would feel less confident that their own subgroup standards and values are prototypical of common in-group identity. Consequently, other subgroups would – by extension of the common in-group identity logic – appear less deviant and out-group differences would become less salient. As a result, out-group bias and prejudice would diminish. Therefore – if social projection is reversed – recategorization into a common, more inclusive group is likely to promote not only *sub*group, but also *out*-group tolerance. The Pilgrims' Paradox could then be explained.

Our records of the pilgrims' impressions and experiences demonstrate how social projection reversal works. Typically, Muslims in the North Caucasus who had never visited majority-Muslim states imagined that there – and particularly in Saudi Arabia, the heart of Islam – most people were ideal Muslims living ideal Muslim lives. With this idealized image as a benchmark for self-evaluation, we found the North Caucasus Muslims critical toward themselves and others living in secular states such as Russia, their homeland. This often enhanced their intolerance of what they saw as incompatible with that idealized image in the everyday life of local North Caucasus Muslims. Those who made the pilgrimage to Mecca, on the other hand, witnessed and interacted with people of diverse character and behaviors representing millions of pilgrims. They inevitably saw alongside religious people of highest morality those people who they believed were dishonest. Actually, most pilgrims whom Sufian interviewed during his participant observation of the Hajj told him they anticipated that in Mecca they would encounter only honest people. Thus, encountering in the Holy Land people the pilgrims perceived as dishonest was usually one of the biggest disappointments and culture shocks. All the pilgrims in the group from Nalchik, in which Sufian was a participant observer, regularly complained about mundane things during the pilgrimage – i.e., the quality of food or accommodations or the onset of illness, etc. A higher taxi price during the busiest hours or at night was something the pilgrims invoked most frequently as a manifestation of "unbelievable injustice." The North Caucasus pilgrims were also surprised to find a lack of manners that they believed would be unconscionable in the Holy Land. One of the pilgrims in his interview spoke with outrage about a man whom he saw spit on a street of Mecca. Another could not contain his anger at a man who, having completed a prayer, refused to yield his place to a fellow believer who needed it during prayer time at the Ka'aba, which was so crowded that many people could not find even a small space on the ground to pray.

Abdul-Aziz Davletshin, the nineteenth-century Russian government official who specially examined the Hajj effects in Russia, summarized the positive prosocial effects of these culture shocks among pilgrims. He could have been the first who expressly – albeit unwittingly – described social projection reversal in action, using the Hajj as an illustration. Davletshin concluded that the Hajj, on balance, while making some older pilgrims more withdrawn into religion, had positive political effects. He found that the pilgrims returned more tolerant of the Russian government and secular regulations after they had chance to observe in their travels the imperfections and the negative aspects of life in the Ottoman Empire, of which Mecca and Medina were a part at the time. He wrote, "We may imply most positively that almost all our pilgrims come back to the homeland with [a] significantly improved worldview, more enlightened, and with [a] more tolerant understanding of our political situation – the [idyllic] colors they used to paint the Muslim Turkey and its Caliph disappeared completely." Davletshin describes in detail how, after encountering "the Turkish rules and the corruption that is common everywhere, our pilgrims return with [an] absolutely different understanding" of the Ottoman Empire; "it astonishes them [pilgrims] how, in the very Heart [Center] of Islam, Bedouins, the compatriots of the Prophet, rob their co-believers arrived with such difficulties to perform the rituals of their common religion"; the pilgrims who "used to imagine [the Arabs] almost as saints observe that they have very light attitude towards the performance of the main rituals of the religion and interest in money prevails in them above other interests"; the pilgrims "find it strange that there is no order and cleanness in the very 'Mother of Cities' [Mecca] and 'the City of the Prophet' [Medina]."[5]

And all this despite the findings we presented indicating the Hajj enhances religious devotion and ignites the passions of faith.

An entry in Sufian's 2009 Hajj diary shows that the same perceptual dynamic persisted among the group of the Kabardino-Balkaria pilgrims he studied:

While walking seven times around the Ka'aba, many pilgrims admitted they could not concentrate on their own inner feelings, because in the crowd of thousands of people someone always pushed them and some particularly fervent pilgrims almost knocked them off their feet. The combined effect of the unexpected sense of helplessness and injustice was also evident in another instance, much talked about among the pilgrims. A taxi ride from the hotel to the Ka'aba typically cost 10 to 15 Riyals. They said a lot of taxi drivers were seasonal labor migrants who bumped up the prices. (Although sometimes, one might get a free ride from local residents who refused to take money from the pilgrims.) Four pilgrims from our group fell victim to one avaricious cab driver. They made a deal with him that he would take them to our hotel for 10 Riyals each. However, upon arrival, the cab driver swore that the pilgrims misunderstood him and that the fee was actually 100 Riyals a person. He started shaming the pilgrims, saying, "Hajj – haram!" (intimating that if they didn't pay the price, their pilgrimage would be considered sinful). The pilgrims gave up and each paid 100 Riyals. All four of them were mad about this daylight robbery to the depth of their souls, yet no one dared refusing to pay. Another example of the pilgrims' rage is when they saw people spit in Mecca. In the Caucasus, spitting is considered insulting, and the pilgrims in our group exclaimed with outrage: "How can one spit on the holy ground?"

However, when returning home, as observations suggest, the hajjis typically reconsidered those grievances. Most of them told us they came to peace with the understanding that everything was not perfect even in Mecca. In their interviews after the Hajj, they reported being no longer preoccupied with those disappointments, even though they still vividly remembered them. Mukhamed, age eighty, said: "A hajji should not stress the inconveniences experienced during the pilgrimage." Chamal, age seventy, recalled how he had problems with food and cold weather at night. Yet, he dismissed these problems as unimportant and summarized his experiences this way upon coming back home: "I departed healthy, performed the Hajj, and came back safe and sound." Chamal, along with most pilgrims we observed and interviewed, had health problems that got worse during the Hajj. However, the pilgrims considered them a positive experience – saying they believed that sickness and pain canceled out misdeeds or sins they may have committed before the Hajj. Batyr, age thirty, said: "Bad deeds fall from the pilgrim during his sickness as fast as the leaves fall from a tree in autumn." Nazir-hajji, the leader of Sufian's 2009 group from Nalchik, said, "Allah forgives the bad deeds of a patient if he does not complain about his sickness."

In our focus groups, the pilgrims voiced a few complaints of this nature, yet overall they got little traction. After seeing that people were not perfect even in Mecca, the Hajj pilgrims became less intolerant of the imperfections of their countrymen and, by extension, of people from other countries. This mindset is indicative of the pilgrims' determination to enhance their tolerance and fortitude in the face of hardship and to reduce proclivity for complaining and scapegoating – thus weakening the all-too-well-recognized perceptual drivers of intolerance and hostility among humans.

Why didn't the opposite obtain or why, upon encountering the unforeseen hardships and disappointments, didn't the pilgrims simply downgrade the Hajj as a ritual? This is where the high intrinsic value of common group identity plays a crucial role – which explains why the Hajj effects would not necessarily obtain in other settings. From the standpoint of Eliade's sacred space and time of origin, doing so would make the pilgrims contemplate the prospect of cognitive and emotional self-destruction. They would have to admit to themselves that the God they worshiped was impure, inadequate, uncaring. But what would that mean, then, for their core individual identity, for their identification with their God? Hence, most individuals in this situation would rather assuage, please, pacify, and solidify their dominant faith.

The pilgrims in our study reconciled their shocks by broadening the perceived boundaries of condonable behavior. They relaxed the boundaries of who qualified to be an ideal Muslim. They realized that many aspects of their own behavior they believed were unacceptable could actually be acceptable to their God. And if so, they realized they could be more tolerant of the views, beliefs, and behaviors they previously thought would be unacceptable in other people. This kind of recategorization meant more than raising the level of abstraction or increasing the comparative fit ratio with one's ingroup. It meant simultaneously identifying more strongly with a superordinate group's identity and extending the conceptual boundaries of that superordinate category – i.e., making that category more inclusive. Thus, almost every hajji in our focus groups, when discussing their reaction to behaviors initially viewed as incompatible with being in the Holy Land, made comments, the gist of which amounts to a statement: "If this happens in the most sacred space, God must be more tolerant, less strict than I thought, so I should be the same." Conversely, during our focus groups the hajjis never discussed whether the initially shocking flaws they encountered on their journey devalued the ideal Islamic state of the Kingdom of Saudi Arabia (KSA) or made their pilgrimage experience less valuable.

In short, the pilgrims reversed social projection.

And that meant the hajjis were identifying more strongly with their common superordinate identity as Muslims while simultaneously extending the conceptual boundaries of that superordinate identity – i.e., making the notion of Muslim more inclusive. To generalize using the vocabulary of social psychology, this is a *de facto* instance of subgroup recategorization into a more outgroup-tolerant common group. It is logical then that the hajjis would view religions outside Islam and social groups not typically associated with Islam with less intolerance than the non-hajjis.

SOCIAL CAPITAL TRANSITIVITY

Repositioning into a high-common-identity-value setting also increases the likelihood of sociability being transitive. Social capital is not only about joining groups, networking, face-to-face contact, communication, and other instrumentally acquired and transportable socialization skills – as the cornerstone theoretical work that we reviewed in Chapter 3 details. We refer here to studies showing that people who join church associations have also been more likely to join civic associations,[6] and that people who socialize more than others with family members are also more likely to socialize – and thus build social capital – with the followers of religions other than their own.[7] And yet, we have also explained that other studies pointed to different outcomes and the debates about social capital transitivity in the mainstream sociological literature remain unresolved.

This is why we felt it would be important to consider the symbolic value of sociability. This latter aspect is not developed systematically in the social capital literature. Yet, once we thought of it, it became clear to us that symbolic value – such as experiencing common Islamic identity at the holy sites of Mecca (i.e., in more general terms, personal proximity to one's *Axis Mundi*) – would help sociability within a group encourage sociability across groups.

This consideration adds to the conversation on social capital transitivity in a nontrivial manner. Seen through the prism of the Hajj experiences we examined, social capital is transitive not only in a sense that the more individuals socialize in one setting (bowling or church) the more they would socialize in other settings (civic associations). It was the first-time socialization in high-common-value settings that we realized was most likely contributing to stronger prosocial views among the hajjis compared to the non-hajjis. More broadly, this would explain why in some contexts, passive or rare or irregular socialization may have as strong prosocial effects as active socialization – the sense of sharing important symbolic values could leave long-lasting impressions and enhance proclivity to socialize even if the pilgrims were, for the most part, non-joiners, non-networkers, or non-socialites and when they didn't cross in-group boundaries to have contact with people of other faiths.

This point is particularly important. Most socialization we observed among pilgrims during the Hajj occurred within their travel groups, typically coming from the same country and region within a country. The pilgrimage set the context in which this socialization acquired special features. The hajjis treasured opportunities to express and live their common identity as pilgrims. The strong sense of common identity value as pilgrims and Muslims set the stage for sharing common experiences, for equitable socialization. It reduced the need for hierarchy within their travel groups. (And, in one study, Robert Putnam argued that religious participation among Catholics in Italy failed to engender actually diminished social capital, because the Catholic Church is hierarchically organized.)[8] The mode of interactions was that of a horizontal network rather than a hierarchy. Sufian's diary recorded the following observations:

Within our group of pilgrims, no one experienced the disruptive sense of defenselessness and injustice from each other. I observed not a single case when one of the pilgrims deliberately took advantage of others. One could feel a special atmosphere within a group. Our group atmosphere felt different than one's typical group solidarity – unlike something that happens when people in a group placed into unknown surroundings become more united in the face of a supposedly hostile environment. In the latter kind of groups, leaders typically emerge and a role hierarchy sets in. In contrast, the atmosphere in our group of pilgrims emanated from the refusal of each one of us to compete for leadership within the group or to set up a hierarchy. In my experience, the most typical catalyst of hierarchy in male groups is the assignment of group chores – such as washing the floor in the common sleeping room, bathroom, or walkways; cleaning up after common meals; and so on. In the army, for instance, when regulations are hard to enforce within living quarters, most servicemen try to avoid the worst chores and some try to assert their dominance by bullying others to do them instead. In our group of pilgrims, quite the opposite, everyone considered helping others an honor, or rather, as something beneficial to one's soul. Sometimes, when someone forgot to clean up in the kitchen or the bathroom, other pilgrims would readily do it for them. Most common, I witnessed readiness to bring food or water to fellow pilgrims. Also, it was as if our group atmosphere reinforced and broadened the old Caucasus custom of serving food and water to the elders. ... Usually, such a disposition to altruism within a group later translates into different views of the hajjis toward colleagues at work, relatives, and friends.

No matter how actively they socialized before the pilgrimage, the hajjis maintained friendship networks with former group members for years. Hajjis typically stay in touch with the leaders of the tour groups, in which they performed the pilgrimage, and through them, with other hajjis. Some may form networks with the local pilgrims who performed the Hajj at other times. The interesting point, given our discussion of the social capital theory, is that these gatherings or contacts within the hajji networks are not necessarily regular or frequent. And yet, the high intrinsic value of common identity comes through when these meetings happen. Interestingly, also, even though the pilgrimage for each of the participants was a deeply personal, emotional, pride-evoking experience, the hajjis allow non-hajjis to take part in their group meetings. One Kabardino-Balkarian non-hajji, Ismail Teppeyev, reported how he felt after one typical hajji reunion in his village: "When we got together, I listened to the amazing stories our old-timers shared. I felt I was flying."[9]

The hajjis who do not live in the same town may have each other's phone numbers and communicate over the phone and also gather on occasions other than reunions, such as funerals. Sufian observed a multi-city hajji network in action while organizing one of our focus groups. His lead contact in putting the group together was his uncle, Chamal, who had constant communication with other hajjis in and outside of his hometown of Nalchik. In fact, Chamal assembled most of the group from out of town, except for one coworker. Our records show that, at the beginning of the focus group, Chamal informed us he communicated with twenty hajjis, inviting them to participate. Those who live in the same town or city typically meet more often, as we could observe with the focus group of the hajji women. Zeynab-hajjiah helped us organize a focus group drawing on her local pilgrim network. They pitched in and prepared a sumptuous welcoming meal. Sufian, who then lived permanently in Kabardino-Balkaria and was used to generous displays of hospitality typical in his culture and who participated in home receptions such as this one with the non-hajjis for his colleagues from within and outside Russia, including the United States, was positively impressed. He commented: "It was enough to feed a wedding." Looking back, we believed we got a good taste – literally – of the fusion between Caucasus hospitality and the spirit of the hajji pride in their accomplishment of the pilgrimage. We felt the special energy of the common in-group identity pride.

* * *

Government-backed Muslim authorities in Kabardino-Balkaria and local branches of the Russian federal government have been known to recognize the importance of the pilgrim status and the influence of their networks in local society. One telling example happened in 2007, when a large group of hajjis from Kabardino-Balkaria experienced problems during their trip and could not return home when they planned. The pilgrims, according to Regnum – the then reputed Russian news agency mostly independent from the Kremlin – publicly blamed the Spiritual Directorate of Muslims of Kabardino-Balkaria (a government-controlled body to oversee local Muslims) for the pilgrims' logistical problems. Partly in response to these public accusations, the government-endorsed *mufti* of Kabardino-Balkaria, Anas Pshikhachev (i.e., chief of the Spiritual Directorate), in June 2008 dismissed the Hajj group leader, the *rais-imam* of the Nalchik mosque, Nazir-hajji, for "failure to carry out official duties." Nazir-hajji took on the official and influential Muslim leader. He filed charges in the municipal court, seeking to reverse his dismissal. The court kept postponing hearings on this case. In the end, Pshikhachev backed down and revoked the dismissal. More than that, the Spiritual Directorate issued a letter of reference to Nazir-hajji, commending him for "a strong contribution to the revival of Islam and the moral and spiritual education of the public." Nazir-hajji nevertheless resigned on his own accord. It is possible that a compromise was reached to avoid public scandal from escalating had the court hearings began.[10] As we learned later, a group of hajjis gathered in Nalchik during the standoff and met with the local authorities and Muslim leaders demanding Pshikhachev's resignation.[11] This kind of peaceful but vocal civic public discussion was rare in Muslim communities in Russia, where everybody was afraid of heavy-handed government and law enforcement interference, fearing unjust accusations of Islamic extremism.

Another example comes from our own experience, when Sufian was making arrangements to undertake the pilgrimage. When he filed the paperwork for his Hajj journey, the local branch of Russia's visa and immigration service processed his travel documents expeditiously. He later learned from other pilgrims and officials that Russia's powerful Federal Security Service (FSB, or the former KGB) monitored travel passport applications and instructed the immigration officials to speedily review all documents filed by prospective hajjis and to make sure they avoid bureaucratic obstacles. When Sufian departed with his group of pilgrims from Nalchik for the nearest international airport at Mineral'nyye Vody – an approximately two-hour drive – local police officers were on board to guard the bus. Overall, the pilgrims commented positively on the Russian government's role in making their Hajj possible. Even the only negative report that reached us had a silver lining. One of the pilgrims revealed privately that he bribed an FSB officer at the Mineral'nyye Vody airport custom service in order to fix a minor issue with his passport. However, this means that in the pilgrim's case, the FSB officer was open to helping him and to accepting a bribe – even though from what the authors learned during their ethnographic work in the region and dealing with visa and registration issues in Nalchik, the FSB officers reviewing visa and immigration issues were not open to bribery. Upon returning from Hajj, some pilgrims were in possession of religious literature that they obtained in the KSA, but that was prohibited in Russia, according to the Federal List of Extremist Materials on the Ministry of Justice of the Russian Federation.[12] The FSB confiscated from the pilgrims about a dozen Russian-language copies of *Obyasnenie Osnov Very* by Muhammad S. Utsaimin, which was listed as extremist literature on the Russian Ministry of Justice's website under number 171; free copies of the book were delivered to the pilgrims' hotel in Mecca by an unidentified person. Also the FSB confiscated, from

Sufian, an English copy of *The Fundamentals of Islam*, by Muhammad S. At-Tamimi (a free copy was given to him at an exhibition in the Prophet's Mosque in Medina), which we could not find on the List of Extremist Materials on the Ministry of Justice's website. The confiscation of those materials at the airport did not have further repercussions for the pilgrims to our knowledge.

* * *

Research outside the North Caucasus also indicates that the socialization effects within the hajji networks stem from the particularly high intrinsic value of common in-group identity. That value is anchored in Eliade's notion of the sacred; it is about reliving the experiencing of the *Axis Mundi*. In this manner, it contributes to positive recategorization – pro-social effects within the group are more likely to apply outside the group. Summarizing the contributions of sixteen scholars to their 2005 edited volume, *Muslim Networks from Hajj to Hip Hop*, Miriam Cook and Bruce Lawrence wrote: "Daily and annually across time and space, the history of Islam flows from Mecca and back to Mecca. It flows through myriad networks. They connect individuals and institutions, at once affirming and transforming them."[13]

These arguments and observations explain a great deal about the results of our focus groups analysis. As we reported in Chapter 2 (Figure 2.1), the non-pilgrims spent most of their discussion time (about 68 percent) on talking about the importance of the uniformity of Islam across social groups. The pilgrims were much less concerned about this issue, devoting just about 14 percent of their conversations to it – i.e., almost five times less than the non-pilgrims did. This finding held when we parsed out our analysis into specific dimensions of Islamic uniformity that comprised distinct discussion segments in focus groups – in personal appearances (based on terms "beard," "shave," "hat," "skirt," "headscarf," "jewelry," "amulet"), in the nature and practice of religious beliefs across different schools of Islam and in relation to other religions (based on terms "Shariah," "*Madhhab*," "Shi'a," "monotheism," "God-abiding," "Bible," "Christian," "Jew," etc.), and in terms of religion's precedence over ethnic rituals (based on terms "ethnic," "tradition," "nationality," "mountain" [people], "Adyge," "Kabardian," "Balkar," "Circassian," "Russian," "Dagestani," etc.). The focus on uniformity among the non-pilgrims is distinctly predominant compared to the pilgrims across age, gender, and associated socioeconomic status differences (Table 5.1).

TABLE 5.1 *Non-Pilgrims in Kabardino-Balkaria Focus Groups Devoted Significantly More Time than Pilgrims to the Importance of Uniformity of Behavior and Beliefs in Islam (as percent of total discussion time within each group).*

	Hajj-1 (older men)	Hajj-2 (older women)	Non-Hajj-1 (younger women)	Non-Hajj-2 (men mixed age)
Islam Uniformity: Looks	0	2	7	6
Islam Uniformity: Beliefs	3	10	39	48
Islam Uniformity: Rituals	7	7	25	12

* * *

We thus witnessed how the interaction effect of common in-group value (the *Axis* effect of repositioning) and exposure to subgroup diversity (the *Mundi* effect) engendered social projection reversal and social capital transitivity – the key aspects of positive, prosocial recategorization. Social projection reversal in particular highlights the key difference between the Hajj model of social tolerance and the conventional inter-group contact model (in which the causal mechanism is friendships and dependencies evolving across any two or more out-groups). This insight is in many ways counterintuitive, yet it makes sense. In the Hajj model, individuals become more tolerant of the outsiders not because they get to like them or need them, or because they idealize them, or because they believe that diversity is a higher common good. Rather, appreciation of diversity emerged out of negative culture shocks – the betrayed expectations of harmony and perfect social behavior in the Holy Land. Its appreciation emerged through overcoming the initial frustration, anger, consternation, worry, puzzlement, and numerous other negative, perplexing feelings. Amenities may not be what one expects. Taxi drivers may cheat. Shopkeepers may rip you off. Listening to some pilgrims passionately complain about these perceived injustices during the Hajj, Sufian wrote in his diary, sometimes made him wonder if they might lose faith in Islam. And yet, this is something he sensed the pilgrims could not contemplate losing – partly because giving it up would mean invalidating their personal deep spiritual and physical involvement in the Hajj journey. They had to make allowance that tolerance of imperfections and inconsistencies – of social diversity – was something divinely validated. And this understanding to them was not something abstract, it was something they lived and felt. The Hajj model thus shows how tolerance may arise not necessarily from one's exposure to positive social contact, but from one's reconciling with negative social contact.

* * *

As we were revising our manuscript in late 2015, Sufian reread this chapter and asked if we could add his impressions about a then recent case involving a pilgrim from the United States. He believed it would be a powerful demonstration of how tumultuous – in this case traumatizing – a path to positive recategorization can be, how social projections may be reversed and re-reversed in complex ways. The case represents a hot issue concerning Islam and tolerance as it is understood in the West. It remains highly controversial. Mikhail wondered if Sufian would be comfortable commenting on it. Sufian had no doubt. His draft notes recording his reactions tell the story.

There is a recent case of Parvez Sharma, a New York-based, gay, Muslim activist from India. A maker of religious reality films, he performed the Hajj at the age of forty-one. Sharma's local Islamic community, including his own mother, stigmatized him because of his sexual orientation. Sharma's mother died of cancer when he was twenty-one. According to the story about him in the *New York Times*, "not long before her death, he came out to her. Her anger was relentless – and so was Mr. Sharma's shame."[14] Reading how a mother rejected a son shocked me to the core.

Sharma's 2007 documentary, *A Jihad for Love*, depicted the struggle of gay Muslims around the world to reconcile their faith with their sexual orientation. The movie had two personal outcomes for Sharma. On the one hand, his movie made him famous and recognizable. In 2008, *Out* magazine named him one of the "Top 100 gay men and women who have helped shape culture." On the other hand, becoming a celebrity raised challenges to his personal security. After his 2007 documentary, many Muslims labeled Sharma "an infidel, and in the intervening years, he has gotten more death threats than he cares to recall," wrote the *New York Times*. However, despite the deadly threats from his fellow Muslims, he decided to perform the Hajj. As the story went, "he felt called to make the pilgrimage – it is considered a duty for all Muslims to perform at least once in their lives – and hoped especially to reconcile his faith with his sexuality."

When making his decision to go to Mecca, Sharma was aware of the personal risks he faced. First, as a gay celebrity, Sharma could be easily recognized during the Hajj. He was afraid that he might get in trouble if his sexual orientation were exposed. As the *Times* wrote, "Mr. Sharma, a soft-spoken man with chiseled features and a trim black beard, said he was 'terrified' that he would die at the hands of the Saudis." Second, he faced danger as a professional filmmaker. He was afraid he might get himself in trouble with the Saudi police for filming during the Hajj. For that reason, he did not take a professional camera with him, and filmed everything with an iPhone strapped to his neck with rubber bands. His video showed that "Mr. Sharma, 41, struggles visibly with his fear, even as he prays." His fears were not ungrounded and indeed, as the *Times* reported, "at one point, officials saw Mr. Sharma recording a prolonged scene, confiscated his phone and destroyed the footage."

The Hajj was a highly personal dramatic experience for Sharma. It was personal and often dramatic also for me and for others in my group, yet his was exceptionally intense. The *Times* quoted him saying, "I cried a lot. I unloaded a lot of baggage there." According to conventional wisdom, I sensed that such a hard experience in his community and during the Hajj would force Sharma to make a choice. The fear and injustice he experienced during the Hajj might become the last straw in his life-challenging, gut-wrenching interactions with other Muslims, including his own mother. I felt Sharma could be torn apart by a powerful urge to reject Islam and convert to another religion or even to turn atheist. Having been through the pilgrimage and having analyzed how it affected me, I could also sense how the intensive religious experience during the Hajj could turn Sharma into an ardently devout Muslim – to the extent that it would not surprise me if he would deny and publicly reject his sexual orientation as inappropriate for Islam to reconcile with his Muslim community.

Indeed, as I learned, Sharma became more devoted to Islam and felt he became a better Muslim as a result of his Hajj. It also allowed him to make peace with the memory of his mother, "during the hajj, in his sleepless, dreamlike state, Mr. Sharma felt her forgiveness – and he, in turn, forgave her." This reminded me of the hajji from my North Caucasus group who felt his pilgrimage put him at peace with his deceased parents who had been conditioned by the Soviet rule to feel uneasy about embracing religion.

Sharma's Hajj, however, didn't make him reject who he was, professionally and sexually. After going through his hard journey in the Holy Land, he embraced even more his own country, the United States, which is tolerant of the gay community. And also he created his new documentary, *A Sinner in Mecca* (2011), where he showed the hardship and spirituality of the Hajj and their complex, often paradoxical interaction.

6

Repersonalization

If social projection can be reversed and social capital is transitive, then we should not necessarily expect common group identification to engender depersonalization. Social psychologists view the latter as an important driver of intergroup bias with individuals placing more emphasis on group identity over personal identity. John Turner defined this process as when "people come to see themselves more as the interchangeable exemplars of a social category than as unique personalities defined by their differences from others."[1] The classic example is enlisting in the armed forces and taking pride in being "a man or a woman in uniform." The sense of pride in this example is transferred from one's personal, unique traits to the unity and uniformity of the institution defending a group. However, stretching this logic, social psychologists argue that depersonalization entails not a loss of self, but a redefinition of self in a way that favors group membership over individuality, with a new, redefined self-identity being just as meaningful to a person.[2] The U.S. Army's recruiting slogan builds on this logic: "Be all you can be." One implication is that in the real world, personal and group identifications overlap and are mixed. Another implication, however, is that regardless of any given real-world mix, moving along the interpersonal-intergroup continuum is a zero-sum process – the more one identifies with a group category (army uniform), the less important individual identity traits (sleeping late or love of poetry) become to a person, even if the two identity types can be mixed (a soldier writing a marching song for his platoon). Of course, an individual may claim that by becoming a better "woman in uniform," she becomes more of an individual, that uniformity is her individuality. Yet, such *post hoc* rationalization does not mean the interpersonal and the intergroup identities of that same individual are truly interactive and interchangeable *by choice* – i.e., that by enlisting an individual may choose to become less of a soldier and more of a civilian, or to follow the commander's orders selectively, etc.

Yet, a different process is plausible. If one's commitment to common superordinate identity such as that of Muslims during the Hajj gets stronger, then one's perceived common in-group boundaries would expand and the importance of subgroup prototypicality is likely to diminish. In that case, an individual could experience an enhanced sense of group commonality and individuality simultaneously. Going back to John Turner's formulation, such a person will no longer face a mutually exclusive choice to be either "unique personalities" or "the interchangeable exemplars of a social category."[3] That person can experience both identifications. We define this phenomenon as *repersonalization* – i.e., when a person develops a stronger sense of both individuality and a more inclusive sense of common group identity. An important part of this process is understanding and coming to value the possibilities for acquiring new personal characteristics and seeing them as complementing one's personal identity as a result of feeling a part of a larger social group (e.g., "Muslims of the world, unite in your diversity!"). This means feeling empowered to analyze, to understand better, and to celebrate one's identity as a unique individual – a theme that has been one of the dominant in our interviews and focus group discussions during the Hajj study. It is the be-all-you-can-be logic within a context where the common group value – unlike in the case of the armed forces – is not explicitly defined in terms of friend or foe with respect to other groups. The resulting self–group identity synergy would then raise the intrinsic value to a person of progressively more inclusive common identities, extending eventually to the most inclusive social category possible – i.e., being human.

The Hajj experiences illustrate this logic and help flesh out ways in which it can be generalized to other contexts. Importantly, the relationship between the intergroup and the interpersonal is fluid and multidimensional. Thinking of oneself as an individual versus as an ideal Muslim is interactive and not zero-sum – i.e., the relationship between individual preferences and ideal-type identity – what is proper or improper, allowed or banned, acceptable or objectionable – is constantly reinterpreted and reimagined. Repositioning and recategorization prime individuals not only to accept differences they observe between themselves and a multitude of other pilgrims, but to make this acceptance an inherent part of their common group identity-building experience (e.g., as Muslims). The Hajj context is the opposite of joining the army example in a sense that a person moves from his or her residence locality where group identity is relatively uniform to a context where identity is by design diverse. In the case of the Hajj, individuals whose Islamic identity is wedded to a rather narrow, parochial, local stereotype join the global celebration of Islam in all its forms under the sanctifying aura of the Holy Land and centuries of tradition.

The Hajj experiences starkly illustrate that the shared sense of humanity in a common group setting is not the only factor in repersonalization. Particularly important in that regard is appreciation that one's sense of belonging to the common group depends on one's personal behavioral choices. In other words, it is a setting where the path to commonality is through individuality – i.e., where these paths can be infinitely diverse and the common group setting makes individuals realize it better, internalize it more deeply. In other words, it is a setting where they internalize the realization of no uniform path to common identity, of there being endless ways to be Muslim, or Christian, or Hispanic, or a Beatles fan.

The specific illustration is the notion of the Hajj acceptance. The pilgrims share a strong belief that individual pilgrims may never know if their Hajj will count or be accepted by God. The common understanding is that this happens strictly on a case-by-case basis. In other words, while everyone shares group-unifying experiences during the Hajj, the ultimate outcome (which is also the ultimate purpose of the pilgrimage) is a strictly personal issue. And only God will eventually judge if every individual pilgrimage was acceptable. The pilgrim may never know the outcome of that judgment, as it is totally in the divine realm. The general belief among Muslims that God may or may not accept their Hajj is typically expressed in their prayers requesting the Hajj to be accepted. The non-pilgrims may show respect for the pilgrims by wishing for them that their Hajj is accepted. One of the focus group participants, Muhammed, age sixty, who had not had the opportunity to perform the Hajj, illustrated this by addressing the pilgrims thus: "To all who performed Hajj, I wish that your Hajj to be accepted."[4] As these wishes are expressed, everyone understands that acceptance depends on each person's own record of deeds, thoughts, and feelings.

Another individuating aspect of the Hajj acceptance norm – particularly strong among Muslims from Russia's North Caucasus – is that acceptance can be shared, depending on the will of the Almighty. In Islam, the pilgrimage may be performed on one's own or on somebody else's behalf. The Hajj may be performed multiple times, but on behalf of only one person at a time. Some pilgrims believe that God may or may not accept the pilgrimages undertaken for somebody else. One of the participants of a focus group, Khasan, sixty-five years old, who performed a second pilgrimage on behalf of his mother, expressed the concept in following way. "I felt that I had to perform Hajj for myself and then for my mother. I was able to achieve that. I hope that God will accept them both."[5]

The norm encourages both self-realization and altruism. A pilgrim may perform the first Hajj only on one's own behalf. In case the pilgrim does not properly perform the next Hajj on someone else's behalf, it is understood that God might withdraw acceptance of the pilgrim's own first Hajj and transfer it to the person on whose behalf the second pilgrimage was performed.

Technically, other four Pillars of Islam – pledging that there is only one God, daily prayers, charity, and fasting – also may or may not be accepted by God because they may or may not be performed correctly. However, the Hajj is understood to require more physical effort, financial resources, and time. Therefore, its acceptance is a particularly sensitive issue. The pilgrims usually avoid claiming that God accepted their Hajj. Only one of the interviewed pilgrims, Hasan, forty-five years old, who was performing his second Hajj, told us during the study that: "A trustworthy believer passed through somebody else the good news to me that God accepted my first Hajj." Usually, the signs of God's acceptance of Hajj are interpreted more generally. Well-known Dagestan Sufi, Said-Affandi Chirkavi, who was killed by a Russian Muslim woman suicide bomber, said: "If the hajji performs no bad deeds after his pilgrimage, that may be interpreted as his Hajj has been accepted by the Almighty."[6]

Preoccupation with acceptance of one's pilgrimage is a persistent mental and emotional trial, a trial of deeper self-exploration. It makes the hajjis look deeper inside themselves and replay their lives' deeds, choices, thoughts, and feelings. And this self-exploration is reinforced through the performance of common rituals and the search for the most optimal common identity – the kind that one could more plausibly associate with the prospect of their Hajj acceptance. This made the Hajj a thoroughly individuating common group experience.

While interacting with the pilgrims during the Hajj, Sufian examined their sense of individuality by reading them poetry. His selections were from a Russian Jewish poet, Osip Mandelshtam, whose work he determined was unknown to the pilgrims – largely because public circulation of Mandelshtam's works during the Soviet era was strictly limited and excluded from the school curricula whereas the popularity of public poetry recitals declined after the collapse of Communism and the rise of new media technologies. Sufian recited several poems – including one in which he expected pithy references to the alleged Ossetian ethnicity of Joseph Stalin to resonate with the sense of common North Caucasus identity among Circassian pilgrims. Yet, that was not the poem that elicited most interest. It was the one titled "Your Image, Tormenting and Unsteady," conveying the sense of personal liberation through proximity to the divine. Apparently, Stalin and the Caucasus ethnic identity failed to excite. While penned by a non-Muslim, the general idea touched Sufian's fellow hajjis deeply. In our translation:

> Your tormenting and unsteady image
> I could not distinguish in the mist.
> "God!" – I uttered by accident,
> Without thinking I would say that.
> The God's name, like a great bird,
> Flew out of my chest.
> Now, a thick mist is curling ahead of me,
> And the empty cage is left behind.

It made us think of how Turner's notion of depersonalization is reversed as the Hajj makes the pilgrims see themselves more "as unique personalities" rather than "the interchangeable exemplars of a social category." The cage is left behind. In social psychological terms, the operative word here is "interchangeable." The hajjis certainly see themselves and other pilgrims as "exemplars of a social category" – but in doing so, they also see a celebration of unity in diversity, a proud celebration of Islam as a world religion. This explains, perhaps, why Sufian, after completing the Hajj, said he could only compare it in terms of the effect on his perceptions of self and the world with his first trip from a closed, authoritarian, post-Soviet Russia to the open Western society of the United States. The two experiences, indeed, have a crucial element in common – a journey from the historically prevalent uniformity to diversity.

Thus, being embedded in what Eliade described as the "sacral space" as well as "the time of origin," the pilgrimage enhances among the hajjis both individuality and a common religious group identity. As Eliade explains: "the religious man wishes to be *other* than he is on the plane of his profane experience. Religious man is not *given*; he *makes* himself, by approaching the divine models."[7] Key to the perceptual micro mechanisms of the repersonalization mechanism is one's immersion into the sacred space as a quest to comprehend what it means to be one's real self, as a path to the axis, or core around which one may orient herself or himself. And so it is through imitating models of ideal divine behavior (as in retracing the deeds of Prophet Mohammad being part of the Hajj) that individuals during the pilgrimage experience more acutely than they otherwise would what it means to be unique as a human, and as an individual. As Eliade formulates this conclusion: "Religious man assumes a humanity that has a transhuman, transcendent model."[8] Repersonalization among the pilgrims thus has a particularly strong effect precisely because it comes out of this paradox of diametrically opposing motivations reinforcing one another. The more closely the pilgrims yearn to imitate and approximate models of divine faith and behavior, the more they experience this imitation as profoundly idiosyncratic acts grounded in their individuality.

To summarize this process in terms of social psychology, we may say that through engaging in intense self-analysis while performing the Hajj rituals, the pilgrims experienced and developed a stronger appreciation for a closer, more intimate identification with the ultimate superordinate social category – i.e., humanity.

* * *

The repersonalization argument has three broad implications. First, it lends support to previous studies showing that religious practice generally enhances sociopolitical tolerance. Second, it specifies broader social conditions under which a stronger identification with common group values may reverse depersonalization supposedly resulting from the latter. Crucial among them is the balance between social equality and individuality, the shared sense of individual choice and responsibility, the understanding of multiple paths leading to common identity, and an intimate self-identification with humanity. The celebratory aspect of common identity is also important. This would suggest, for example, that voluntary associations would improve relations among participating racial, ethnic, social, or religious subgroups more so than compulsory associations – e.g., why intergroup relations may improve significantly more in contract armies than in conscription armies. While both would train for uniform behavior, the sense of individual choice and responsibility – and hence, the appreciation of multiple paths to commonality among fellow servicemen and women – would be stronger in voluntary armies or in National Guard units.

Third, and perhaps paradoxically, the sense of equality during the Hajj when thousands of pilgrims spend the night under the open skies in the same white robes may be a key factor in the relationship between religious behavior and support for political democracy. It is based on the same logical foundation as Alexis de Tocqueville's finding that Roman Catholics in the nineteenth-century United States showed a stronger political advocacy for civil rights and individual freedoms than Protestants. It significantly undermines arguments that Islam is doctrinally and procedurally incompatible with democracy. In fact, it suggests that one of Islam's central rituals may rather enhance intrinsic democratic orientation among individuals. De Tocqueville traced this apparent puzzle to the social-theological practices of Catholicism. Whereas in no sense implying that Islam is the same as Catholicism as a religious faith, De Tocqueville's observations point out a social dynamic inside the religious ritual among Catholics in America that strongly resonates with the practice of individuality in equality that the pilgrims experience during the Hajj in the Kingdom of Saudi Arabia:

In the Catholic Church the religious community is composed of only two elements: the priest and the people. The priest alone rises above the rank of his flock, and all below him are equal. On doctrinal points the Catholic faith places all human capacities upon the same level; it subjects the wise and the ignorant, the man of genius and the vulgar crowd, to the details of the same creed; it imposes the same observances upon the rich and the needy; it inflicts the same austerities upon the strong and the weak; it listens to no compromise with mortal man, but reducing all the human race to the same standard, it confounds all the distinctions of society at the foot of the same altar, even as they are confounded in the sight of God.[9]

More than a century and a half after these observations, Kabardino-Balkaria pilgrims reported in the same Tocquevillean terms what impressed them the most about the Hajj. In essence, they testified that the Hajj reproduced the same democratizing effects of religious practice that impressed De Tocqueville about the practice of Catholicism in the United States. Prominent in our interviews and focus group conversations was the expression of empowerment the pilgrims felt to analyze, to understand better, and to celebrate their identities as unique individuals. With everyone wearing white *Ihram* robes made of sheets to walk around the Ka'aba and to spend a night in the open air at Muzdalifah, the hajjis reported the rising sense of common humanity.

Khizir, age fifty, eloquently summarized these impressions of the North Caucasus hajjis: "And so imagine millions of people in white robes gather in one location and praise their Creator, the Almighty Allah.... With their arms up in the air they beg him for mercy, for forgiveness, for the blessings, for the bliss. And as they do it, the air above that land is trembling. And undeniably, when I saw all that for the first time, it left an indelible impression in my memory and in my heart and soul."[10]

In addition to memories about the impression of equality, we had the opportunity to interview pilgrims during the Hajj. When asked about his impressions while in the Arafat valley during the Hajj, Magomet, age twenty-nine, made a comment reflecting the sentiment of most of his fellow pilgrims we interviewed about their journeys:

I felt today the equality of all people. No matter what [social] category they belong or their status in life, they all are equal today – I felt that! We are all clothed in the same *Ihram* robes. ... And I feel that when we need it, I feel as we all become brothers and help each other out. ... We often heard about the Judgment Day and I feel as if today is that day and we all are equal and waiting for that judgment. He will ask us [about our deeds] and we will not be able to lie to Him.[11]

Another pilgrim, Mukhametkhan, age forty-eight, expressed being over-whelmed with the sense of common humanity in Mecca, "I am absolutely equal with you at this holy place. Here we are equal with you. Absolutely. We sleep in similar beds. We pray the same way. We pray to the same Almighty Allah. What is the difference between us then? There is no difference."

Atmir who by then had performed the pilgrimage seven times, verbalized his impressions emotionally: "The most important feeling from the Hajj is the feeling that arouses when you comprehend the greatness of those several days in Mecca when you see millions of people from all over the world, of different social status who fall on their knees with one expression "Allah Akbar!" [The God is Great]. Presidents and commoners alike perform Hajj. Where else can we be equal with presidents?!"

In his Hajj diary, Sufian recorded his firsthand impressions of these experiences:

We arrived in Muzdalifah around 10 pm, when most of the pilgrims already were there, lying on the ground, preparing for sleep. Buses had been taking the pilgrims to Muzdalifah since 6 pm. The bus I was on drove through big torrents of in-comers walking around people who staked out places on the ground. Everybody was dressed the same, and the men were just wrapped in two pieces of cloth. I feel as if it were a campsite where people arrived from all over the world of their own free will. "This is the sight that makes the biggest impression on me during the Hajj. We also will be passing with crowds in front of God on Judgment Day," said Atmir, another pilgrim from my group. The scene of the pilgrims' gathering in Muzdalifah stunned me. I thought that the only way to rationally explain this chaos would be to imagine it was, indeed, the Doomsday rehearsal. The event would be inspiring and powerful, but also overwhelming. An immense noise stayed in the Valley. ...

It should be noted that the logistics of moving millions of pilgrims through Muzdalifah was very well organized. Via a perfect road through the valley busses brought new groups of pilgrims one after another. People in uniform were everywhere and maintained order. However, even in such an organized event I felt the underlying chaos. Many groups could not find a place on the bare ground to settle down for the night. Our group was one of them and we had to wait for almost two hours to find a spot, as we kept watching endless rows of men and women settling down on the ground.

* * *

Repersonalization would explain why the pilgrims in our focus groups were significantly less animated than the non-pilgrims to discuss the importance of uniformity in Islam (as we showed in Chapter 5, Table 5.1). Additionally, we found through content analysis of focus group conversations that the pilgrims were more confident than the non-pilgrims to talk about state–religion relations and engagement in secular public activities. The hajjis were much more accepting than the non-hajjis of Muslims participating in secular public life. One may also treat this as a greater willingness on the part of the pilgrims to expose oneself to secular experiences and to accept diversity secular views. As indicators of this aspect of repersonalization we marked conversations on four themes: (1) church–state relations (with key terms featuring "state," "government," "law," "rules," "police," "education," etc.); (2) social equality ("income," "rich," "poor," "cost," "price," "status," etc.); (3) the appropriateness of self-expression in public (such as being photographed, filmed, or interviewed – that fundamentalists in Islam typically consider a social taboo) and interest in civic/public life ("media," "program," "television," "Internet," "conference," "public speech"); and (4) foreign travel preferences based on countries one would like to visit the most. One distinct subtheme we identified as part of the latter in the first focus group we held (which was among the male hajjis) was interest in how people live in and also in traveling to the United States. We noted this since the United States has a secular form of government whose foreign policy the locals had frequently perceived as hostile to Islam and to Russia. As in our earlier illustrations, our indicator of topic salience was discussion duration measured as the percentage of word count per subtheme relative to the total theme word count in each focus group.[12] Also, we broke down the analysis by group to control for age, gender, and concomitant socioeconomic differences.

The results show a significant difference (Table 6.1). The hajjis were particularly more willing than the non-hajjis to talk about religion–state

TABLE 6.1 *The Pilgrims in Kabardino-Balkaria Focus Groups Were Significantly More Open to Discussing Secular Issues and Engagement in Public Life (as percent of total discussion time within each group).*

	Hajj-1 (older men)	Hajj-2 (older women)	Non-Hajj-1 (younger women)	Non-Hajj-2 (men mixed age)
Church–State Relations	39	15	3	4
Social Equality	3	4	0	5
Participation in Secular Public Life	9	6	1	5
Interest in the United States	1.1	6	0	0.6

relations. They spoke a lot about government regulations that could make the practice of Islam easier for believers. In doing so, the pilgrims did not demand that Russia turn into a theocracy, nor did they challenge the secular government's political authority or complain about current government policy. They mostly proposed specific, community-level, constructive solutions such as improved access to the existing mosques or availability of prayer space in public buildings. The pilgrims were more open to discussing social equality, as well as the media and public activism. They were, on the whole, more open to discussing the possibility of traveling to and living in the United States. And despite differences among the hajjis across gender regarding attention to religion–state relations and travel to the United States, the pilgrims devoted more time to these topics than any of the non-pilgrim focus groups. In other words, the likelihood of a group of pilgrims discussing these issues was significantly higher than of a group of non-pilgrims of similar age, gender, and related socioeconomic status. (We present more detailed control tests of these factors in our conclusion to Part II.)

Consistent with their greater engagement with church-state issues and openness to participate in civic life, the pilgrims in our focus groups also showed a greater propensity than the non-pilgrims to draw on their own experiences and interpretations of faith. More specifically, when the pilgrims expressed their views they felt less compelled than the non-pilgrims to back them up with references to the primary sources of Islamic faith. In other words, the non-pilgrims were more likely to make judgments with reference to what they believed was the one and only set of canonical sources – understanding it was unlikely they themselves could possibly have the time to thoughtfully and profoundly study every word in

TABLE 6.2 *Frequency of References to the Primary sources of Islamic Faith (Allah, Prophet, Qur'an, Sunnah, and Hadith) Proportionate to Total Discussion Time in Each Focus Group (number of references per 1,000 words).*

Hajj-1 (older men)	Hajj-2 (older women)	Non-hajj-1 (younger women)	Non-hajj-2 (men mixed age)
10.3	7.1	21.3	20.0

those sources and to verify their significance with the most learned Muslim theologians. This reminded us of Sufian's thoughts and observations during the Hajj when he came to a realization that prior to embarking on the journey to Mecca most would-be pilgrims had preconceived, idealized notions of what constituted an ideal Muslim – all grounded in their understanding that it was uniquely consistent with the primary sources of Islam. And this, in turn, suggests they sought justification and validation in the primary sources of rather uniform images of ideal Muslims that may or may not have necessarily been consistent with the Islamic canon. The pilgrims had the wisdom of their experiences to take a broader, more flexible view. They did not need to mention Allah, the Prophet, the Qur'an, the Sunnah, or the Hadiths as often as the non-pilgrims did to make and validate their arguments. In actual focus group conversations, the pilgrims made references to these specific sources not even half as often as the non-pilgrims did (Table 6.2). Overall, this translated into the pilgrims being more open to considering alternative opinions in our focus group discussions.

By implication, this means repersonalization should entail defundamentalization of one's beliefs, whether religious or secular. One important implication of our content analysis in this regard is that the hajjis would be less likely to be swayed by someone who would claim to be a real authority on Islamic faith and/or who would claim a reputation for practicing or living the ostensibly pure and fundamental Islamic faith unadulterated by innovation. In other words, the hajjis would be less prone than the non-hajjis to falling under the influence of individuals such as *amirs* in the North Caucasus who claimed to be the authority on pure Islamic faith and would recruit and oversee groups of young Muslim followers. It was something that Sufian observed and recorded in his diaries during the Hajj and that impressed him much. As we discussed these findings, we concurred on one important implication. The defundamentalization should, in theory, make the hajjis less likely to be influenced or recruited by local militant Islamist activists who typically present themselves as the authoritative practitioners of pure or cleaner Islam in the North Caucasus. (However, for theoretical reasons we ascertained earlier, we are not claiming here that performing the Hajj completely inoculates one from turning to radical or violent militancy or becoming an insurgent or terrorist, since the psychological motivations for the latter are more complex and substantially different than the logic of socialization and faith we analyze in this study.)

Finally, we believe it is important to report one non-textual finding from our focus groups illustrating repersonalization among the pilgrims relative to the non-pilgrims. The latter declined our requests to have the discussions videotaped and to have individual or group pictures taken after the sessions. The hajjis agreed to both. In fact, Islam does not condone taking photos, but it never prohibits it either. Those who went to Mecca could see how pilgrims from all over the world took pictures to remember their Hajj experiences and to share them with others back home. It transpired in our focus group conversations and interviews that most hajjis made photo albums – in hard copy or/and electronic format – about the Hajj. They often downloaded pictures of their Hajj experiences onto their cell phones.

THE 3 R'S MODEL SUMMARY AND THE BIG PICTURE OF FOCUS GROUP CONVERSATIONS

Going back and forth between theory and empirics made us realize that the Pilgrims' Paradox is more than the observation of the initial condition (Hajj) and the outcome (tolerance), but also and primarily about the *paths* to tolerance. These paths are in crucial respects counterintuitive at each of the three R stages – and this is where we felt something important could be added to conventional wisdoms in social sciences and Islamic studies. And so, repositioning engendered prosocial effects not because the pilgrims anticipated and prepared themselves to experience ethno-cultural diversity in Mecca, but because they anticipated and prepared themselves to experience the deeds and emotions of connecting in person with the unifying group symbols of their monotheistic religion. It was through anticipation of unity, not diversity, that diversity amazed them once they experienced it. It was not exposure to diversity *per se*, but exposure to diversity under the expectation of uniformity that made the pilgrims we observed and interviewed open up their minds to different ways of practicing uniformity. It was this kind of mind opening that contributed to diversity appreciation rather than a simple observation of different people. And this kind of mind opening also set the stage for recategorization – i.e., rethinking of intergroup boundaries within and outside Islam. Recategorization, in turn, became possible not because exposure to diverse ethno-cultural groups generated positive views of these groups, but because it generated negative and often shocking experiences, the kind of experiences that made the pilgrims wonder how certain kinds of behavior were possible in the Holy Land. Yet, no matter what those negative behaviors were, the pilgrims ultimately learned to tolerate them, because otherwise they would have to challenge the foundations of their faith and the sanctity of Islam itself. In a sense, diversity evolved like scientific knowledge does – not so much through accumulation of confirming evidence, but through ruling out of the falsifying evidence. The pilgrims emerged from the Hajj with more tolerance not necessarily through immersion in bliss, but through overcoming the pain.

Repersonalization also worked counterintuitively, in many ways as an opposite to the way repositioning worked. Exposure to the unity of the pilgrims at Muzdalifah after the initial exposure to ethno-cultural diversity of the pilgrims in Mecca had the most striking effect in the regard. In other words, repositioning worked through the pilgrims anticipating uniformity and then experiencing diversity. Repersonalization worked through the pilgrims anticipating diversity and then experiencing uniformity. Repositioning meant embracing unity through diversity. Repersonalization meant embracing diversity through unity.

Thousands of words and hundreds of conversation segments in our focus groups among the pilgrims and non-pilgrim Muslims in Kabardino-Balkaria illustrated these counterintuitive findings systematically. It is important to emphasize here that the unit of our analysis was not a focus group (we held four), but a thematic text segment (of which we have hundreds). It was a large-N analysis where textual segments represented cases. Pulled together graphically (Figure 6.1), the focus group content data cogently summarize our principal findings and arguments. Repositioning effects come through in the pilgrims devoting significantly more discussion time to the sacred nature of the pilgrimage and its global diversity (*Axis Mundi* themes). Recategorization effects come through in significantly less time the pilgrims spent than the Muslim non-pilgrims discussing the importance of uniformity in Islamic beliefs and the behavior of Muslims. Repersonalization effects come through in the pilgrims' greater willingness than the non-pilgrims to talk about religion–state relations, participation in secular public life, and travel prospects to the United States.

This summary content analysis is a check on our interpretative findings from ethnographic observations and interviews. The former turned out to be consistent with the latter on all major themes except one – the discussion of socioeconomic equality. The pilgrims and the non-pilgrims devoted approximately the same share of focus group time to this issue. It is also notable that this theme was one of the least prominent in focus group discussions overall. The participants talked about it approximately as much as they did about traveling to the United States – the latter being in response to a wrap-up question asking participants to briefly list foreign countries where they desired to travel. Whereas we do not find the dearth of social equality discussion as confounding, it adds a nuance to our conclusions. It notably suggests that social identity and social capital effects on tolerance that we examined result more from social interactions than from social status.

Pooling the data on all major discussion themes also enabled us to examine some important alternative explanations of our findings. What if the differences between the pilgrims and the non-pilgrims that we identified were due first and foremost to differences in the participants' age, gender, or socioeconomic status?

We checked on this in two ways. First, we compared how much the mean share of discussion time per theme differed between the two Hajj groups and between the two non-Hajj groups. Figure 6.1 makes this easy to do by comparing the total length of the solid (Hajj) versus patterned (non-Hajj) stacked columns and the length of the lighter versus darker shaded part of each column within each theme. Themes are separated by vertical gridlines. So, what if the differences between the pilgrims and the non-pilgrims are *less* pronounced than the differences among the pilgrims and among the non-pilgrims on any particular theme? If that were the case, we should be able to find instances where in a cluster of two stacked columns on any given theme a darker portion of the overall taller column is shorter than a darker portion of the shorter column, or vice versa. The same should also be observed with the lighter column portions. Yet, we find no such instances in Figure 6.1 for all themes discussed a different amount of time by the pilgrims versus the non-pilgrims, with the possible exception of social equality.[13] On every theme, if the total discussion time was longer among the pilgrims or non-pilgrims, it was also longer in any of the two pilgrim groups compared to any of the two non-pilgrim groups. For example, on the *Axis* theme, the Hajj-1 group spent about 34 percent of its discussion time and the Hajj-2 group about 46 percent, for a total of 80 percent (solid color column). The non-Hajj-1 and non-Hajj-2 groups

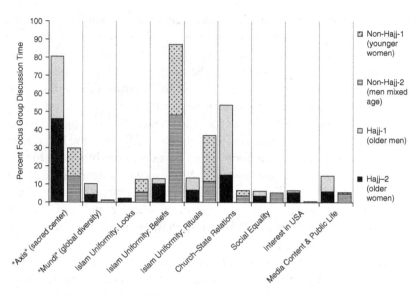

FIGURE 6.1 Principal Themes in Kabardino-Balkaria Focus Groups.

each spent approximately 15 percent of discussion time, for a total of 30 percent (the patterned column). The combined share of discussion time for the Hajj total is larger than for the non-Hajj total *and* the discussion time percentage for either Hajj-1 or Hajj-2 is larger than for either non-Hajj-1 and non-Hajj-2. In theory, however, the same totals for Hajj versus non-Hajj group discussion time could be a result of different time distributions by individual focus group. For example, what if we observed the Hajj-1 discussion time at 5 percent, Hajj-2 at 75 percent, with non-Hajj-1 at 10 percent and non-Hajj-2 at 20 percent? It would mean that whereas one Hajj group spent disproportionately more time on the theme than the non-Hajj groups, the latter *both* spent more time on it than the other Hajj group. It would then suggest that the chances of any Hajj group spending more time on the topic than any non-Hajj group would be 50–50. Something other than the pilgrimage would then plausibly explain the difference across groups. In Figure 6.1, we do not observe such asymmetric between- versus within-group time distribution on prominent discussion themes.

We also checked more closely for age and gender differences. We found they were unlikely to have anywhere near as strong an impact on discussion content differences across focus groups as the participation in the Hajj did. First, all hajjis in our groups – across gender – discussed the Hajj as *Axis Mundi*, the mass media, public life, and the United States more than twice as long as the non-hajjis did. Relative to the non-pilgrims, the pilgrims spent more than nine times as much time talking about church–state relations, but less than a fifth of the time discussing the importance of Muslims adhering to uniform standards concerning their faith, rituals, and personal appearance (cf. Figures 6.2a and 6.2b showing near-identical data patterns).

Second, when we held age and pilgrimage constant (Figures 6.2c and 6.2d), we saw gender making a marginal difference among the non-hajjis and some sizeable difference among the hajjis – yet the latter is nowhere near as pronounced as the difference on the same themes between the pilgrims and the non-pilgrims overall (Figure 6.2a).

Third, some important differences by gender across groups actually testify more to the effects of the pilgrimage than gender *per se*. Comparing Figures 6.2c and 6.2d shows that women pilgrims spent almost the same amount of time as men discussing issues related to repersonalization (the media, public life, and the United States) – a particularly notable finding among older women in a society where by tradition those topics are considered the prerogative of men. (In fact, if age mattered more, we would expect this particular theme to be significantly more salient among younger women in the non-pilgrim group.) Women in the Hajj group also spent a significant amount of time discussing another traditionally male conversation topic – church–state relations. In the non-pilgrim groups, by contrast, women practically did not discuss those two themes and men discussed them less than the men among the hajjis. In fact, women pilgrims spent more time than men non-pilgrims discussing these two themes (Figures 6.2b and 6.2d).

To sum up, differences by age and gender were not associated with the group discussion duration on these key themes when we held participation in the Hajj constant as strongly as the difference between the pilgrims and the non-pilgrims was associated with theme salience when we held constant gender and (to the extent the design allowed us) age differences (Figure 6a and 6b versus Figure 6c and 6d). We looked for but failed to observe distinct patterns of discussion duration on key themes of interest one would expect to obtain if age and gender differences were stronger than the Hajj/non-Hajj differences. We did observe this pattern, however, on a theme we used as control – a discussion of interpersonal relationships such as dating and love. This theme was (sometimes in conjunctions with the matters of faith) more prevalent in discussions among younger and female participants and less popular among older and male participants.

(a)

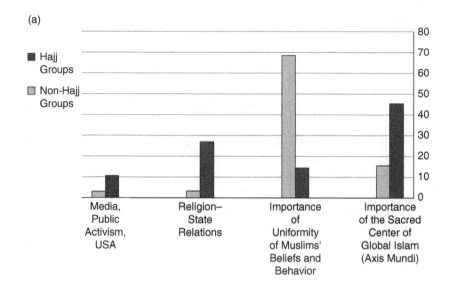

(b)

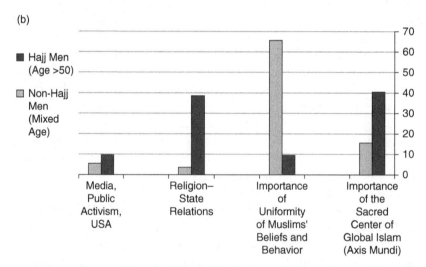

FIGURE 6.2 Age and Gender Effects Not Decisive in Focus Groups (% word count by group).

*These results are near identical for the Hajj women (over age 50) versus non-Hajj women (under age 45).

The topic consumed about 10 percent of group discussions among older women, 18 percent among the men of mixed age, and 33 percent among younger women. In the male pilgrim group where all men were over fifty, this topic was not raised at all. (This is not to say that family relationships

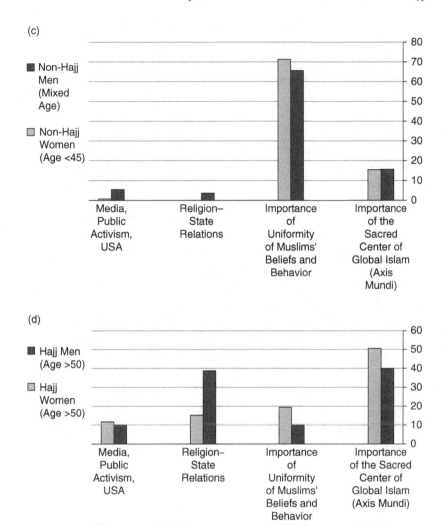

FIGURE 6.2 (cont.)

more broadly defined were not raised in that group. They were, but only in the context of the conversation on government policy, the media, and education.) Importantly, this pattern of theme salience clearly was not in evidence when it came to the three R themes of interest in this study.

* * *

The findings we have presented – reflecting on hundreds of field observations and verbal statements in interviews and focus groups – indeed appear paradoxical. The Hajj is a massive ritual of great fervor. It is physically demanding. It is imbued with monumental symbolism. It is relatively expensive for most Muslims from the North Caucasus and often requires financial sacrifice. It takes place in the heart of a turbulent region, in what once was Osama Bin Laden's home country. With all these and many more other factors, one would expect that performing the Hajj would stiffen the religious identities of the pilgrims. One would also expect them to come out of it with an inflated sense of Islamic superiority or Islamocentrism – and, consequently, to become more intolerant to religious and social others and more alienated from and hostile to secular governments and civic life. But contrary to this logic, the North Caucasus hajjis about whom we learned through our research came out as more prosocial and more tolerant to outgroups than the equally devout local Muslims who desired to perform the Hajj but had no opportunity to do so. The pilgrims, as we understood, did not necessarily become this way because during the Hajj they actively explored Islamic doctrine and actively sought out and found its embedded potential for sociopolitical tolerance – replicating the arguments of Islam experts like John Esposito or prominent Islamic reformers in the West such as Tariq Ramadan.[14] And we have also seen that they did not become this way through mere exposure to intergroup diversity or building cross-cultural social capital. The logic of repositioning, recategorization, and repersonalization was crucial to make these factors matter in the pilgrims' path to tolerance.

PART III

BEYOND THE HAJJ

7

Islam's Social Spaces: Europe versus the United States

INTRODUCTION

Does the Hajj model of social tolerance apply outside the Hajj? To what extent does the logic of repositioning, recategorization, and repersonalization apply in other settings? These are crucial questions to explore. And while we may disappoint some who are eager to see us rigorously test our findings out of sample, we hope to encourage most readers by casting the exploratory searchlight to new ideas for further inquiry and debate. Of particular value is to examine some intriguing prospects the Hajj model suggests for improving intergroup relations writ large. Two important points have to be made, however, before we continue.

First, by investigating our 3 R's model implications outside the Hajj, we in no way challenge the uniquely and fundamentally sacred meaning of the Hajj as a Pillar of Islam. Nor do they mean that if tolerance may arise from similar socializing experiences outside Islam, the special value of the Hajj would be somehow diminished. This is not a trivial concern and not lip service to cross-cultural correctness. It was raised by Sufian, who understands acutely how our academic analysis may be misinterpreted by Muslims who strongly feel the Hajj experience is part and parcel of their personal identity. In fact, Sufian's concern once again unintentionally validated the important point we made earlier about the high intrinsic value of the pilgrimage to Muslims. We strongly feel it is important to acknowledge this concern and keep it in mind. Yet, we also concluded, after an involved and at times emotional discussion, that in the final count, elaborating the lessons of the Hajj model of tolerance and applying them in other contexts, both religious and secular, actually enhances the value of the pilgrimage as a humanizing experience. Metaphorically, our examination of the Hajj effects on individuals is akin to astronomers investigating a particularly bright star while the examination of the Hajj *model* effects outside the Hajj context is akin to investigating how far its light may reach and what new worlds it may illuminate.

Second, when it comes to tolerance, it is imperative to keep in mind the distinction between the Hajj effects and the Hajj model effects. The latter is derived from our investigation of the former, but it does not mean the two are identical. One is not reducible to the other. Just as one may reasonably expect that experiencing the Hajj could affect people in ways we have not discussed, one may also reasonably expect that experiencing the Hajj model effects – i.e., from exposure to in-group diversity in high common in-group value contexts – could affect people regardless of whether they performed the Hajj or not. We are not concerned here – though it would be a good future research question – with whether and under what conditions some Hajj model effects on tolerance may be stronger or weaker than the Hajj effects *per se*. But just the same way as we approached our investigation of the *actual* Hajj effects, our focus in this plausibility probe of the Hajj *model* effects is primarily not on correlating the outcomes, but on exploring the *process*, on tracing the perceptual and behavioral pathways to improving tolerance. If the latter takes place in Hajj-like settings outside the Hajj and outside Islam – to what extent and how does the logic of repositioning, recategorization, and repersonalization matter? In doing so, we move from exploring what studying society can tell us about studying religion to what studying religion can tell us about studying society.

THE HAJJ MODEL OF SOCIAL TOLERANCE

Two principal generalizable conditions that are key to physical and symbolic repositioning during the Hajj make these socio-psychological effects benign, or prosocial. The first is the *Axis* effect – the intrinsic common in-group identity is highly valued. The second is the *Mundi* effect – social diversity within this common ingroup is high. The important condition of repositioning is that the value of common in-group identity to participants must be superordinate (higher) vis-à-vis their subgroup values. In the case of the Hajj, this happens through the pilgrimage celebrating a common identity as Muslims, which supersedes individual subgroup identities such as being Circassian or a rural-based female. As we have argued based on our findings, under these two conditions social recategorization and social capital effects become transitive – as inclusive views inside a group extend to outgroups.

The *Axis Mundi* effect has nontrivial – though somewhat counter-intuitive – lessons on how to improve relations across social groups of any kind. This possibly amounts to a significant conceptual reorientation of intergroup conflict resolution. Widely used practices to promote social and political tolerance are embedded in conventional wisdom emphasizing the importance of exposing individuals to diversity of views and behaviors through gathering together people representing different social groups and promoting intergroup understanding through discussion forums, conferences, educational exchanges, festivals, sporting events, and the like. These are all valuable methods, but they may not be sufficient and not necessarily the best solutions. The point here is not about *if* it is important to bring diverse groups into contact, but *how*.

This is where the *Axis Mundi* logic offers added value. Let us suppose we seek to improve relations between two ethnic groups. The conventional approach would suggest facilitating maximum contact and interaction between them by bringing together as many representatives of each group as possible in different formats. One would be maximizing *across-group* interaction. The *Axis Mundi* approach would additionally recommend to bring together representatives of the same ethnic group that represent as many subgroup identities as possible – in other words, to maximize *within-group* interaction. The important condition is that diverse subgroup members interact in settings encourage them to honor or celebrate or recognize or experience in any other form a positive and inclusive common in-group identity. Events in the United States such as the National Council de la Raza gatherings or Cinco de Mayo parties that celebrate the common Hispanic cultural heritage and, in doing so gather together multiple groups and associations as well as diverse individuals would serve as one example of the *Axis Mundi* model. Caucasian, African, Asian or Native Americans holding similar events to celebrate each group's common identity would be another example and stand to enhance ethno-racial tolerance. One could also expect socially variegated mass congregations of Catholics to attend the Pope's visits and addresses to improve the participants' religious and social tolerance. Again, it is important to stress here that these events must aim to celebrate, but not to make unique and exclusive, the common in-group identity. Promoting within-group contact and interactions needs to be based on positive and benign identity affirmation and to avoid claims of preponderance or superiority over other groups – including references that may denigrate and make feel inferior the participating subgroup members. As a reverse example, affirmation of exclusivity and superiority of common in-group identity – combined with low social diversity – would feed social and political intolerance, hostility, and intergroup conflict (one may consider social settings among the KKK in the South of the United States and militant *jihadist* groups in Afghanistan).

We demonstrate the significance of the Hajj model in two ways. First, we present a mini-case study on Muslim integration in predominantly secular societies, drawing, in part, on mass survey data. We then show how the Hajj tolerance model could be extended, hypothetically, outside Islam and outside religion – in particular to improve relations among ethnic groups.

INTEGRATING MUSLIMS: AMERICA VERSUS EUROPE

Acceptance of social and cultural diversity as well as civic engagement are critical issues when it comes to integration of Muslims into predominantly secular mainstream societies in Western Europe and North America – particularly considering people's increasing global mobility. As an expert on American Islam, Paul Barrett, defined it, pivotal to such integration are "respect for democracy, the Constitution, and other laws; tolerance of other faiths and of secularism; and some basic interaction with the larger society."[1] In other words, the emphasis here is on sociopolitical integration, which is of primary interest to us.

Before we proceed, remember the point we just made about the distinction between the Hajj effects (arising from completing the pilgrimage) and the Hajj model effects (arising from socializing in broader social contexts that have essential elements of the Hajj experiences, not necessarily religious in nature). In this plausibility analysis, we are not going to examine the former, only the latter. Specifically, we will not be examining whether the number of Hajj pilgrims from a country affects sociopolitical tolerance levels in that country. To do so, first of all, would be empirically fruitless. The number of Hajj pilgrims from a country is set by the Kingdom of Saudi Arabia (KSA) and typically amounts to about 0.1 percent of the estimated Muslim population of a country (Saudi Arabia is an exception). Proportionately few Muslims outside North Africa and the Middle East had ever performed the Hajj. One may think of it this way. Even if the Hajj quota stays unchanged (under a probably unrealistic assumption that Saudi Arabia will be able to constantly expand the pilgrimage infrastructure to accommodate the continuing growth of global Muslim populations) and even if no pilgrim in any given year is repeating the Hajj (which actually happens frequently), it would still take thirty years for most countries to see the proportion of hajjis in their Muslim populations reach just 3 percent assuming no pilgrims die in the meantime. One could get around this problem if survey data were available for the United States and Europe that would be similar to the 2009 Clingingsmith, Khwaja, and Kremer survey in Pakistan. Yet, as far as we have ascertained, it is not. Without this kind of individual-level data one cannot compare the *actual* Hajj effects in the United States versus Europe. But even if such data existed, analyzing them would still only allow one to examine the actual Hajj effects in different contexts, but it would not allow one to systematically examine the Hajj-*model* effects. For the same reason, we are not concerned in Chapter 8 about investigating whether certain religious experiences based on Catholicism or Protestantism might have been the decisive factor in the formation and evolution of the Hispanic immigrant associations in the United States. Doing so would mean examining the actual effects of religious ritual participation whereas we take up these cases to examine the effects of different types of socialization – one resembling the Hajj pattern more closely than the other. Besides, our reading of the literature does not suggest that religion-based effects could have accounted for the profound differences we found between America's leading Hispanic immigrant associations.

Second, at the theoretical level, we felt it is important to avoid the temptation of naïve falsifications. The news of the day offered us a potent illustration. The front pages of the *New York Times* at the time of writing had been filled for several days with sad, heartbreaking reports of the shooting rampage in San Bernardino, California, in which Syed Rizwan Farook, age twenty-eight, and his wife, Tashfeen Malik, age twenty-nine, killed fourteen people and wounded twenty-one. With the names of Middle Eastern origin, the FBI declaring the case a terrorist act, and the radical Islamic State's (ISIS) radio station claiming responsibility for the attack,[2] it is understandable that some people who knew about this book project commented along the lines: "I guess these two perpetrators never performed the Hajj." This kind of question is precisely what we mean by the impulse for naïve falsification or confirmation. It is naïve, for one, because it implies that intolerant views are qualitatively the same social phenomena as mass rampage shootings – or homicides or bombings or other terrorist acts or psychotic outbursts of violence or any violent behavior, for that matter. But they are not. This is a well-established finding in social sciences that we referenced earlier. This kind of Hajj-pegging question is also naïve because it implies the Hajj effects would obtain regardless of multiple intervening variables – such as policing capacity or availability of informers or technology – that one wouldn't consider studying the pilgrimage effects on perceptions. Thus, the Hajj effects – or, more precisely, their absence – cannot help us explain terrorism and not even jihadist militancy. But the Hajj *model* analysis can help us identify localities – from global regions to countries to neighborhoods – where communal intergroup (ethnic, religious, or other) conflict is more likely than in others.

* * *

The comparison of Europe and America we undertake is telling precisely from the standpoint of the Hajj model of tolerance. Not only has it helped us better understand the model's causal mechanisms, but it also shed light on important debates on the nature of immigrant integration. One argument with a long academic pedigree is resource determinism. From this standpoint, sociopolitical integration, like cultural integration, would primarily result from higher levels of income and education among outgroup members, regardless of other differences, including religion. The underlying logic is that wealthier and better-educated people are more likely to feel successful in society and therefore would want to belong in it. They would have the incentive to be more tolerant.[3] Exemplifying this perspective, Joselyne Cesari argued in her 2004 book, *When Islam and Democracy Meet*, that Muslims became more sociopolitically tolerant in the United States than in Europe due to being wealthier and better educated.[4] And, as we noted in Chapter 2, prominent scholars in debates on Islam's compatibility with Western-style democracy – such as John Esposito and Olivier Roy – generally take this view for granted. Indeed, economic determinism would suggest that Islamic faith is not the principal barrier to integration of Muslims in the West.

On the other hand, a more recent cross-national statistical analysis of survey data indicates that individual resources do not necessarily explain cultural integration. In an ongoing study, social scientists Justin Gest of George Mason University and Richard Nielsen of the Massachusetts Institute of Technology have been examining the data from face-to-face random-probability-sample surveys of Muslims and non-Muslims in the United States in 2010 and in the United Kingdom and France in 2008. The samples included 475 Muslims and 2,683 non-Muslims in the United States; 529 Muslims and 976 non-Muslims in Great Britain; and 541 Muslims and 978 non-Muslims in France. In a quasi-experimental approach, they first estimated opinion differences across countries and, indeed, found that Muslims in the United States generally held more sociopolitically tolerant views than Muslims in Britain and France. In particular, they were more likely to accept people of different religion becoming their neighbors and to have more confidence in the media, judiciary, and elections. They then held income, education, age, gender, and neighborhood type constant across samples. The results were practically the same, indicating that individual resources did not explain sociopolitical assimilation.[5] Moreover, in his 2010 book, *Apart: Alienated and Engaged Muslims in the West*, Gest found that, among immigrants to the United States, individual resources could cause frustration and alienation instead of sociopolitical integration due to rising expectations.[6]

When we examined Sufian's reports from the Hajj and our focus groups conversations, socioeconomic differences did not appear decisive. As we reported in Chapter 2, our focus groups in particular offered several ways to compare the views of Muslims of different occupations, income levels, and education. We saw much deeper differences between the pilgrims and the non-pilgrims than across these socioeconomic characteristics of participants.

And so we asked whether differences between sociopolitical integration of Muslims in the United States versus Europe could be explained not by the differences in their resources, but in social and political contexts. In particular, we examined to what extent these contexts may differ on the key characteristics of the Hajj model of tolerance – notably, exposure to intra-Muslim social diversity? We examined this exposure and its effects first by comparing ethnonational demographics in the United States and Europe and then by comparing the organization of key socialization venues for Muslims – mosques and religious associations.

ETHNONATIONAL DEMOGRAPHICS

Since the 1960s, the size of Muslim populations has increased significantly in both Europe and the United States. At the same time, the immigration push and pull factors as well as domestic political and socioeconomic differences resulted in a divergent pattern of Muslim demographics in these two regions. Whereas the exact size and composition of Muslim populations are hard to ascertain in each region, one difference is striking. Diversity within the Muslim populations is significantly higher in America. In the United States, no single group among Muslims – by sect, ethnicity, race, or national origin – is dominant. In a 2011 mass survey, the Pew Research Center found that foreign-born Muslims (comprising about 63 percent of Muslims in the United States) came from seventy-seven

TABLE 7.1 *Racial Composition of Muslim Population in the United States (based on the Pew Research Center 2011 American Muslims Survey).*

	Total	Foreign Born	Native Born	General Public
	%	%	%	%
White	30	38	18	68
Black	23	14	40	12
Asian	21	28	10	5
Other/Mixed	19	16	21	2
Hispanic	6	4	10	14

countries. No single country of origin accounted for more than one in six Muslim immigrants and for more than one in ten of America's Muslims. The largest number of first-generation immigrant Muslims in the United States was born in Pakistan (14 percent). Iran, the Palestinian Territories, Bangladesh, Yemen, and Jordan each accounted for approximately 5 percent and Iraq for 4 percent of foreign-born Muslims. The remaining 57 percent of America's immigrant Muslims represented seventy countries, with no single country among them accounting for more than 3 percent. This demographic dispersal is even thinner if one considers the second- and third-generation Muslims who also include a significant number of native-born African American converts. In the general population, seventy-one countries of origin account for 73 percent of America's Muslims, with no single country accounting for more than 2 percent.[7]

The diversity of origin translates into ethno-racial diversity. The Pew Research Center data show that no single ethnic or racial group is dominant among Muslims in the United States. In the 2011 Pew survey, based on a nationally representative sample of 1,033 Muslims in the United States, about 30 percent identified themselves as white, 23 percent as black, 21 percent as Asian, 6 percent as Hispanic, and 19 percent as ethno-racially other or mixed.[8] Diversity among the foreign- and native-born Muslims is also high – and higher overall than in the general population (Table 7.1).

* * *

In Western Europe, Muslim populations are also predominantly immigrant. But in contrast to the United States, large majorities of Muslims in most Western European countries come from only one or two countries. In Germany, approximately 79 percent of Muslim immigrants since the 1950s have come from Turkey. In France, nearly 70 percent are from

Algeria and Morocco. In Great Britain, 78 percent are from Pakistan and Bangladesh (formerly, Eastern Pakistan). In Spain, nearly 80 percent are from Morocco. In the Netherlands, 68 percent are from Turkey and Morocco. As a consequence, Muslim populations within most countries in Western Europe have clearly dominant ethno-racial groups. Thus, the Muslim population in France is predominantly North African Arab, in Germany it is predominantly Turkish, and in Britain it is predominantly South Asian.[9]

This divergence of Muslim demographics across the Atlantic resembles the divergence of Muslim demographics between those who get exposed to the Hajj and those who do not – i.e., between a high-subgroup-diversity and low-subgroup-diversity common group environment. The high Muslim population diversity in the United States is akin to the high Muslim population diversity that has so much impressed the pilgrims during the Hajj. The low Muslim population diversity in most of Western Europe (relative to the United States) resembles the generally low Muslim population diversity that the non-pilgrims typically experience as a given. The contrast between the socialization contexts arising from this divergence is similar to the one that characterizes repositioning versus non-repositioning, as we discussed in Chapter 4. Socialization context among Muslims in North America broadly reflects the social interaction model in Figure 4.2(b) and among Muslims in Western Europe – Figure 4.2 (a) (Chapter 4). Given this divergence, the Hajj model of tolerance would predict that overall America's Muslims stand a better chance than Western Europe's Muslims to be constructively integrated into society and polity.

Subgroup diversity does not automatically translate into tolerance and social integration. High diversity is pivotal, however, as a stage-setter for socialization among Muslims in common group settings, or in situations where they recognize, affirm, celebrate, promote, or develop their common identity as Muslims. Though they are nowhere near as symbolically, doctrinally, and experientially important as the Hajj, it is precisely in such settings that the Hajj effects reveal themselves. Recall that the benign repositioning effects in the Hajj model of tolerance arise from a combination of intrinsic value of common group identity and subgroup diversity within that group. High-value, high-diversity socialization is the key. We present two examples of this logic in the lives of Muslims in the United States and in Europe.

ARCHITECTURAL AXIS MUNDI

The first example is socialization among Muslims to design and build mosques. The mosques – coming from *masjid* in Arabic – are important symbolic spaces where Islamic belief and practice are one. They represent important common values in Islam. A meeting or, rather, a series of meetings and discussions about the construction or remodeling of a mosque could be legitimately considered a high common group value setting. The issue is also potentially divisive. Islamic canonical texts and traditions do not prescribe a universal mosque design aside from certain basic elements such as running water for ablution before prayer and a prayer space oriented toward the *Qibla* (the direction of Mecca). According to Akel Ismail Kahera, a professor at the Prairie View A&M University School of Architecture in Texas who specializes in architecture and community development, "There is no prescription for a mosque in the holy text in the Qur'an."[10] *The Architect*, the magazine of the American Institute of Architects, a trade association, notes: "Historically, the mosque aesthetic has varied dramatically from region to region. The Muslim world extends from Spain and Africa to Asia, resulting in seven distinct regional styles – from open courtyard plans in Spain and North Africa to the pyramidal roof construction of Southeast Asia and the massive central domes of Turkey."[11]

This means the diversity of regional subgroups within Islamic communities stands to make a difference. From the standpoint of our Hajj model, under conditions of high regional diversity, the debate on mosques is likely to gravitate toward issues least divisive with respect to the common Islamic identity, something that would cut across regional differences. In fact, a report on Islam in America by *The Economist* magazine suggests this is largely the case: "Different traditions get squashed together." Christopher B. McCoy – an architect from Kentucky who has designed seven mosques in the United States since 1998, including the two-story, 13,810-square-foot Islamic Center of Elizabethtown, KY – told *The Economist* that regional architectural preferences were hardly the central issue among local Muslim communities. Whereas lamenting that some of his elderly clients "often wanted to stick a minaret on their mosques to make them look like something from back home," overall, he said: "the question is usually not whether we should have an Indian- or a Saudi-style dome but, can we afford a dome?"[12] This is understandable. In a context in which many groups may want to prefer architectural solutions that looks like back home, there is likely to be a greater understanding that no group has sufficient numbers to claim that their ancestral identity is more prototypical and therefore deserves to be architecturally honored more than others.

In another indication of the prosocial effects of common identity affirmation in high-diversity settings, McCoy was reported as calling the present "an exciting time for the architectural commission of mosques."[13] The first decade of the twenty-first century witnessed a rapid rise in the number of new Islamic cultural centers in the United States. According to a survey conducted by a University of Kentucky professor of Islamic studies, Ihsan Bagby, the United States had more than 2,100 mosques in 2013 – 74 percent more than in 2000. He estimated also that purpose-built new mosques accounted for nearly a third of this increase.[14] Given his experience with local communities requesting the new Islamic centers, McCoy felt America's Muslims were moving in the direction of developing their own distinctive architectural designs – a reflection of how freedom in practicing Islam reflects innovative self-expression in a maturing of Muslim American culture. As he told *The Architect*:

Muslims moved to the United States en masse 40 years ago, and architecturally, the first mosques were in adapted or rented structures. What you are seeing now are groups who have grown out of those first homes as well as a new generation of American-born Muslims desiring their own purpose-built space. ... Domes and minarets are beautiful architectural symbols, but not Islamic by themselves. Similar to the way Shakers used their faith to guide the manner in which they built, Muslims can expose the inner beauty of a local vernacular in a uniquely Islamic way.[15]

In Britain, the mosque design evolved differently, reflecting the presence and the influence of the dominant South Asian ethno-cultural group in the Muslim population. Shahed Saleem, the author of *The British Mosque: A Social and Architectural History* and founder of the architectural firm Makespace Architects, specializing in mosque design, emphasized the importance of ethnic cultural heritage in shaping the prevalent mosque architecture in Britain: "A mosque has an exceptionally simple programme. ... This means that every formal and architectural representation of the mosque we see beyond this is a cultural accretion accumulated across time and culture."[16] What Saleem calls "the Brit-Mosque" evolved over 120 years representing ecological and architectural adaptations around the central features of Indian Mughal and Pakistani mosques. Saleem's next statement illustrates how ethno-cultural group dominance reveals itself in the evolution of the Brit-Mosque: "In theory, it can take on any architectural form and express almost any visual language. What we generally see, however, and especially in the post-war era of mosque building, is the continuous return to known architectural motifs, domes, minarets and pointed arches. One explanation for this is that the mosque in Britain is relied upon to represent the religious and cultural identities of its commissioners in an immediate and assertive way."[17]

This sounds predictable, if we apply the Hajj model perspective: big *Axis*, small *Mundi*.

And the *Axis Mundi* perspective also explains the following paradox. While one may assume that debates about the mosque design would be limited by shared cultural understandings of the dominant ethnic group among British Muslims and the reported assertiveness of Islamic community leaders, these debates appear to be more intense and acrimonious than those Christopher McCoy observed in the United States. According to Saleem, in England, "Mosques are perhaps the most contested building type in the city, provoking debate – sometimes fierce – on issues of identity, social change, race, politics, style, and taste."[18] One outcome of these debates, as Saleem's studies imply, is not diversity, but the assertion and reproduction of cultural and religious stasis, if not social alienation: "The mosque remains a conceptually static space, unable to diversify from its conservative role as a place for the preservation and perpetuation of religious ritual."[19] Another plausible implication of the combination of acrimony and dominant-group assertiveness is that in the United States, Muslims have been commissioning a significantly larger number of purpose-built mosques relative to the total number of mosques in a country. Experts estimated that the total number of mosques in America and Britain around 2013 was approximately the same – 2,100 and 2,000, respectively. However, in the United States, just since 2000, purpose-built mosques accounted for nearly 25 percent of the total. In Britain, mosques purpose-built over 120 years still accounted for just more than 13 percent of the total.[20]

This difference is not only about architecture or religious expression or cultural demographics, but also about socialization. Almost from their beginnings to the present, mosques have played important social functions far beyond the original meaning of *masjid* as a "worship place" or "prostration in prayer." One may conceive of a mosque as the multiple intersection of the sacred and profane (or secular) in Islamic life. In the United States in particular, mosques are typically part of cultural centers with ancillary rooms or buildings where visitors may meet socially and engage in scholarship or commerce. As architect Christopher McCoy explained: "The Islamic Center is more of a hub of cultural and community events containing other elements such as multipurpose rooms and halls, meetings rooms, offices, and gymnasiums."[21] From the standpoint of our Hajj 3 R's model of tolerance, the mosque is a microcosm of *Axis Mundi* – suggesting that in America, they are more likely to be a conduit for Muslims developing inclusive views, prosocial behavior, and stronger civic engagement than they would in Western Europe. That being said, we also understand that the case of mosques is a window on how the Hajj model may apply outside the Hajj context, an illustration of how our central findings and lessons from empirical analysis could apply out of sample. We do not claim the mosques case offers systematic empirical proof, only that it illuminates important aspects of the *Axis Mundi* process – and that means they are worth exploring further.

TRANSITIVE SOCIALIZATION

Our second example of the *Axis Mundi* effects is Islamic associations or societies – voluntary public forums bringing together Muslims in a nation or region, typically to discuss common problems and their solutions so as to improve the well-being of the community. In the United States, the case in point is the Islamic Society of North America (ISNA). According to *The Encyclopedia of Muslim-American History*, the ISNA by 2010 was "the largest Muslim-American coalition in the United States, with a membership of more than 400 mosques and Islamic Centers." Since it was founded in 1983, the ISNA's membership has increased from just over 5,000 to nearly 25,000 members in 2007, and its operating budget has grown from $1.1 million to $3.7 million. By that time, its principal role became to serve "as an authoritative voice in influencing – though never formally regulating – the relationship of Muslim Americans to one another and to larger American institutions, including the U.S. government and the media."[22] In this sense, the ISNA illustrates the relationship between in-group and out-group socialization. Its experience shows that the accommodation and affirmation of diversity within a common group united by a high-value identity could indeed translate into more inclusive outgroup attitudes and prosocial behavior.

The reporter of *The Economist* who covered the 2014 ISNA annual convention had no clue about our theory. And thus, the resulting selection of vignettes from the convention that clearly impressed the reporter amounts to a richly detailed unwitting testimony of the *Axis Mundi* effects at work. It is worth quoting in full, since it colorfully and seamlessly illustrates the in-group-to-out-group transitivity of positive socialization effects:

[T]he Islamic Society of North America's gathering, which took place in Detroit over the Labour Day weekend, served as a reminder of how well America is assimilating a religious minority that has often struggled to feel at home in Europe. The conference hall was filled with Muslims of different races wearing clothes that identified them with different traditions. The Islamic Boy Scouts had a stand, as did a Muslim liberal-arts college from California. People discussed how to erect mosques without infringing America's arcane building regulations, or swapped business cards in the food court. The star turn was a Southern Baptist, Jimmy Carter. . . . The only overt hostility to Israel came from two Hasidic Jews in fur *shtreimel* hats, who had come from Brooklyn to announce their solidarity with the people of Gaza.²³

The description first lays out the key dimensions of subgroup diversity under the umbrella of common group identity – different races, different clothes, different traditions, the Muslim Boy Scouts, and the Muslim liberal arts students. It also conveys the dynamism of socialization among these diverse subgroups, as in "people discussed" and "swapped business cards." Then, the report details prosocial out-group behavior and civic engagement – the participation of a noted Southern Baptist and Hasidic Jews, and dealing with "America's arcane building regulations."

The Economist report reflected substantive changes in the ISNA since the mid-1990s, which addressed the then growing problems of declining membership, funding, and association newspaper circulation following public opposition to the 1990 Gulf War. The turning point was in 1993, when a new ISNA leadership adopted what essentially was an *Axis Mundi* approach. Instead of predominantly focusing on projects and services targeting small local Muslim communities, the association "engaged in national collaborative efforts." Key to these efforts was a strategy designed "to incorporate Muslims from a variety of backgrounds" – i.e., increasing subgroup diversity within a high common value group – "in both its activities and leadership structure."²⁴

The strategy succeeded on both counts. From 1993 to 2007, the number of attendees of the ISNA's annual convention increased from 6,000 to 35, 000. The circulation of the ISNA's newspaper, *Islamic Horizons*, also increased manifold, reaching 50,000. Increasing grassroots diversity brought in vibrancy and increased intergroup socialization among members. More than 500 business set up booths at the 2008 convention. Diversity, socialization, and civic engagement promotion continued to increase – a trend that positively impressed *The Economist* reporter in 2014. In 2007, the ISNA generated an agreement between Shi'a and Sunni Muslim Americans, seeking to forego discord and to promote intra-Islamic unity. It was a successful response, addressing concerns arising from the growing sectarian conflict in Iraq. (Initiatives such as this almost certainly are part of the explanation as to why mass and brutal violent sectarian conflicts in Iraq and Syria – particularly with ISIS waging war against the Iraqi government at the time of writing – have not resulted in sectarian clashes in the United States over the issues dividing the Shi'a and the Sunnis in the Middle East.) Meanwhile, the ISNA also set up departments to get its members to engage with issues such as marriage, domestic violence, conflict resolution, nonprofit management, refugee resettlement, banking and finance, Internet use, education, leadership, public communication, and community outreach – a clear evidence of promoting civic activism.[25]

The association's leadership structure also diversified significantly. In the late 1990s, three women were elected to the ISNA board. In 2005, one of them, Ingrid Mattson, got elected as the ISNA's first female president. A white Muslim American and an African American Muslim were elected vice presidents of ISNA. National Islamic leaders with their own followers were also elected to the board – notably, W. D. Mohammed and Jamil Abdullah al-Amin. The ISNA joined the National Consultative (Shura) Council that, in addition to these two leaders, included other large Muslim associations, such as the Islamic Circle of North America, CAIR, MAS, and the Muslim Public Affairs Council.

Embracing a burgeoning ethno-racial, intrareligious, and social diversity of its members and affiliates while promoting the unity of Muslim Americans as a high-value goal, the ISNA also expanded outreach to non-Muslim groups and associations. In a broader theoretical sense, these developments illustrate how inclusiveness within a common group leads to inclusiveness of outgroups. Thus, ISNA partnered with the National Council of Churches and established the Office of Interfaith and Community Alliances. In 2007, the association signed the "A Common World between Us" declaration, joining more than 300 Christian and 138 Muslim scholars and organizations that sought to improve relations between Christians and Muslims. At the same time, ISNA adopted a goal of becoming "a Muslim Rev. Billy Graham" to the federal government and started participating in interfaith events. The latter included taking part in the National Prayer Breakfast to mark the presidential inauguration of Barack Obama in 2009.

Since 2007, the ISNA has participated in efforts to improve Muslim–Jewish relations within and outside North America. Each year, the association joined The Foundation for Ethnic Understanding, presided by Rabbi Marc Schneier, in the annual Weekends of Twinning to build partnerships between synagogues, mosques, and other Jewish and Muslim groups on issues of common concern, such as hunger and poverty relief. In 2011, the ISNA reported, "thousands of people from over 250 synagogues, mosques and Muslim and Jewish groups took part in the Weekend of Twinning in 16 countries around the world." Thousands of Muslims and Jews joined to feed hungry and homeless people and to discuss the shared moral imperative in Islam and Judaism to provide this form of aid.[26]

In Western Europe, one finds no functional equivalent of the ISNA on the same scale, even though formally Muslim societies and associations abound in Europe and many of them declare intent to improve relations among Muslims and between Islam and other faiths. *The Economist* quote cited earlier reflects this absence whereby attending the annual ISNA convention makes the journalist marvel "how well America is assimilating a religious minority that has often struggled to feel at home in Europe." The story of the Muslim Council of Cooperation in Europe (CMCE) – one plausible candidate to play the role of the ISNA in the EU – is a good illustration. It was founded in 1996 in response to the realization that the Muslim population in Europe was increasing and its claims for accommodation would have to be addressed. The European Commission president, Jacques Delors, invited a few Muslims leaders, notably Mohammed Arkoun and Mohammed Boussouf, who had been active before with European institutions to serve as permanent liaison between the EU and local Muslim organizations. While CMCE leaders worked on important grassroots initiatives and concerns such as the construction of a big mosque in Strasbourg, the organization failed to evolve into a polymorphic and vibrant vehicle for the assimilation of Muslims into European societies, the way the ISNA did in the United States. Almost two decades after being founded, the CMCE's main Internet presence – a link from its Wikipedia page accessed – was about a half-page of turgid officialese on the web page of the Dialog with Religions Archives of the European Commission's Bureau of European Policy Advisers. Its homepage link in Wikipedia led to the advertisements of the Australian UGG sheepskin boots in Finnish when we researched this issue in December 2015.

The CMCE programmatic documents and activities reveal the far-reaching effects of the presence of dominant ethnonational groups among Muslims in major Western European states. The strongest of these effects, most likely, was an emphasis on Islamic identity assertiveness within each country – which translated into the push for recognition of the uniqueness and special status of Islamic identity at the European level rather than into a push for integration of Islam. The very terms used to describe Muslim populations by the CMCE and the ISNA reflect this conceptual distinction. Unlike the ISNA, which since the early 1990s promoted the concept of "Muslim Americans" (stressing unity in diversity), the CMCE has promoted the concept of "European Muslims" (implying ethnonational specificity of Muslim communities). The conceptualization of "European Muslims" was the cornerstone of the "Muslim Charter" which the CMCE published in 2002, based on the Charter of the Central Council for Muslims in Germany (ZMD). Having analyzed this document, an expert on European Islam, Berengere Massignon, concluded:

The CMCE document set forth a list of ambitious demands in favour of European Muslims in terms of recognition, both symbolic and financial. These demands aim at an equality with the historic religions as well as a recognition of the specificity of Islam. ... On the basis of this text, it appears that the logic of Europeanization advocated by the CMCE does not fit in with a *strategy of assimilation* but with the *assertion of identity* in a context of sedentarisation of the European Muslims and their access to national, and therefore European, citizenship.[27]

The assertion of identity approach is exemplified by the CMCE's emphasis on the prospectively growing number of Muslims within the EU as the main reason why Islamic identity needed to be asserted and recognized as special, deserving exceptional treatment on the part of European institutions. Massignon found it "characteristic" of European Muslim associations to argue that "some Muslims add the number of European Muslim immigrants to the population of those Muslim-majority countries that may join the Union, in order to highlight the weight of Islam in Europe."[28] This formulation implied that the emphasis was on the recognition of Islamic uniformity across EU states rather than on bringing Europe's Muslims together to celebrate and benefit from the diversity of their communities. A notable example of this position was the Report of the High-Level Advisory Group established at the initiative of the president of the European Commission, "Dialogue between Peoples and Cultures in the Euro-Mediterranean Area," in September 2003. The report noted that eastward enlargement would bring into the EU 10 percent of Bulgaria's Muslims, followed by the Muslim majority of Bosnia-Herzegovina, and – potentially – Turkey's 80 million Muslims.[29]

At the national level, the dominance of ethnonational groups within Muslim populations translated into fragmentation of Muslim associations along intrareligious, socioeconomic, or ideological lines. In Britain, for example, debates on Islamic doctrine and practice between the Barelvis and the Deobandis split up the dominant South Asian Muslim population. Divisions among the tribal Biraderi networks have hampered the integration of Pakistani Muslims into social and political life.[30] Major Muslim associations explicitly positioned themselves to prioritize serving specific ethnic populations. The Islamic Society of Britain and the Muslim Burial Council said they would first and foremost address the needs of "non-Arab Sunni Muslims," whereas the Muslim Association of Britain oriented itself toward "Arab Muslims."[31] One member of the influential Muslim Council of Britain (MCB) interviewed in 2007 described this fragmentation:

We have major ego trappings and sectarian divides; you will not go to that mosque because that other mosque has a particular united image and particular Muslim identity. Our key problem is trying to keep everyone happy. So the Deobandis who are mainly Pakistani and the Gujaratis run their particular organization and are different to Salafis, yet they have the common identity of the Shahada [testimony of faith].[32]

Fragmentation along ethno-regional lines has also been characteristic of Muslim associations in France. The *Yearbook of Muslims in Europe* – a compilation of contributions from European scholars specializing in Islam – concluded in 2009 that "the main Muslim organizations in France reflect countries of origin." Thus, the Grande Mosquee de Paris (www.mosque-de-paris.org) represents the Algerians; the Federation Nationale des Musulmans de France (FNMF) and its more recent spinoff the Rassemblement des Musulmans de France (RFM) represent the Moroccans; and the Comite de Coordination des Musulmans Turcs represents the Turks.[33]

In the context of the dominant ethnic group demographics, the one plausible cross-ethnic umbrella organization in France – l'Union des Organisations Islamiques de France (UOIF, www.uoif-online.com) – has remained relatively marginal in scope. Instead of uniting Muslims across ethnonational backgrounds, it targeted minority Arab Muslim groups in France that also happened to be distinct from the majority Algerians and

Moroccans on ideological grounds – emphasizing the goals resembling those of the Muslim Brotherhood of Tunisia and Egypt. The debate also emerged about UOIF radicalism and anti-Semitism.[34] When the French government in 2003 facilitated the establishment of the French Council of the Muslim Faith (Conseil français du culte musulman, CFCM), the dominant ethnonational groups – the Moroccans and the Algerians – exploited the rule whereby the election of the council leadership is based on the size of prayer space in its member organizations' mosques. In the unstated *de facto* recognition of Moroccan dominance, the French interior ministry made sure that the voting in the first two elections in 2003 and 2005 favored the rector of the Paris Grand Mosque, Dalil Boubakeur, as the Council president.[35] The resulting intergroup rivalries undermined the council and no ISNA equivalent emerged in France. Similar organizational and doctrinal issues – traceable to the ethnonational group dominance within Muslim populations – also precluded the Central Council for Muslims in Germany (Zentralrat der Muslime in Deutschland, ZMD) and the Islamic Commission of Spain (Comisión Islámica de España) to develop strong integrationist orientation and capacity as did the ISNA in North America.

Of course, the reality is more complex. In the United States, for example, as Peter Skerry of Boston College argued in 2011, other Islamic associations – notably, the Muslim Public Affairs Council (MPAC), the Islamic Circle of North America (ICNA), and the Council on American Islamic Relations (CAIR) – make the picture of Muslim American integration considerably more "muddled," with the kind of emphasis on Islamic values, religious conversion, and Islamism that is largely absent in the ISNA.[36] In Western Europe, the CMCE and some national associations have also promoted, in part, the agenda of social and political integration and assimilation. Yet, on the whole, the contrast between the *Axis Mundi* dynamic exemplified by the ISNA and the dominant group dynamic exemplified by the evolution of Islamic organizations in Europe is distinct and telling.

MELTING POT MATTERS

Academic analysis shows that integration of immigrants – or any minority outgroups – in mainstream society can be construed as both agreement and achievement. The former means sharing predominant social attitudes and behaviors. The latter means achieving around average individual resource levels, such as income, education, and residence type.[37] They may also be viewed as predominantly cultural versus economic integration. Both aspects could be viewed in terms of the classic push-pull dichotomy of social forces driving immigration – with the "push" being an indicator of an outgroup members' effort to integrate and the "pull" being an indicator of the host state and society's openness or "welcomeness" to minority out-group integration. In fact, both would reflect the push-pull interaction. The synergy may be positive – with migrants being more eager to integrate into more acceptant host societies and with the host societies likely to become more accepting upon witnessing migrants' constructive efforts to integrate and contribute. Or it may be negative – if the reverse pattern obtains. For instance, if migrants are segregated through certain settlement policies yet provided with welfare assistance, they may have less incentive to integrate. In mainstream society, this lack of incentive could be viewed as unwillingness to integrate culturally and economically, stoking exclusionist sentiments. Typically, as a significant body of literature shows, migrants gradually change their attitudes to conform to those prevalent in the rest of their receiving societies or communities – though not straightforwardly, with migrant community structures and destination social contexts playing a crucial role and with agreement resulting in more positive or more negative social attitudes.[38]

On both agreement and achievement measures, through multiple complexities and caveats, Muslims in America have been doing considerably better than in Europe – suggesting a more positive push-pull integration synergy.

AGREEMENT

Systematic comparative analysis of public opinion shows that Muslims in the United States are significantly more likely to have more inclusive and moderate political and social views – views more consistent with the logic of the "melting pot" that has converted millions of immigrants from all over the world into civic Americans since the founding of the United States. In a sense, one may argue, the *Axis Mundi* effects are registered in individual views. They are not only about society, but they are also about the mind.

In 2006 and 2007, the Pew Research Center polled more than 3,500 Muslims in Britain, France, Germany, and Spain and more than 1,000 Muslims in the United States, using sophisticated sampling techniques to account for the demographics of predominantly Islamic populations in these countries. One of the central findings – based on the indicators of social integration extensively tested across cultures and over time – was that the U.S. Muslims were more socially mainstream than the European Muslims. Fewer than half (48 percent) of Muslims in the United States reported considering themselves first as Muslim rather than American compared to almost two-thirds of respondents on average in the four European countries (Table 7.2). In three of the four European countries surveyed by the Pew Research Center, a significantly larger number of respondents said they felt they were Muslims rather than citizens of each respective state – i.e., 81 percent in Britain, 66 percent in Germany, and 69 percent in Spain. Only in France the numbers were about the same (46 percent).[39] Also, Muslim Americans showed greater sensitivity to the problems facing the integration of women into Islamic societies, with significantly more of them than in Europe saying life was better for women in the United States than in Muslim countries. Far more Muslims in the United States than in Europe expressed their opposition to religious extremism – about 51 percent, compared with the average of 36.5 percent for Europe's four surveyed nations (Table 7.2). Only in Britain, the number was approximately the same (52 percent).[40] In addition, a significantly smaller number of Muslim Americans bought into anti-American conspiracy theories and acknowledged that Arabs carried out the 9/11 attacks on New York and Washington, DC. Related to that, fewer Muslims in the United States than in Europe said that suicide bombings against civilians could be often or sometimes justified in order to defend Islam from its enemies (Table 7.2).[41]

In another survey four years later, the Pew Research Center asked a broader range of questions in the United States, confirming these integrative trends. About 56 percent of respondents said they wanted to adopt "American customs and ways of life" compared to only 20 percent who insisted on remaining distinct from the larger American society. And whereas on average Muslim Americans were less willing to display an American flag at home than the general public (44 percent versus 59 percent), their attitudes on key dimensions of social integration showed significant convergence with the mainstream. Only 31 percent said that being Muslim made them feel in conflict with modern society (exactly the same as the number of Christians in the United States). About 33 percent reported working with others to fix neighborhood problems and participating in other social events compared to 38 percent in the general public. Given the combined margin of sampling error in surveys that produced these findings, this difference is not greater than chance. Similarly within the statistical margin of error from the general public was the number of Muslim Americans saying they saw no difference

TABLE 7.2 *Muslims Were More Socially Mainstream in the United States than in Europe (percent respondents in the Pew Research Center surveys).*

	USA 2007	Europe*(2006)
Feel they are Muslim, not American/ European	48	65.5
Life is worse for women in Muslim countries	62	54
Very concerned about Islamic extremism	51	36.5
Believe Arabs carried out 9/11 attacks	40	33.25
Believe suicide bombings of civilians can be justified**	8	13.5

* Average for Britain, France, Germany, and Spain – in that order in formula
** Sum of often, sometimes, or rarely (to defend Islam from its enemies)

between women and men as political leaders (68 percent versus 72 percent) and reporting that their community was a good or an excellent place to live (79 percent versus 83 percent). On other important measures, the difference was wider, yet not prohibitively large. This concerns respondents who said they were registered voters (66 percent among Muslims versus 79 percent among the general public), voted in the 2008 presidential election (64 percent versus 76 percent), followed government and public affairs all or most of the time (70 percent versus 79 percent), and believed in evolution (45 percent versus 52 percent). In addition, where the data were available for 2007 and 2011, one finds Muslim Americans feeling better integrated into American society on practically all indicators. Thus, the number of Muslim Americans who felt the U.S. government effort to combat terrorism was sincere rose from 26 percent to 43 percent. The number of those opposing Islamist extremism (i.e., concerned about it), went up from 51 percent to 60 percent. The number of Muslim Americans saying their community was a good or an excellent place to live increased from 72 percent to 79 percent and the number of those saying homosexuality should be accepted by American society jumped from 27 percent to 39 percent (a particularly impressive gain in just four years).[42]

ACHIEVEMENT

In immigration studies, economic attainment has long been considered one of the cornerstones of out-group integration in host states and societies.[43] The integration literature strongly indicates that socioeconomic attainment is not necessarily related to cultural integration (further undermining the argument of resource determinists with respect to differences in Muslim integration in America versus Europe). In a multilevel regression analysis of data from five waves of the European Values Surveys (from 1981 through 2005), Pippa Norris and Robert Inglehart found that the biggest determinant of Muslims' stance on gender equality, divorce, abortion, homosexuality, and democratic values was the difference between prevailing views on these issues in their countries of origin and countries of destination. On the whole, European Muslims' social views were about midway between the former and the latter. Individual income levels mattered somewhat, but nowhere near as much as relocation to and residence in a European destination country. In fact, cutting-edge, multimethod experimental research on immigrant integration in France indicates that it is not that economic opportunities open the gates for cultural integration, but that it is culturally exclusionist views that close the gates to economic opportunities of migrants. Reporting in the authoritative *Proceedings of National Academy of Sciences of the United States of America*, Claire Adida, David Laitin, and Marie-Anne Valfort showed with a correspondence test that in the French labor market, Muslims faced a significant barrier to entry – other important socioeconomic characteristics being equal, a job applicant with a name associated with Muslim heritage was two and a half times less likely to be invited for a job interview than an applicant with a name associated with Christian heritage.[44] In the United States, a similar experiment found that hiring discrimination against Muslims compared to Christians was less widespread. It was most likely in ten states with the most significant Republican Party majorities around 2012 presidential election and nonexistent in ten states with the most significant Democratic Party majorities around that time (with the latter accounting for a larger share of the U.S. population than the former).[45] These societal barriers to integration through economic achievement also come through in comparative polling data – scarce though it is. According to Pew Research Center mass opinion surveys, about half of Muslims polled in Great Britain (46 percent), France (52 percent), Germany (56 percent), and Spain (55 percent) in July 2006 identified unemployment as one of their principal worries. In the United States, a similarly designed Pew Research Center found in May 2007 that only 2 percent of Muslims identified jobs and financial problems as their biggest problems. (These surveys provide the most closely matching questions at the most similar point in time to compare the perceptions of Muslims in Europe versus the

TABLE 7.3 *Income Disparities between Muslims and General Public in Advanced Democracies (Pew Research Center polls, 2007).*

	Muslims	General public	Difference
United States	%	%	
$75,000 or more	26	28	−2
$30,000–$74,999	39	39	0
Less than $30,000	35	33	+2
	100	100	
France			
€29,500 or more	20	32	−12
€17,500–€29,499	35	41	−6
Less than €17,500	45	27	+18
	100	100	
Spain			
€21,500 or more	7	26	−19
€14,500–€21,499	20	24	−4
Less than €14,500	73	50	+23
	100	100	
Germany			
€30,000 or more	12	26	−14
€18,000–€29,999	35	39	−4
Less than €18,000	53	35	+18
	100	100	
Great Britain			
£40,000 or more	13	23	−10
£20,000–£39,999	26	38	−12
Less than £20,000	61	39	+22
	100	100	

Pew Research Center noted that exactly comparable income ranges were not available across countries.

United States on this issue.) The difference on this issue between Europe and the United States persists even if one assumes that in the United States' Pew Center poll, respondents who said their main problem was discrimination, racism, and prejudice did so because they felt it prevented them from achieving higher income or social status. In that case, one may consider that 21 percent of American Muslims worried about achievement barriers – still a 30 percent smaller share of Muslims than in Europe.

With these considerations, other Pew Center surveys indicate that social integration of Muslims in America has been paying off economically, with the difference between integration of Muslims in the United States and Europe in that sense well-pronounced. As Table 7.3

shows, most Muslim Americans report about the same household income as any American. This is not the case in the four European countries where the Pew Center surveyed Muslims. There, on average, more than 20 percent more Muslims than country residents in general were likely to be in the bottom third income group nationally. Conversely, nearly 14 percent of European Muslims were less likely to be in the country's top third income earners.[46]

* * *

Given all these divergent trends, two caveats must be kept in mind. First, our comparison does not imply that integration of Muslims into European societies is unlikely – for all the problems, some of them with tragic endings in mass violence. A significant number of individual Muslims and leaders of Muslim associations in Europe desire and work to promote integration. As the U.S. envoy to Muslim communities, Farah Pandith, observed in 2007: "Muslims in Europe are working hard to try to find ways to educate their own communities and talk about the balance between being Muslim and Western, not Muslim or Western."[47] Second, socialization dynamics within religious communities are not the only – and, in their own right – not necessarily the most important and crucial factor that drives integration. Immigration and citizenship policies, social welfare policies, public opinion among social majorities within states, cultural traditions, and many other factors play a part. Yet, they all, in important ways, work through rather than aside from socialization processes. In other words, understanding these forces would not necessarily reduce the importance of looking at in-group socialization, but is likely to give one a more nuanced understanding how this socialization works.

8

The *La Raza* Axis: Hispanic Integration in North America

THE HAJJ MODEL BEYOND THE SACRED

As we explored the social effects of the Hajj in the North Caucasus and Islamic socialization in Europe and North America, one big question came up in our conversations: Is the *Axis Mundi* effect unique to religious practice? Consequently, does this benign effect of symbolic in-group socialization obtain only with religious identity, or could religious experiences also shed light on group identity formation and intergroup relations outside religion?

Mircea Eliade's seminal work, which initially informed our theoretical interpretations of Sufian's experiences during the pilgrimage, draws a strong distinction between the sacred and the profane in human nature. This distinction is the spatial, perceptual, and behavioral bedrock of religious identity. What distinguishes every sacred space, Eliade argues, is "a hierophany, an irruption of the sacred that results in detaching a territory from the surrounding cosmic milieu and making it qualitatively different."[1] And yet, the beauty and power of Eliade's insight is that it offers us much more than a strict, black-and-white, sacred-profane dichotomy. On the one hand, Eliade masterfully dissects the perceptual-behavioral essence of hierophany as the power of religion to meaningfully center the individual. The profane space is homogenous and thus decentered. The sacred space is nonhomogeneous because it is organized around a centering symbol, the *Axis Mundi* of the imaginary world, of the *imago mundi*. The *Qibla*, the iconostasis, the temple threshold, the skyward opening of shaman's yurt, come through as the *Axis* of the human cognitive-emotional universe and in doing so they sacralize life.

On the other hand, the threshold of a place of worship serves not only as a powerful symbol of the sacred-profane distinction, but also as

172

a symbol of the interconnectedness between the two: "The threshold is the limit, the boundary, the frontier that distinguishes and opposes two worlds – and at the same time the paradoxical place where those worlds communicate, where passage from the profane to the sacred world becomes possible."[2]

The sacred and profane in the real world meaningfully interact. The following passages from Eliade illustrated to us the importance of using insights gained from the study of religious identity to examine nonreligious social identities and relations:

[A] profane existence is never found in its pure state. To whatever degree he may have desacralized the world, the man who has made his choice in favor of a profane life never succeeds in completely doing away with religious behavior. ... Even the most desacralized existence still preserves traces of a religious valorization of the world ...

... this experience of profane space still includes values that to some extent recall the nonhomogeneity peculiar to the religious experience of space. There are, for example, privileged places, qualitatively different from all others – a man's birthplace, or the scenes of his first love, or certain places in the first foreign city he visited in youth. Even for the most frankly nonreligious man, all these places still retain an exceptional, a unique quality; they are the "holy places" of his private universe, as if it were in such spots that he had received the revelation of a reality other than that in which he participates through his ordinary daily life. ... A similar ritual function falls to the threshold of the human habitation, and it is for this reason that the threshold is an object of great importance. Numerous rites accompany passing the domestic threshold – a bow, a prostration, a pious touch of the hand, and so on.[3]

In fact, as we considered this point, we realized that both of us still follow a seemingly meaningless profane ritual in our daily lives rooted in superstitions widespread in Russia: we do not shake hands across the threshold. Many times while in America, we have either invited a person who extended a hand in greeting inside or we stepped outside to shake their hand. In doing so, we unwittingly sought to avoid violating the once sacred valorization of the threshold that we still observed without giving ourselves an account of its religious meaning.

Thus, our big take from Eliade was that religion has symbolic power, not only because it offers uniquely powerful symbols tied into personal visualizations of the beginning and the end of life, but because this powerful symbolism is something that transcends religious experiences. Eliade's own work, we decided, is powerful precisely because it uses insights from our understanding of religion to make us think about the world outside religion. It is powerful because it has discerned and clearly defined, or qualitatively operationalized, the concept of symbolic centering, the *Axis Mundi* effect, that transcends the sacred and profane and clarifies the vast differences and innate similarities between the two. The micro foundations of this underlying and transcending effect are preeminently social – the *Axis Mundi* is a cognitive and emotional dynamic that organizes or defragments any life, any experience, the sacred and the profane alike. It is ultimately about how individuals identify with the outside world in general and with other individuals in particular. It must, therefore, be part of the emergence, formation, and transformation of collective identities, whether religious or not – even though one would also expect, based on Eliade, that discerning the *Axis Mundi* effect outside religion is more complicated. This is what we decided to examine in our last chapter with an illustrative case of Latino immigrant integration in the United States. We have no illusion that we are making a definitive case, but we hope we have an informatively suggestive, thought-provoking, illustrative case that could spark new approaches to the analysis of entrenched theoretical and empirical puzzles concerning intergroup relations.

LATINO IMMIGRATION AS AN ILLUSTRATIVE CASE

Immigrant integration is a perfect case to probe the extension of Eliade's *Axis Mundi* logic outside predominantly religious experiences. First, immigration typically involves a radical change of individuals' spatial orientation, or one may call it re-spacing. It is akin in many ways to what we discussed earlier in this book as repositioning. Familiar thresholds and poles are left behind and new axes of orientation are sought. Second, immigrants need to redefine themselves, to ask who they are in the new world they are entering. They need to rethink, to recontextualize their identities. Observers of immigrants have a good vantage point to study individual identity in formation. In this manner, they in fact explore what we have earlier termed as *recategorization* and *repersonalization*. Third, immigration offers a harder test of our three R's logic because here we are dealing with fluid and multiple prospective *Axis* symbols (social, economic, ethnic, linguistic, religious, and others). Fourth, the case of Latino immigration is particularly interesting because it has been historically diverse. Thus, the Latino immigrants have a common in-group identity available to them as Latinos, but they also epitomize in-group diversity by country of origin, social status, ethnic makeup, language usage, mode of entry, etc. Finally, this case is close to home – particularly for Mikhail, who has written most of his contributions to this book at his apartment in San Diego, California, about twenty miles from the U.S.–Mexico border crossing at San Ysidro, which happens to be the world's busiest. In fact, Mikhail wrote the sentence you are reading now on a city bus in San Diego sitting next to two Mexican women as they conversed in Spanish. Not all Americans, however, would treat Mikhail's experience as a benign manifestation of culturally enriching diversity of their country.

LATINOS AND INTERGROUP THREAT

In an influential book on patriotism in the United States, a sociology professor at the University of Michigan and the University of Chicago, Morris Janowitz, claimed that Mexican migration into the United States threatened "a bifurcation in the social-political structure of the United States" – a social split that would undermine America's democracy.[4] In the early 2000s, Janowitz's colleague Samuel Huntington, a Harvard political scientist and the author of the "clash of civilizations" theory, made a sweeping argument in a popular book and in journal articles that Mexican and other Hispanic migration into the United States would destroy "the American Creed" – with its cornerstone civic liberties and work ethic – mainly because the Hispanics would allegedly fail to assimilate. With great alarm, Huntington regarded the data on somewhat slower acquisition of English among Hispanic migrants as well as reports about Hispanic Americans cheering for the Mexican national soccer team when it Played against the United States, salsa selling better than ketchup across the United States, and "José" outpacing "Michael" as the most popular newborn boys' name in Texas and California as evidence of the coming "hispanization" of the West and the Southwest of the United States. Huntington warned about exclusively Hispanic linguistic and cultural enclaves proliferating in the United States and Hispanic voters changing the course of domestic and foreign policy in a way that would lead to a precipitous decline of the United States as a world power.[5]

Systematic social research, however, fails to sustain these alarmist views. The same year that Huntington's *Who Are We?* book made an alarmist splash about America's "Hispanization," one of the world's preeminent experts on the topic, Columbia University professor Rodolfo de la Garza, published an exhaustive review of empirical studies on Latino migration in the United States, in a 2004 issue of *Annual Review of Political Science*, a respected scholarly journal. The studies showed unambiguously that Hispanics were not resisting assimilation and not developing any civic creeds as an alternative to the American Creed. Non-English-speaking Hispanic communities were not proliferating and getting entrenched. On the whole, intermarriage between Mexicans and non-Mexicans continued apace. Mexican Americans viewed bilingual education – which Huntington interpreted as a sign of "Hispanization" – predominantly not as a way to retain Spanish, but as a way to learn English. Second-generation Hispanic teenagers in Miami, Florida, and San Diego, California – the biggest magnets of Latino migration in the United States – were practically all speaking English, but only half of them still spoke Spanish.[6]

Fast forward to our writing in April 2016, and we notice no Latino People's Republics in Florida. In Texas, the Mexican immigrants have not been reclaiming the Alamo. In California, immigration experts have been talking on the local public radio station about more Mexicans leaving than arriving in the Unites States. Across the board, the persistence of high levels of ethnic identification among Latinos has not resulted in the formation of ethnic Latino parties – something we would have observed if Huntingtonian premonitions were valid. Like European immigrant groups – such as the predominantly Catholic Irish and Italians a century or so ago – whose integration into American society few would dispute now, most Latinos developed a strong political identification with one of the two main American parties (the Democrats) while some others (notably the Cubans in Florida) have identified with the other mainstream party. Using mass surveys of Latino adults in the United States, political scientists Matt Barreto and Francisco Pedraza showed that, in fact, strong mainstream party identification strengthened among Latinos over four generations.[7] This is hardly a sign of ethno-political "bifurcation." Something that could pass for a Latino ethno-political party – the La Raza Unida Party founded in 1970 as part of the Chicano movement – declined by 1980. According to Jose Angel Gutierrez, a leading expert on Hispanic social and political movements in the United Sates, La Raza Unida declined based on the political logic embedded in the American political system: "like most third political parties in the United States, it ended as quickly as it had begun."[8]

Moreover, it appears that political mobilization of Latino identity has in itself been conditioned by mainstream party identification. Across America's political spectrum, party affiliation has mattered more than co-ethnic contact in support for public policy and candidates. In a study of October 2004 polls among 1,600 registered Latino voters, Matt

Barreto and Stephen Nuno found that using co-ethnics to contact Latinos helped win the latter's support for party agendas and candidates among Republicans, but not among Democrats.[9] Summarizing a large body of social research, political scientists Luis Fraga, John Garcia, Rodney Hero, Michael Jones-Correa, Valerie Martinez-Ebers, and Gary Seguro found that political mobilization among Latinos typically arose not out of the sense of Latino ethnocentrism or cultural distance from other groups – in other words, not out of some kind of civilizational chasm – but out of a sense of discrimination against them as a group (notably from the passing of anti-immigrant propositions in California and some other states).[10] This mobilization dynamic has been central for many other groups in the United States – something principally indicative of mainstream political integration rather than ethno-political "bifurcation." We by no means imply race and ethnicity are inconsequential, only that they matter socially and politically in ways contradicting the clash of civilizations view. Latino racial views appear to have evolved the same way – sharing many of the same racial resentments as the whites (particularly toward African Americans), but not translating those resentments into meaningful political choices. Using 7,500 interviews with Latino registered voters nationally and in critical states at twelve points in time from March 2007 through August 2010, Barreto, Segura, and Ali A. Valenzuela found that mean responses among Latinos on items gauging racial prejudice were statistically indistinguishable from those of non-Hispanic whites and – moreover – those Latinos who expressed strong racial resentment were no less likely than others to vote for Barack Obama in the 2008 presidential primaries.[11]

A TALE OF TWO ASSOCIATIONS

American society has been proving Huntington wrong for many reasons. The *Axis Mundi* model puts one of them in the spotlight. And it is a reason – or rather, a process – that otherwise might be overlooked. It has to do with Hispanic-American *socialization* – particularly the socialization of Hispanic-American community leaders and organizers, opinion leaders, and other notables. Those are precisely the actors who could have and would have paved the way for the establishment and sedentarization, as well as the cultural and civic consolidation of Hispanic territorial enclaves across the United States in opposition to the American Creed – and from there to a deeper social bifurcation across America, of which Janowitz and

Huntington warned. The *Axis Mundi* logic suggests that one of the mechanisms that precluded the Huntingtonian denouement must have been socialization among Hispanic community notables in *high-common-group-value* yet *high-diversity* settings. Does the story of Hispanics in the United States offer plausible evidence that, indeed, this may have been the case?

One place to cast the Hajj model searchlight is the evolution of Hispanic or Latino[12] public associations in the United States – particularly the most prominent ones among them, the League of United Latin American Citizens (LULAC) and the National Council of La Raza (NCLR). LULAC is the older of the two with the largest network of grassroots affiliates, while NCLR has the largest constituency base and is by far the best-funded and most politically influential Hispanic association in the United States. Both espouse highly valued common principles – the pursuit of civil rights and freedoms in safeguarding and promoting Hispanic identity. In other words, both serve as umbrella organizations representing large and diverse segments of the United States' Hispanic population and both promote high intrinsic identity-related values for America's Hispanics. Yet both evolved differently. These differences illuminate the *Axis Mundi* effect. Of particular importance are both associations' perspectives on diversity – both doctrinal and organizational – within their ranks.

THE LEAGUE OF UNITED LATIN AMERICAN CITIZENS: UPS AND DOWNS OF IN-GROUP DIVERSITY

LULAC originated in 1929 in south Texas, in part, to safeguard not only the rights, but the security and the lives of local Mexican Americans. In a tragically ironic way, one may see it emerging in response to developments that Huntington was predicting in the early 2000s – yet this happened almost a century earlier. As a senior staff member of LULAC explained in an interview with Deirdre Martinez, a scholar specializing in Hispanic associations in the United States:

If you go back to the beginning of LULAC, there was actually a minirevolution going on in Texas in which Mexicans in Texas were actually trying to secede from the union – this was put down violently by the Texas Rangers. In fact, LULAC talks about how more Hispanics were killed in the Southwest than African Americans were lynched in the South. So it was pretty violent and ugly and so the LULAC leaders saw this and thought the better strategy might be to emphasize our American-ness and ask for the rights given to other Americans.[13]

In advocating full access to the rights of American citizens for Hispanics, LULAC made important advances. In the late 1940s and early 1950s, LULAC took an active part in two successful lawsuits against segregation and racism in schools – *Mendez v. Westminster* (1945) in California and *Delgado v. Bastrop Independent School District* (1948) in Texas.[14] In 1950, lawyers and their staff volunteering for LULAC filed more than a dozen suits or complaints against school districts in America's Southwest – building up to the victory of the anti-segregation argument in the landmark 1954 U.S. Supreme Court *Brown v. Board of Education* case.[15]

However, LULAC's pursuit of American-ness in the fifty to sixty years that followed resulted – in all probability unintentionally – in significant constraints on social diversity within the association. The association's leadership emphasized precisely the social values that Huntington believed were quintessential to the American Creed – in particular, individualism and capitalism. The underlying rationale was that by adopting these values, Mexican Americans would appeal to the core values of the majority white population of the United States and that the latter would, in turn, be more likely to support the inclusion of Hispanics in America's sociopolitical mainstream. However, the long-term unintended consequence of this approach was *de facto* narrowing of the association's social diversity. This happened in several ways, three of them being particularly illustrative. First, the appeal to individualism restricted the ideological diversity within LULAC clearly favoring middle-class conservatives and, over the years, becoming associated with Republican partisanship. Second, the emphasis on "Anglo-Saxon" rational-legal principles and English language use restricted social and age diversity within the association, as LULAC prioritized the interests of members who were U.S. citizens already. This made LULAC less attractive to new migrants – in fact, precisely the populations that could have benefited from stronger integrationist policies the association formally espoused. Third, LULAC's assertions that Hispanics were white Caucasians – believing that in claiming whiteness they would be granted civil liberties faster than African Americans – undermined ethno-racial diversity within the group.[16] Paradoxically, the emphasis on ground-up representation added to these constraints on ethno-racial diversity, favoring sedentary Mexican populations. And as it happened, the shift of the public mood in the United States in the 1960s in favor of civil liberties, racial integration, and more socially inclusive values overall, as well as the rising new waves of Hispanic migration from Mexico, Cuba, and Latin America coincided with stagnation and the significant decline of LULAC membership and influence. The constraints on in-group diversity particularly at that time made LULAC less adaptable to social change that favored intergroup diversity. And so, by the early 1970s, the association was on the brink of extinction. The number of its dues-paying members dropped from about 3,300 in 1951 to 2,500 in 1962 to just about 1,000 in 1972.[17]

The 1980s, however, saw the reversal of this decline alongside significant changes in the association's philosophy favoring greater social inclusiveness. This is evident in what LULAC considers its historic milestones of that decade. In 1980, the LULAC website asserts, it "fought to get better coverage of Latinos in the media" – suggesting a more inclusive ethno-racial definition of its membership. In 1986, the organization claimed successfully lobbying a Texas State Senate subcommittee to kill the English Only resolution before it reached the Senate floor. This was a significant reversal compared to the association's traditional insistence on using English among Hispanics in the United States. In 1987, LULAC filed a class action suit against the INS to process illegal applicants eligible for amnesty. This marked a significant change in the association's stance, opening up to new immigrants and embracing the problems of illegal immigrants. Along the way, LULAC was also becoming more open to gender diversity, leading in 1994 to the election of Belen Robles as its first woman president.[18] Along with these major shifts in orientation, active membership rebounded, reaching approximately 10,000 by 2005.[19]

THE NATIONAL COUNCIL OF LA RAZA: THE IN-GROUP IDENTITY-DIVERSITY SYNERGY

The story of the other major Hispanic public association in the United States, the National Council of La Raza, illustrates how organizational emphasis on inclusiveness and intergroup compromise contributed to successful institutionalization, integration of diverse elites within a common (Hispanic) identity group, and successful interaction and partnering with other ethnic and racial groups. NCLR was launched almost forty years after LULAC – in 1968, with financial support from the Ford Foundation, the National Council of Churches, and the United Auto Workers. The socially diverse funding sources dovetailed with NCLR's programmatic emphasis on nonpartisanship and service to "all Hispanic subgroups in all regions of the country."[20]

The focus on embracing diversity among Hispanics – i.e., subgroup diversity within a common identity group – also reflected the principal goal of NCLR's founders. That goal was to increase the national visibility of all Hispanics, without which, the founders believed, "legislation such as the Civil Rights Act of 1964 and the Economic Opportunity Act of 1964, while creating enormous change in other areas of the country, had relatively little impact on the Hispanic community."[21] They envisioned an umbrella Hispanic/Latino institution of the kind they believed was "critical to the success of the Black civil rights movement, and around which they could rally, unify, and organize."[22]

Aside from nonpartisanship, another crucial, foundational move toward that goal was NCLR's revision of its bylaws in 1973, mandating that its governing board should consist of an equal number of men and women. This was followed by bylaws requiring that "identifiable constituencies" be represented by at least half the board – effectively meaning that the association's governing bodies could not be dominated by the demographically most numerous Mexican Americans (who make up approximately 65 percent of Hispanic population in the United States). Had the organizational rules merely reflected grassroots demographics, then NCLR would not be what it became. It would then have a dominant ethnic subgroup within its ranks – a recipe, in terms of the SIT, for that group claiming greater prototypicality to common identity and thus increasing negative inter-subgroup bias.[23]

Perhaps some may find it paradoxical, but in-group diversity promotion and the top-down approach to identifying and fighting for issues of greatest concern to the inclusive common-identity community have been the key factors in making NCLR in the early 2000s the largest Hispanic public association in the United States. Summarizing the association's evolution, Deirdre Martinez noted: "Its thirty-year history reveals a few peaks and valleys but an overall growth and formation of a solid reputation on the national scene."[24] The *Axis Mundi* approach worked. By 2006, the NCLR had an estimated $90 million in assets, a $28 million budget, a staff of 125, a central office in Washington, DC, and eight affiliates covering major regions of the United States.[25]

As it has focused for more than forty years on social and political empowerment of America's Hispanics, as well as on practical issues, such as education and health care, NCLR also evolved as the largest *de facto* common group-gathering forum for diverse Hispanic subgroups. In the scope of social diversity, vibrancy, and color, the annual conventions of NCLR resemble those of ISNA with respect to America's Muslim community. These conventions – as well as regional and thematic conventions, meetings, camps, and other forums under the NCLR

umbrella – serve as precisely the high-value, high-diversity, nondiscriminatory, identity-affirming social settings. Whatever the political disputes
and controversies the associations may be part of, its socio-organizational
environment *per se* is likely to have promoted prosocial and integrationist
tendencies among America's Hispanics in the same way as the Hajj has
promoted more socially and politically tolerant views among millions of
Muslims around the world.

The across-group and within-group diversity-maximizing approaches
need not be mutually exclusive. Whether one is more successful than the
other and how the two may interact appears to be a theoretically promis-
ing and substantively important avenue of social research.

* * *

This may seem counterintuitive, but we felt when assessing the implications of the Hajj model of tolerance outside the Hajj and outside
religion – exploring how far and how bright our conceptual searchlight could reach – that the logic of more tolerant, prosocial, inclusive,
cosmopolitan, respectful, compassionate, understanding, inspiring, and
empowering social effects during the Hajj resonates with the logic of
immigrant nation-building, the one epitomized in the cornerstone
principle of American social and political organization – the principal
of "E pluribus unum" ("out of many, one"). This resonance is complementary. The Hajj logic of tolerance we examined could be summarized as "in one, many" – it is the conceptual yin of the "E pluribus
unum" yang. This insight came to us after we almost finished this
chapter, reviewing in detail the micro-case of Hispanic public associations in the United States and the Islamic associations in the United
States and Europe. After Sufian completed the Hajj and returned
home, he told Mikhail that in terms of depth and strength of impact,
only one other experience in his life was similar to the Hajj. It was
visiting the United States for the first time a few years earlier. And so
we conclude with Sufian's extended comments on this realization.
They recap the *Axis Mundi* effects at a personal level, through his
very own repositioning, recategorization, and repersonalization.

When we arrived in Jeddah airport, I had a feeling that I encountered an absolutely
different civilization. Two basically unusual things caused that feeling – prayer
places were everywhere and men had white long dresses rather than trousers.
Later, traveling and staying in Medina and Mecca, that feeling was enhanced by
other things – locals eating with their hands and sitting on the floor, the view of the
desert as if deprived of life, store hours that corresponded to the five-time-a-day

prayer schedule, and the architecture of the flat-roofed buildings, including big flat umbrellas at the Grand Mosque in Medina (the roofs and umbrellas did not need to be pointed at the top because of the absence of rains).

Already upon arrival in Jeddah, I recalled how I had felt once before, encountering a new civilization upon arriving for the first time in the United States of America. Right after deplaning at the JFK airport, I felt as if I discovered a different species of people – and that despite the fact that I met many Americans before my trip. I remembered how I felt that American people were unusually friendly when compared to reserved Russians. I experienced an imperceptible sense of freedom. My first impression was that Americans were freer with using their bodies – I could observe people sitting on the floor, or using their mouth, as if it were a third hand, to carry a pen or a newspaper. Later, I came to appreciate the feeling of living in a democratic society in the United States. It grew on me. I thought often how hard, how downright impossible it would be to imagine and to feel democracy living in Russia. It impressed me the most after experiencing life in the United States how non-invasive the state was in everyday life compared to Russia, and how the people, the individuals, were not perpetually scared of the state. Banks, shops, universities, airlines, newspapers, TV and radio channels in the United States looked very private and not oppressed by the state. It seemed as if the state authorities were minding their own business and did not interfere with the civil society. It was very different from the feeling I developed growing up in the USSR and later living in Russia, where I felt the presence of the state everywhere and every day, and thought of the state like a mighty and scary ancient god that always interferes with peoples' lives. Everything in the United States seemed to be designed to give more freedom and opportunities to the people and discourage the authorities from interfering in the life of the civil society. The very existence of the civil society in the United States apart from the state was unusual for me because I was used to the situation in the USSR and post-Soviet Russia where all nongovernment organizations were dependent and linked to the state institutions. In Russia, I always felt that serving the state was the only way to succeed in life and the Russian civilization was designed to provide social lifts to get promoted to bureaucratic positions.

In the KSA, I had a feeling that the life of its society was designed to make it as easy as possible to conduct religious duties. The mosques were open 24/7 and were built so that everybody could walk to a neighborhood mosque after the call for prayer and to arrive there five minutes ahead of time. The public places had water fountains and cabins with showers where you could wash yourself before the prayer. At the same time, I felt the strong presence of the state that built and sustained that entire religious infrastructure.

Conclusion

Islam and the West, Islam and democracy, Islam and terrorism. As we wrap up this book, these questions continue to resonate in America's public discourses from Washington, DC, where Sufian now lives, to California, Mikhail's home. They implicitly permeated any discussion of the big international news that unfolded while we were working on this book – from the downing of the Russian tourist charter jet over Egypt to the mass deadly terrorist attacks in Paris to the rampage shooting at a community center in San Bernardino, California, and to the election of Donald Trump as president of the United States. We explicitly stated in our introduction that our book is not principally about these questions. We warned about making naïve linkages. And yet, when all is said and done, these issues are important to a lot more people than those who may be interested in the Hajj or in the North Caucasus or in Islamic associations in America and Europe or in integration of Hispanics into American society or in theories of social and political tolerance, or all of these combined. And so, of course, we asked ourselves: Where do we stand on these issues, on the big debates?

We have to make it clear from the outset. We did not find anything in our study that would indicate that Islam *per se*, as a faith, is a barrier to democracy. Our analysis of the Hajj impacts shows that one of the Five Pillars of Islam, a fundamental ritual of Islamic faith, is likely to enhance sociopolitical tolerance. The latter is, in turn, a quintessential democratic value, a pillar of civil liberties, and a social foundation of democratic praxis. This finding therefore makes it harder to argue that Islam is an ideational and social basis of authoritarianism, intolerance, and terrorism. Our results thus also go against assertions that Islamic beliefs and practices *per se* undermine the separation of the state and religion.[1] In our extensive observations and content analysis, the hajjis were less insistent than the non-hajjis that Muslims must understand and follow Islamic standards and values in public life and politics as strictly as possible and as contingent on immutable principles. In other words, the hajjis were more likely to recognize Islam as a living religion – potent to embrace social change and to thrive as human society develops – a notion doctrinally and ritualistically embedded in the *Axis Mundi* of Islamic faith.[2] In this sense, we are on the same page with the leading scholars of Islam – such as John Esposito, Olivier Roy, Juan Cole, Tariq Ramadan, and many others.

But we also make a different point. In fact, the core of our work sets us apart from these scholars. We have to conclude that Islam could contribute to democratic discourse and values not only – and not necessarily even as much – through Muslims internalizing and acting on doctrinal concepts like consultation (*shura*), consensus (*ijma'*), independent interpretive judgment (*ijtihad*), or natural law (*istislah*),[3] but more so through socio-psychological effects of religious identity-affirming practices such as the Hajj. To put it simply, if bluntly, the religious content of Islam is probably immaterial to whether Islam is compatible with democracy and Western values.

Let us revisit our study on this particular point. What distinguished the pilgrims from the non-pilgrims in our conversations and focus groups the most? It was certainly not that the pilgrims spoke with enthusiasm about notions such as *shura* or *ijtihad* – or any of the dozens if not hundreds of related concepts and pronouncements in the holy texts or in the influential *fatwas*, etc. – while the non-pilgrims spoke with caution or apprehension or suspicion about them. The fact was that neither group evoked any such concepts *at all*.

Nor was it that the pilgrims and the non-pilgrims differed in expressing the depth of their faith and in emphasizing the positive messages in Islam. They all talked about it as a religion of peace and compassion; they all believed it encouraged the best qualities in people, such as altruism and helping those less fortunate. They all denied it engendered radicalism or terrorism.

The crucial difference was not even how much, but simply *how* they discussed core religious symbols and principles. And the biggest difference in that *how* reflected more than anything else the difference in personal experiences, in the *practice* of the pilgrimage. The hajjis stood out through a significantly more pronounced sense they conveyed of *personalization* and *socialization* of their religious experience. If you recall, it was the synergy of personal emotions and high religious symbolism that accounted for the pilgrims discussing Islam's sacred spaces longer, more expressively, and in more detail than the non-pilgrims. Performing the Hajj made Islam more personalized to them and made them more deeply socialized in Islam. It repositioned them. It made them open their minds so they could recategorize outsiders as someone more acceptable. It repersonalized them, making them more open to civic engagement. And we do need to put in a word of caution here – we are probably talking more about latent perceptual and behavioral predispositions rather than active public diversity-championing or enlisting in a movement for Islamic reformation. The pilgrimage doesn't automatically turn any Muslim into a reformer like Tariq Ramadan or Ali Shariati, but it most likely makes them more amenable to their messages of Islam's *capacity* for self-development and adaptation to the changing world.

* * *

Writing conclusions is helpful. It made us think with greater clarity about something that directly flows from the previous discussion. It made us realize our study is also distinct from the existing work on Islam, society, and politics in a broader – we can call it meta-theoretical – sense. The big question we ask and explore is not if Islam can contribute to democracy or tolerance. Rather, by studying Islam's ritualistic *practices* and making theoretical generalizations about our findings, we hope to help ourselves and others ask, explore, and understand new ways in which individuals and groups could improve their tolerance and acceptance of others, engage in constructive social contact, build more positive social capital across multiple divides – ethnic, religious, class, gender, etc.

And this is where our theoretical assessment of our Hajj investigation is critical. The theoretical heart of our Hajj model of tolerance is what we called the *Axis Mundi* effect – arising from physical and symbolic repositioning of pilgrims into Islam's sacred *Axis Mundi*, through ritualistic behavior, perceptions, emotions, and cognition. Critical for generating these effects is a combination of high intrinsic common group identity (*Axis*) and high subgroup diversity within that same common group (*Mundi*). Another important condition was that the common group value (e.g., pilgrims or Muslims) must be higher to individuals than any of their individual subgroup values (e.g., doctors or Circassians). With the *Axis Mundi* effect, we traced how more inclusive views of Islam among pilgrims extend to more inclusive views of other religions and social groups. In other words, we traced how social recategorization and social capital became transitive.

We have also explored the nontrivial, if counterintuitive recommendations for improving intergroup relations arising from our theoretical explanation of the Pilgrims' Paradox. We followed the *Axis Mundi* logic outside the Hajj experiences and outside Islam. Our principal insight is generalizable as follows: to improve tolerance across social groups, intergroup contact needs to be supplemented by inter-subgroup contact within each conflicting or divergent group. Build bridges not only over *across-group* divides, but also over *within-group* divides. We suggested that such across-difference socialization within an internally diverse common group is likely to be transitive – i.e., to improve socialization outside the common groups.

Our probe of social integration of Muslims in the United States and Western Europe and of Hispanic immigrants in the United States suggests this argument is at least plausible. One may call it the Hajj effect, or the *Axis Mundi* effect, or the *La Raza* effect – in reference to our study of the National House of la Raza's role in the affirmation and transformation of the cultural identities of Hispanics in the United States through in-group socialization. These observations suggest, in turn, not only a new avenue of social inquiry, but also new approaches to conflict resolution, tolerance-building, and social integration of minorities and migrants into the social and political mainstream. The *Axis Mundi* effect may well be expected to help minority populations not only to ease into more frequent and benign interactions with majority populations, but to make the majority populations see minorities as less threatening and more acceptable as individuals sharing a state and/or a national identity.

Finally and most importantly, in our discussions over a mutually acceptable synergy of red wine for the author from California and nonalcoholic beer for the author from the North Caucasus, we agreed to emphasize the point that the *Axis Mundi* effect was not replacing, but complementing a more traditional across-group approach to conflict resolution. The two, we felt, have a great potential to be mutually complementary, not mutually exclusive. The bottom line for this study thus is not to say that a previous conception was wrong and we offer something new and better, but to say that while existing wisdom is important, new insights could enrich it and help improve intergroup relations.

* * *

In 1678, John Bunyan published his famous Christian allegory *The Pilgrim's Progress from This World to That Which Is to Come.*

In a prefatory essay to the book's 1957 edition, Alexander Witherspoon, a professor of English at Yale University, called it "the most influential religious book ever written in the English language."[4] The giants of English literature alluded to this title in their works to draw attention to explorations of human identity change through journeys in space and time. Charles Dickens subtitled his *Oliver Twist* (1838) – an imaginary travel into childhood – "The Parish Boy's Progress." Mark Twain's 1869 exploration of cultural differences in a travelogue, *The Innocents Abroad*, had an alternative title, "The New Pilgrims' Progress." C. S. Lewis titled his autobiographical journey from religious childhood through a philosophical landscape in search of the pagan island of his adulthood's desires *The Pilgrim's Regress* (1933).

Coming from a different cultural background, neither of us thought of the *Pilgrim's Progress* as we researched and wrote this book. Our principal motivation arose from intellectual curiosity, honed in long discussions in one of the authors' Soviet-era cubicle-size kitchen in Nartkala over tea and local treats. The inspiration came from the counterintuitive, from wondering if ardor, passion, fervor, elation could lead to serenity, wisdom, tolerance, generosity. It came from the anticipation of paradoxes and from recognizing the value of paradoxes for generating new knowledge. During one of these long kitchen conversations, we recalled an old popular Soviet monthly science television show called *The Incredible Obvious* (*Ochevidnoye – Neveroyatnoye*). Each program when we watched it regularly back in the 1970s and the 1980s started with a quote from Russia's classic poet, Alexander Pushkin – "Oh, how many incredible discoveries are prepared for us by the spirit of enlightenment, and by experience – the offspring of hard mistakes, and by genius – a friend of paradoxes."

In retrospect, somewhat like in Bunyan's allegory, the Muslims we studied performed a holy pilgrimage from their symbolic "City of Destruction" (we can think of the legacy of Soviet ideology) to what they imagined as the "Celestial City" and Mount Zion (the religious environment of Mecca and Medina and Mount Arafat, the rediscovery of the one's *Axis Mundi*). However, unlike Bunyan's pilgrim who "progresses" straightforwardly to heaven, our hajjis returned home transformed by their religious experience and became more tolerant toward their own "City of Destruction" and toward its fellow denizens with whom they desired to work for a better life. In that sense, somewhat similar to C. S. Lewis's characterization of his novel as "a kind of Bunyan up to date," our study has probed the sociopolitical impacts of the Islamic pilgrimage in today's world. At the same time, as our exploration of rich and systematic studies of the role of religion in society and politics has revealed earlier in this volume, that is not how many contemporary writers and researchers may interpret the impact of the Hajj on Muslims. To draw attention to these debates and controversies – which we believe are pivotal to generate new knowledge on these important issues – we called the focal point of our investigation "The Pilgrims' Paradox." We are far from claiming we have conclusively resolved these controversies – and we hope we have not. More than anything else, we hope to inspire further exploration of the ideas we have and have not yet generated and of paradoxes we have and have not yet identified.

Notes

INTRODUCTION

1. Robert R. Bianchi. *Islamic Globalization: Pilgrimage, Capitalism, Democracy, and Diplomacy*. Singapore: World Scientific, 2013.
2. As in valuable studies such as Coleman, Simon, and John Elsner, eds. *Pilgrimage: Past and Present in the World Religions*. Cambridge, MA: Harvard University Press, 1995.
3. John L. Esposito. *Future of Islam*. Oxford: Oxford University Press, 2010, pp. 47–48; John L. Esposito. *Who Speaks for Islam: What a Billion Muslims Really Think*. New York: Gallup Press, 2007, pp. 15–16; John L. Esposito. *Islam: The Straight Path*. New York: Oxford University Press, 2005 (revised 3rd edition), pp. 91–93.
4. Esposito, *Islam*, pp. 212–213.
5. Adam Robinson. *Bin Laden: The Inside Story of the Rise and Fall of the Most Notorious Terrorist in History*. New York: Arcade Publishing, 2011.
6. Peter Mandaville. *Global Political Islam*. New York: Routledge, 2007, pp. 289–291.
7. M. Steven Fish, Francesca R. Jensenius, and Katherine E. Michel. "Islam and Large-Scale Political Violence: Is There a Connection?" *Comparative Political Studies*, 43(11) (November 2010), 1327–1362.
8. Charles Kurzman. *The Missing Martyrs: Why There Are so Few Muslim Terrorists*. New York: Oxford University Press, 2011; Charles Kurzman, David Schanzer, and Ebrahim Moosa. "Muslim American Terrorism since 9/11: Why so Rare?" *The Muslim World*, 101(3) (July 2011), 464–483.
9. Olivier Roy. *Globalized Islam: The Search for a New Ummah*. New York: Columbia University Press, 2004, p. 9.
10. Ibid.
11. Ibid.
12. Ibid., p. 10.
13. Juan Cole. *The New Arabs: How the Millennial Generation Is Changing the Middle East*. New York: Simon and Schuster, 2014; Juan Cole. *Engaging the Muslim World*. New York: Palgrave Macmillan, 2009.

14. E.g., the Religious Orientation Scale in Gordon W. Allport and John M. Ross. "Personal Religious Orientation and Prejudice." *Journal of Personality and Social Psychology,* 5 (1967): 432–443; Religious Fundamentalism Scale in Bob Altemeyer and Bruce Hunsberger. "Authoritarianism, Religious Fundamentalism, Quest and Prejudice." *International Journal for the Psychology of Religion,* 2 (1992): 113–133; and Christian Orthodoxy Scale in J. Timothy Fullerton, and Bruce Hunsberger. "A Unidimensional Measure of Christian Orthodoxy." *Journal for the Scientific Study of Religion,* 21 (1982): 317–326.

15. We earlier introduced these three key terms (3 R's) in Mikhail A. Alexseev and Sufian N. Zhemukhov. "From Mecca with Tolerance: Religion, Social Recategorisation and Social Capital." *Religion, State, and Society* 44(1) (2016): 371–391.

1 RUSSIA'S NORTH CAUCASUS: THE STATE, THE HAJJ, AND THE REVIVAL OF THE SACRED

1. "V Kabardino-Balkarii Vzorvan Avtomobil' S Militsionerami [In Kabardino-Balkaria a Police Car Has Been Blown Up]." *Kavkazskiy Uzel,* April 30, 2010. www.kavkaz-uzel.ru/articles/168269/ (accessed November 12, 2015); "V Kabardino-Balkariia: Khronika Vzryvov, Obstrelov I Teraktov [Kabardino-Balkaria: The Chronicle of Explosions, Shootings, and Terrorist Acts]". *Kavkazskiy Uzel,* November 10, 2015. www.kavkaz-uzel.ru/articles/172027/ (accessed November 12, 2015).

2. Sufian N. Zhemukhov. "One Thousand Years of Islam in Kabarda: An Experiment in Periodization." *Anthropology and Archaeology of Eurasia,* 49(4) (2011): 54–71.

3. Stars on the Circassian flag symbolized the Circassian principalities that sought national unification.

4. For the Russian conquest of the North Caucasus, see Charles King. *The Ghost of Freedom: A History of the Caucasus.* New York: Oxford University Press, 2008; Michael Khodarkovsky. *Bitter Choices: Loyalty and Betrayal in the Russian Conquest of the North Caucasus.* Ithaca, NY: Cornell University Press, 2011.

5. Thomas M. Barrett. "The Remaking of the Lion of Dagestan: Shamil in Captivity." *The Russian Review,* 53(3) (1994): 353–366.

6. Oliver Bullough. *Let Our Fame Be Great: Journeys among the Defiant People of the Caucasus.* New York: Basic Books, 2010, p. 318.

7. King, *The Ghost of Freedom,* p. 80.

8. Bullough, *Let Our Fame Be Great,* p. 318.

9. Sufian N. Zhemukhov. "The Birth of Modern Circassian Nationalism." *Nationalities Papers* 40 (Spring 2012): 502–524.

10. For a more detailed account of Russian imperial politics toward the Hajj, see Eileen Kane. *Russian Hajj: Empire and the Pilgrimage to Mecca.* Ithaca, NY: Cornell University Press, 2015; Tugan Kumykov, ed. *Problemy Kavkazskoi Voiny I Vyselenie Cherkesov V Predely Osmanskoi Imperii (20–70-ye gg. XIX v.). Sbornik Arkhivnykh Dokumentov. [Problems of the Caucasus*

War and the Deportation of the Circassians to the Ottoman Empire (from the 1820s to the 1870s). Compilation of Archival Documents]. Nalchik, Russia: Elbrus, 2001, p. 429.

11. For the role of Islam in the post-Soviet Central Asia see: Eric McGlinchey. *Chaos, Violence, Dynasty: Politics and Islam in Central Asia.* University of Pittsburgh Press, 2011.

12. Chen Bram and Moshe Gammer. "Radical Islamism, Traditional Islam and Ethno-nationalism in the Northern Caucasus." *Middle Eastern Studies*, 49(2) (2013): 300.

13. Igor M. D'jakonov, *Kniga Vospominanii* [Book of Memories]. Saint-Petersburg, Russia: Evropeiskii Dom, 1995, pp. 736–737.

14. Marat Shterin and Akhmet Yarlykapov. "Reconsidering Radicalisation and Terrorism: The New Muslim Movement in Kabardino-Balkaria and Its Path to Violence." *Religion, State and Society*, 39(2–3) (2011): 309.

15. V'iachslav Akhmadulin. "Deiatel'nost Sovetskogo Gosudarstva Po Organizatsii Hadzha Sovetskikh Musul'man V 1944–1991 gg. [Soviet State's Management of Organizing of Soviet Muslims' Hajj in 1944–1991]." *Khadzh Rossiiskikh Musulman: Ezhegodnyi Sbornik Putevykh Zametok o Khadzhe [Russian Muslims' Hajj: Annual Journal of Travel Notes about Hajj]*, 5 (2013). N. Novgorod, Russia: Medina Publishing House, 2013. www .idmedina.ru/books/history_culture/?5773 (accessed November 12, 2015).

16. Ibid.

17. For a detailed analysis of the transition of the North Caucasus after the Soviet era, see Georgi M. Derluguian, *Bourdieu's Secret Admirer in the Caucasus: A World-Systems Biography.* Chicago: University of Chicago Press, 2005.

18. Olivier Roy. *Globalized Islam: The Search for a New Ummah.* New York: Columbia University Press, 2004, pp. 125, 134.

19. Larisa Shadueva. "Interview with the Head of Spiritual Directorate in Kabardino-Balkaria, A.M. Pshikhachev." *Kabardino-Balkarskaia Pravda*, February 11, 2006.

20. Mikhail A. Alexseev. "Russia's 'Cold Peace' Consensus: Transcending the Presidential Election." *Forum of World Affairs* 21(1) (Winter/Spring 1997): 33–50.

21. On the consolidation of revolutionary ideological opposition in Russia, see Henry E. Hale. *Patronal Politics: Eurasian Regime Dynamics in Comparative Perspective.* New York: Cambridge University Press, 2015; Stephen E. Hanson. *Post-Imperial Democracies: Ideology and Party Formation in Third Republic France, Weimer Germany, and Post-Soviet Russia.* New York: Cambridge University Press, 2010.

22. Boris Sokolov. *SSSR I Rossiia na Voine: Lyudskie Poteri XX veka [The USSR and Russia at War: People's Casualties in the Twentieth Century]* (Moscow: Yauza, 2014), 104, www.litmir.net/br/?b=211468&p=104 (accessed November 12, 2015).

23. "Russia: Chechen Official Puts War Death Toll at 160,000." *Radio Free Europe*, August 16, 2005, www.rferl.org/content/article/1060708.html (accessed November 12, 2015); Bullough, *Let Our Fame Be Great*, p. 403.

24. Shterin and Yarlykapov, "Reconsidering Radicalisation and Terrorism," p. 321; Arsen Kanokov, "President Kabardino-Balkarii Arsen Kanokov – *Gazete*

[President of Kabardino-Balkaria Arsen Kanokov's Interview to *Gazeta*]." *SK-News*, October 13, 2006. https://sk-news.ru/news/analitic/7428/ (accessed July 26, 2016); "Russia: Nalchik Raid Leaves a Painful Legacy." *Radio Free Europe*, October 12, 2006, www.rferl.org/content/article/1071996.html (accessed November 12, 2015).

25. Timur Doktorov. "KBR: 'politicheskii kotel' nagrelsia do predela ['Political Cauldron' Got Hot to the Maximum Degree]." *Vek*, September 9, 2010. https://wek.ru/kbr-politicheskij-kotel-nagrelsya-do-predela (accessed July 26, 2016).

26. Mikhail A. Alexseev. "Local vs. Transcendent Insurgencies: Why Economic Aid Helps Lower Violence in Dagestan, but Not in Kabardino-Balkaria." In William Ascher, Natalia Mirovitskaya, and Jay Heffron, eds. *Economic Development Strategies and Inter-group Violence*. New York: Palgrave/MacMillan, 2013, pp. 277–314.

27. Nikolai Sergeev. "V Raslpedelenii Khadzh-Turov Nashli Priznaki Extremizma [Signs of Terrorism Have Been Found in Distribution of Hajj Tours]." *Kommersant*, July 20, 2012, www.kommersant.ru/doc/1984193 (accessed November 12, 2015).

28. "Mikhail Babich: My Budem Vyzhigat' Terrorizm Kalenym Zhelezom [Mikhail Babich: We Will Burn Out Terrorism with a Hot Iron]." *Polnomochnii Predstavitel' Prezidenta Rossiiskoi Federatsii v Privolzhskom Federalnom Okruge [The Full Representative of the President of the Russian Federation in the Volga Federal District]*, July 20, 2012, www.pfo.ru/?i d=56137 (accessed November 12, 2015).

29. Bullough, *Let Our Fame Be Great*; Bram and Gammer, "Radical Islamism"; King, *The Ghost of Freedom*; Shterin and Yarlykapov, "Reconsidering Radicalisation and Terrorism."

30. Shamil Dzhigkayev. "Edut Volchata Na Khadzh [Little Wolves Perform Hajj]." *Makh Dug*, 7 (2008), 14, www.iarir.ru/node/17.

31. Olga Alenova and Zaur Farniev, "Poeticheskii Krizis [Poetic Crisis]." *Kommersant*, June 23, 2011, www.kommersant.ru/doc/1655370.

32. Paul J. Murphy. *The Wolves of Islam: Russia and the Faces of Chechen Terror*. Dulles, VA: Brasseay's Inc., 2005.

33. Ibid.

34. "Imam Musulmanskoi Obshiny Vladikavkaza Provedet Poltora Goda V Kolonii-Poselenii [Imam of the Vladikavkaz Muslim Community Is Sentenced to a Year and a Half in a Colony]," *Regnum*, October 4, 2011, http://regnum.ru/news/1452287.html (accessed November 12, 2015).

2 THE PATHS OF THE PARADOX: FROM PASSION TO TOLERANCE

1. Alexseev to Zhemukhov, e-mail message, July 10, 2008.

2. David Clingingsmith, Asim Ijaz Khwaja, and Michael Kremer. "Estimating the Impact of the Hajj: Religion and Tolerance in Islam's Global Gathering." *The Quarterly Journal of Economics*, 124(3) (2009): 1133–1170.

3. Data assembled for Mikhail A. Alexseev. "Local vs. Transcendent Insurgencies: Why Economic Aid Helps Lower Violence in Dagestan, but Not in Kabardino-Balkaria." In William Ascher, Natalia Mirovitskaya, and Jay Heffron, eds. *Economic Development Strategies and Inter-group Violence*. New York: Palgrave/MacMillan, pp. 277–314.

4. Their few statements were not coded and did not change the flow of the conversations from topic to topic.

5. Robert Plomin. "Commentary: Why Are Children in the Same Family so Different? Non-shared Environment Three Decades later." *International Journal of Epidemiology*, 40(3) (June 2011): 582–592; *Nursing Schools*. "15 Fascinating Scientific Facts about Siblings." *Nursing Schools*, May 15, 2011, www.nursingschools.net/blog/2011/05/15-fascinating-scientific-facts-about-siblings/ (accessed November 19, 2015).

6. Most of Kabardino-Balkaria's Muslims belong to Hanafi Madhhab. In the pilgrims' group from Nalchik, in which Sufian was a participant observer in 2009, 86 out of 109 Muslims adhered to the Hanafi Madhhab and 23 to the Shafi'i Madhhab. The Shafi'i adherents were allowed an option to perform the rituals following the less restrictive Hanafi rules of Hajj-Tamattu. Several pilgrims from the Nalchik group we observed took that option.

7. E.g., John L. Esposito. *Future of Islam*. New York: Oxford University Press, 2010; Olivier Roy. *Globalized Islam: The Search for a New Ummah*. New York: Columbia University Press, 2004.

8. "Circassia and the Circassians." *The Penny Magazine*. London: Charles Knight & Co, April 14, 1838, pp. 137–139, https://archive.org/stream/TheP ennyMagazineOfTheSocietyForTheDiffusionOfUsefulKnowledge/ThePenny MagazineOfTheSocietyForTheDiffusionOfUsefulKnowledge1838#page/n1 47/mode/1up (accessed November 12, 2015); James Minahan. *One Europe, Many Nations: A Historical Dictionary of European National Groups*. Westport, CT: Greenwood, 2000, p. 354.

9. Wikipedia. "Eid Al-Adha." *Wikipedia*, https://en.wikipedia.org/wiki/Eid_al-Adha#cite_note-4 (accessed November 20, 2015).

10. Pilgrims may also encounter differences of religious practice between the Sunni and Shi'a Muslims. For example, among the latter, one popular notion is that the Prophet did not use any sun cover and therefore the pilgrims should abstain from using head gear and should ride in buses with no roofs, regardless of health hazards. For more details, see Akeel Ibrahim Al-Ken, "The Hajj: Past, Present, and Future. The Communication Aspect." PhD, Leeds, UK, University of Leeds, 1995. http://etheses.whiterose.ac.uk/523/1/uk_bl_e thos_341805.pdf (accessed July 26, 2016).

11. Roy, *Globalized Islam*, pp. 109, 111.

12. Roy, *Globalized Islam*, p. 110; Bernard Lewis and Dominique Schapper, eds. *Muslims in Europe: Social Change in Western Europe*. London: Pinter, 1994.

13. After counting and identifying in the text each of the search terms, we then marked text segments as pertaining to these terms and the corresponding themes and subthemes.

14. We separately coded four content elements: (1) the authors' statements or comments; (2) remarks of the two non-pilgrims who were present during parts of the first pilgrims' focus group (marginal with respect to the total group discussion volume); (3) speech acts representing formulaic praise of Islam and Allah unrelated to the discussion of the Hajj and related themes; and (4) digressions into talking about romantic relationships, love, and dating. We excluded the first three elements from the total word counts. We used the word count on the fourth theme as partial control for age and gender effects across groups, since it clearly correlated with the number of females and average age in a group. Excluded from this theme's word count were remarks contributed by the authors and the non-pilgrims.

3   THE HAJJ AS SOCIAL IDENTITY AND SOCIAL CAPITAL

1. Tom Postmes and Nyla R. Branscombe, eds. *Rediscovering Social Identity.* New York: Psychology Press, 2010; Henri Tajfel and John C. Turner. "The Social Identity Theory of Inter-group Behavior." In Stephen Worchel and William G. Austin, eds. *Psychology of Intergroup Relations.* Chicago: Nelson-Hall, 1986, pp. 7–24; John C. Turner, Penelope J. Oakes, Alexander S. Haslam, and Craig McGarty. "Self and Collective: Cognition and Social Context." *Personality and Social Psychology Bulletin,* 20(3) (1994): 454–463.
2. Ann Bettencourt, Kelly Chapman, Nancy Dorr, and Deborah Hume. "Status Differences and In-Group Bias: A Meta-analytic Examination of the Effects of Status Stability, Status Legitimacy, and Group Permeability." *Psychological Bulletin,* 126(3) (2001): 1411–1445; James Habyarimana, Macartan Humphreys, Daniel N. Posner, and Jeremy Weinstein. "Why Does Ethnic Diversity Undermine Public Goods Provision?" *American Political Science Review,* 101(4) (2007): 709–725.
3. Juan M. Falomir-Pichastor and Natasha S. Frederic. "The Dark Side of Heterogeneous Ingroup Identities: National Identification, Perceived Threat, and Prejudice against Immigrants." *Journal of Experimental Social Psychology,* 49(1) (2013): 72–79.
4. The principal problem being excessive emphasis on real-world differences between deductively defined "civilizations" and lack of attention to differences within those "civilizations."
5. Samuel P. Huntington. *The Clash of Civilizations and the Remaking of World Order.* New York: Simon & Schuster, 1996.
6. Donald L. Horowitz. *Ethnic Groups in Conflict.* Berkeley: University of California Press, 1986.
7. Emile Durkheim. *The Elementary Forms of the Religious Life.* New York: Free Press, (1912) 1947.
8. Jeffrey R. Seul. "'Ours Is the Way of God': Religion, Identity, and Intergroup Conflict." *Journal of Peace Research,* 36(5) (1999): 553–569, 560.
9. Anthony Gill. "Religion and Comparative Politics." *Annual Review of Political Science,* 4 (2001): 127.

10. Deborah L. Hall, David C. Matz, and Wendy Wood. "Why Don't We Practice What We Preach? A Meta-analytic Review of Religious Racism." *Personality and Social Psychology Review*, 14(1) (2010): 126–139; Robert A. Levine and Donald T. Campbell. *Ethnocentrism: Theories of Conflict, Ethnic Attitudes, and Group Behavior*. Oxford: Wiley, 1972.

11. Pippa Norris and Ronald Inglehart. *Sacred and Secular: Religion and Politics Worldwide*. Cambridge: Cambridge University Press, 2004.

12. Steven L. Neuberg, Carolyn M. Warner, Stephen A. Mistler, Anna Berlin, Eric D. Hill, Jordan D. Johnson, Gabrielle Filip-Crawford, Roger E. Millsap, George Thomas, Michael Winkelman, Benjamin J. Broome, Thomas J. Taylor, and Juliane Schober. "Religion and Intergroup Conflict: Findings from the Global Group Relations Project." *Psychological Science*, 25(1) (2014): 198–206.

13. Matthias Basedau, Birte Pfeiffer, and Johannes Vüllers. "Bad Religion? Religion, Collective Action, and the Onset of Armed Conflict in Developing Countries." *Journal of Conflict Resolution*, 60(2) (2016): 226–255; Joshua Gubler and Joel S. Selway. "Horizontal Inequality, Crosscutting Cleavages, and Civil War." *Journal of Conflict Resolution*, 56(2) (2012): 206–232; Frances Stewart. *Horizontal Inequalities and Conflict: Understanding Group Conflict in Multiethnic Societies*. Basingstoke: Palgrave Macmillan, 2008; Joel S. Selway. "Cross-cuttingness, Cleavage Structures and Civil War Onset." *British Journal of Political Science*, 41(1) (2011): 111–138.

14. Jonathan Fox. *Religion, Civilization, and Civil War. 1945 through the New Millennium*. Oxford: Lexington, 2004; Susanna Pearce. "Religious Rage: A Quantitative Analysis of the Intensity of Religious Conflicts." *Terrorism and Political Violence*, 17(3) (2005): 333–352; Isak Svensson. "Fighting with Faith: Religion and Conflict Resolution in Civil Wars." *Journal of Conflict Resolution*, 51(6) (2007): 930–949.

15. Monica Duffy Toft. "Getting Religion? The Puzzling Case of Islam and Civil War." *International Security*, 31(4) (2007): 97–131.

16. Bettencourt et al., "Status Differences and In-Group Bias."

17. John T. Sidel. *Riots, Pogroms, Jihad: Religious Violence in Indonesia*. Ithaca, NY: Cornell University Press, 2006; Hans G. Kippenberg. "Searching for the Link between Religion and Violence by Means of the Thomas-Theorem." *Method and Theory in the Study of Religion*, 22 (2010): 97–115.

18. Sascha Helbardt, Dagmar Hellmann-Rajanayagam, and Rudiger Korff. "Religionization of Politics in Sri Lanka, Thailand, and Myanmar." *Politics, Religion & Ideology*, 14(1) (2013): 36–58.

19. Jonathan Fox. "World Separation of Religion and State into the 21st Century." *Comparative Political Studies*, 39(5) (2006): 537–569.

20. Vyacheslav Karpov. "Religiosity and Tolerance in the United States and Poland." *Journal for the Scientific Study of Religion*, 41(2) (2002): 267–288.

21. Sonia Roccas. "Religion and Value Systems." *Journal of Social Issues*, 61(4): 747–759.

22. Harvey Whitehouse and Brian McQuinn. "Ritual and Violence: Divergent Modes of Religiosity and Armed Struggle." In Mark Juergensmeyer, Margo Kitts, and Michael Jerryson, eds. *The Oxford Handbook of Religion and Violence*. New York: Oxford University Press, 2013; Candace S. Alcorta and Richard Sosis, "Ritual, Religion, and Violence: An Evolutionary Perspective." In Mark Juergensmeyer, Margo Kitts, and Michael Jerryson, eds. *The Oxford Handbook of Religion and Violence*. New York: Oxford University Press, 2013.

23. David Clingingsmith, Asim Ijaz Khwaja, and Michael Kremer. "Estimating the Impact of the Hajj: Religion and Tolerance in Islam's Global Gathering." *The Quarterly Journal of Economics*, 124(3) (2009): 1133–1170.

24. Daniel Nilsson DeHanas. "Of Hajj and Home: Roots Visits to Mecca and Bangladesh in Everyday Belonging." *Ethnicitiesm*, 13(4) (2013): 457–474.

25. Sergei Gradirovski and Neli Esipova. "Russian Muslims: Religious Leaven in a Secular Society." *Harvard International Review*, 30 (Spring 2008): 58–62.

26. John Kantner and Kevin J. Vaughn. "Pilgrimage as Costly Signal: Religiously Motivated Cooperation in Chaco and Nasca." *Journal of Anthropological Archaeology*, 31 (2012): 66–82.

27. Eileen Kane. *Russian Hajj: Empire and the Pilgrimage to Mecca*. Ithaca, NY: Cornell University Press, 2015; Abrul-Gaziz Davletshin. "Otchet Stabs-Kapitana Davletshina o Komandirovke v Khidzhaz [Captain Davletshin's Report about His Trip to Khijaz]." *Khadzh Rossiiskikh Musulman: Ezhegodnyi Sbornik Putevykh Zametok o Khadzhe [Russian Muslims' Hajj: Annual Journal of Travel Notes about Hajj]*, 2 (2009). N. Novgorod, Russia: Medina Publishing House, 2009. www.idmedina.ru/books/history_culture/hadjj/2/glava-5.htm (accessed November 12, 2015).

28. Brian D. McKenzie. "Religious Social Networks, Indirect Mobilization, and African-American Political Participation." *Political Research Quarterly*, 57 (4) (2004): 621–632; Robert D. Putnam. *Bowling Alone: The Collapse and Revival of American Community*. New York: Touchstone, 2000; Alexis de Tocqueville. *Democracy in America*, translated by Gerald Bevan. London: Penguin Classics, (1835) 2003; Sidney Verba, Kay Lehman Scholzman, and Henry Brady. *Voice and Equality: Civic Volunteerism in American Politics*. Cambridge, MA: Harvard University Press, 1995.

29. Thomas F. Pettigrew and Linda R. Tropp. "A Meta-analytic Test of Intergroup Contact Theory." *Journal of Personality and Social Psychology*, 90(5) (2006): 751–783.

30. Putnam, *Bowling Alone*, p. 66.

31. Nancy Tatom Ammerman. "Organized Religion in a Voluntaristic Society." *Sociology of Religion*, 58 (1997): 203–215; Pui-Yan Lam. "As the Flocks Gather: How Religion Affects Voluntary Association Participation." *Journal for the Scientific Study of Religion*, 41(3) (2002): 405–422; David O. Moberg. *The Church as a Social Institution: The Sociology of American Religion*. Englewood Cliffs, NJ: Prentice-Hall, 1962; John Wilson and Thomas Janoski. "The Contribution of Religion to Volunteer Work." *Sociology of*

Religion, 56(2) (1995): 137–152; John Wilson and Marc Musick. "Who Cares? Toward an Integrated Theory of Volunteer Work." *American Sociological Review,* 62(5) (1997): 694–713; Robert Wuthnow. "Mobilizing Civic Engagement: The Changing Impact of Religious Involvement." In Theda Skocpol and Morris P. Fiorina, eds. *Civic Engagement in American Democracy.* Washington, DC: Brookings Institution Press, 1999, pp. 331–363.

32. Robert D. Putnam and David E. Campbell. *American Grace: How Religion Divides and Unites Us.* New York: Simon and Schuster, 2010.
33. Andrew Greeley. "Coleman Revisited: Religious Structures as a Source of Social Capital." *American Behavioral Scientist,* 40(5) (1997): 587–594.
34. Ani Sarkissian. "Religion and Civic Engagement in Muslim Countries." *Journal for the Scientific Study of Religion,* 51(4) (2012): 607–622.
35. Fawaz A. Gerges, "The Islamist Moment: From Islamic State to Civil Islam?" *Political Science Quarterly,* 128(3) (2013): 389–426; Robert W. Hefner. *Civil Islam: Muslims and Democratization in Indonesia.* Princeton, NJ: Princeton University Press, 2000.
36. Alfred Stepan. "Rituals of Respect: Sufis and Secularists in Senegal in Comparative Perspective." *Comparative Politics,* 44 (July 2012): 379–401.
37. Agnieszka Halemba. "National, Transnational or Cosmopolitan Heroine?: The Virgin Mary's Apparitions in Contemporary Europe." *Ethnic and Racial Studies,* 34(3) (2011): 454–470.
38. Charles Kurzman, David Schanzer, and Ebrahim Moosa. "Muslim American Terrorism since 9/11: Why so Rare?" *The Muslim World,* 101(3) (July 2011): 464–483, 478.
39. Clingingsmith, Khwaja, and Kremer, "Estimating the Impact of the Hajj."
40. Ibid., p. 25.
41. Methal R. Mohammed-Marzouk. "Knowledge, Culture, and Positionality: Analysis of Three Medieval Muslim Travel Accounts." *Cross-Cultural Communication,* 8(6) (2012): 1–10.
42. Putnam and Campbell, *American Grace.*
43. Carol Delaney. "The "Hajj": Sacred and Secular." *American Ethnologist,* 17 (3) (August 1990): 521.
44. Putnam, *Bowling Alone,* p. 119.
45. Sarkissian, "Religion and Civic Engagement in Muslim Countries," p. 617.
46. Dag Wollebaek and Per Selle. "Participation in Social Capital Formation: Norway in a Comparative Perspective." *Scandinavian Political Studies,* 26(1) (2003): 67–91.
47. Norris and Ingelhart, *Sacred and Secular,* p. 189.
48. Eric Patterson. "Religious Activity and Political Participation: The Brazilian and Chilean Cases." *Latin American Politics and Society,* 47(1) (2005): 1–29.
49. David E. Campbell. "Acts of Faith: Churches and Political Engagement." *Political Behavior,* 26(2) (2004): 155–180.
50. Fox, *Religion, Civilization, and Civil War,* p. 539.
51. James D. Fearon and David D. Laitin. "Ethnicity, Insurgency, and Civil War." *American Political Science Review,* 97 (2003): 75–90; Paul Collier

and Anke Hoeffler. "Greed and Grievance in Civil War." *Oxford Economic Papers*, 56(4) (2004): 563–595.

52. Robert M. Kunovich and Randy Hodson. "Conflict, Religious Identity, and Ethnic Intolerance in Croatia." *Social Forces*, 78(2) (December 1999): 643–668.
53. Robert A. Pape. *Dying to Win: The Strategic Logic of Suicide Terrorism.* New York: Random House, 2005.
54. Gill, "Religion and Comparative Politics."
55. Said-Affandi Chirkavi. *Sokrovishnitsa Blagodatnykh Znanii* [*Treasures of Blessed Knowledge*]. Moscow: IKHLAS, 2002, pp. 75–76.
56. Susan O'Brien. "Pilgrimage, Power, and Identity: The Role of the Hajj in the Lives of Nigerian Hausa Bori Adepts." *Africa Today*, 46 (Summer 1999): 11–40.
57. Fred Burton and Scott Steward. "The Hajj: Challenges and Opportunities." *Security Weekly*, Stratfor, December 5, 2007, www.stratfor.com/weekly/haj ji_challenges_and_opportunities (accessed November 12, 2015).
58. FBI. "Most Wanted Terrorists: Usama Bin Laden," September 29, 2010, www.fbi.gov/a-z-index/wanted/wanted_terrorists/usama-bin-laden (accessed November 19, 2015).
59. Kris Alexanderson. "A Dark State of Affairs: Hajj Networks, Pan-Islamism, and Dutch Colonial Surveillance during the Interwar Period." *Journal of Social History*, 47(4) (2014): 1021–1041; Michael Christopher Low. "Empire and the Hajj: Pilgrims, Plagues, and Pan-Islam under British Surveillance, 1865–1908." *International Journal of Middle East Studies*, 40 (2) (2008): 269–290.
60. Clingingsmith, Khwaja, and Kremer, "Estimating the Impact of the Hajj," p. 1134.
61. *Telegraph.* "Hajj Pilgrimage 2011: By Numbers," November 3, 2011, www .telegraph.co.uk/news/worldnews/middleeast/saudiarabia/8867639/Hajj-pil grimage-2011-by-numbers.html (accessed November 19, 2015).
62. Oliver Bullough. *Let Our Fame Be Great: Journeys among the Defiant People of the Caucasus.* New York: Basic Books, 2010, p. 318.

4   REPOSITIONING OR THE AXIS MUNDI EFFECT

1. Mircea Eliade. *The Sacred and the Profane: The Nature of Religion.* New York: Harcourt, 1987.
2. The Hajj is a form of bidirectional migration that has not been modeled in studies of social identity and intergroup contact. Most of the latter represent either static intergroup situations or unidirectional intergroup movement. The most obvious example of the former is when different ethnic groups that have long resided in the same location interact with each other (e.g., African Americans and Caucasians in a housing complex or neighborhood). One may also consider an intergroup situation as static when members of one non-migrant group view members of other non-migrant groups regardless of their location (e.g., when engineers think what differentiates them from

doctors). The unidirectional group movement is about relationships and interactions between host communities and incoming migrant groups from within or outside the state.

3. Eliade, *The Sacred and the Profane*, pp. 80–84, 87.

4. Ibid., pp. 88–89.

5. Mir Muhammad Ibrahim. *Sociology of Religions: Perspectives of Ali Shariati.* New Delhi, India: Prentice-Hall, 2008, p. 221.

6. Venetia Porter, ed. *Hajj: Journey to the Heart of Islam.* Cambridge, MA: Harvard University Press, 2012.

7. Qur'an 3:97.

8. Francis E. Peters. *The Hajj: The Muslim Pilgrimage to Mecca and the Holy Places.* Princeton, NJ: Princeton University Press, 1994.

9. See also: Jonathan Brown. *The Canonization of Al-Bukhari and Muslim: The Formation and Function of the Suni Hadith Canon.* Leiden, The Netherlands: Koninklijke Brill NV, 2007.

10. Focus group with younger non-pilgrim Muslim women, April 30, 2010, Nalchik, Russia.

11. Sufian's Hajj diaries and observations, November 2009.

12. Juan Eduardo Campo, ed., *Encyclopedia of Islam.* New York: Infobase Publishing, 2009, p. 283.

13. "Record Number of Pilgrims Arrive for Hajj," Royal Embassy of Saudi Arabia in Washington, DC. December 6, 2008. www.saudiembassy.net/affairs/recent-news/news12060801.aspx; "2,521,000 Pilgrims Participated in Hajj 1430," Royal Embassy of Saudi Arabia in Washington, DC. November 29, 2009. www.saudiembassy.net/latest_news/news11290904.aspx; "2.8 Million Pilgrims Participated in Hajj 1431." Royal Embassy of Saudi Arabia in Tokyo. November 18, 2010. www.saudiembassy.or.jp/En/PressReleases/2010/20101118.htm; "2,927,717 Pilgrims Performed Hajj this Year." Royal Embassy of Saudi Arabia in Washington, DC. November 6, 2011. www.saudiembassy.net/latest_news/news11061102.aspx; "3,161,573 Pilgrims Perform Hajj this Year." Royal Embassy of Saudi Arabia in Washington, DC. October 27, 2012. www.saudiembassy.net/latest_news/news10271201.aspx; "1,379,531 Pilgrims from 188 Countries Arrived for Hajj." Royal Embassy of Saudi Arabia in Washington, DC. October 13, 2013. www.saudiembassy.net/latest_news/news10131302.aspx; "Small Increase in Foreign Pilgrims." Royal Embassy of Saudi Arabia in Washington, DC. October 2, 2014. www.saudiembassy.net/latest_news/news10021401.aspx; "1,384,941 Foreign Pilgrims Participated in Hajj." Royal Embassy of Saudi Arabia in Washington, DC. September 22, 2015. www.saudiembassy.net/latest_news/news09221501.aspx (accessed July 14, 2015).

14. Pew Research Center. "The Global Religious Landscape." *Pew Research Center's Forum on Religion & Public Life.* December 18, 2012. www.pewforum.org/2012/12/18/global-religious-landscape-muslim/ (accessed November 19, 2015). Historically, the country and ethnic composition of the pilgrims have fluctuated as a result of Muslim politics played within and across national boundaries – for long-range historical data and the discussion of the role of big politics and big business in shaping these trends, see Robert

R. Bianchi. *Guests of God: Pilgrimage and Politics in the Islamic World.* Oxford: Oxford University Press, 2004.

15. Eliade, *The Sacred and the Profane,* p. 30.
16. Malcolm X and Alex Haley. *The Autobiography of Malcolm X.* New York: Grove Press, 1965.
17. As in the Figure 4.1 data, we excluded short discussions of routine logistics unrelated to performing the Hajj as a ritual – e.g., obtaining visas or arranging bus rides.
18. Tamar Mayer and Suleiman A. Mourad, eds. *Jerusalem: Idea and Reality.* New York: Routledge, 2008, p. 87.
19. Johanan Friedmann. *Tolerance and Coercion in Islam: Interfaith Relations in the Muslim Tradition.* Cambridge: Cambridge University Press, 2003, p. 31.
20. Qur'an 2:144.
21. William Montgomery Watt. *Muhammad: Prophet and Statesman.* New York: Oxford University Press, 1974, pp. 112–113.
22. Qur'an 2:142.
23. Qur'an 2:143.
24. At-Tirmidhi, Abu 'Isa Muhammad. Jami` at-Tirmidhi. Vol. 5, Book 44, Hadith 2975, https://sunnah.com/urn/639670.
25. Alexandre Papas, Thomas Welsford, and Thierry Zarcone, eds. *Central Asian Pilgrims: Hajj Routes and Pious Visits between Central Asia and the Hijaz.* Islamkundliche Untersuchungen, Band 308. Berlin: Klaus Schwartz Verlag, 2012.
26. Interview with Nazir-hajji on October 20, 2009; See also: Fatima Tikaeva, "Obschestvo Na Puti Konsolidatsii [Society on Its Way to Consolidation]." *Islam V Evrazii,* January 23, 2009. http://islamvevrazii.ru/obsh274.php (accessed November 19, 2015).

5 RECATEGORIZATION

1. Samuel L. Gaertner and John F. Dovidio. *Reducing Intergroup Bias: The Common Ingroup Identity Model.* Philadelphia, PA: Psychology Press, 2000; for a review, see John F. Dovidio, Samuel L. Gaertner, Nurit Shnabel, Tamar Saguy, and James Johnson. "Recategorization and Prosocial Behavior: Group Processes, Ingroup Relations, and Helping." In Stefan Sturmer and Mark Snyder, eds. *The Psychology of Prosocial Behavior: Group Processes, Intergroup Relations.* Oxford: Wiley-Blackwell, 2009, pp. 191–207.
2. John C. Turner, Michael A. Hogg, Penelope J. Oakes, Stephen D. Reicher, and Margaret S. Wetherell. *Rediscovering the Social Group: A Self-Categorization Theory.* Oxford: Blackwell, 1987.
3. Alexander S. Haslam. *Psychology in Organizations.* London: SAGE Publications, 2001.
4. Amélie Mummendey and Michael Wenzel. "Social Discrimination and Tolerance in Intergroup Relations: Reactions to Intergroup Difference." *Personality and Social Psychology Review,* 3 (1999): 158–174.

5. Abrul-Gaziz Davletshin. "Otchet Stabs-Kapitana Davletshina o Komandirovke v Khidzhaz [Captain Davletshin's Report about His Trip to Khijaz]." *Khadzh Rossiiskikh Musulman: Ezhegodnyi Sbornik Putevykh Zametok o Khadzhe [Russian Muslims' Hajj: Annual Journal of Travel Notes about Hajj]*, vol. 2. N. Novgorod, Russia: Medina Publishing House, 2009. www.idmedina.ru/books/history_culture/hadjj/2/glava-5.htm (accessed November 12, 2015).

6. Andrew Greeley. "Coleman Revisited: Religious Structures as a Source of Social Capital." *American Behavioral Scientist*, 40(5) (1997): 587–594; Ani Sarkissian. "Religion and Civic Engagement in Muslim Countries." *Journal for the Scientific Study of Religion*, 51(4) (2012): 607–622.

7. Robert D. Putnam and David E. Campbell. *American Grace: How Religion Divides and Unites Us*. New York: Simon and Schuster, 2010.

8. Robert D. Putnam. *Making Democracy Work: Civic Traditions in Modern Italy*. Princeton, NJ: Princeton University Press, 1993.

9. Focus group with elder Muslim men who performed the Hajj, April 27, 2010, Nalchik, Russia.

10. "Imama Nal'chika Uvolili, Vosstanovili Na Rabote, Ob'avili Blagodarnost' I Snova Uvolili [The Imam of Nalchik Was Fired, Restored in His Position, Commended for Good Service, and Let Go Again]." Regnum. August 8, 2008. www.regnum.ru/news/cultura/1042786.html (accessed November 19, 2015).

11. "Rais-imam Nalchika: Mufti Kabardino-Balkarii Prenebregaet MVeruyuschikh [Nalchik Rais-Imam: The Mufti of Kabardino-Balkaria Dismisses the Opinion of Muslims]." Regnum. April 23, 2008. http://regnu m.ru/news/991435.html (accessed November 19, 2015).

12. "Federal'nyi Spisok Ekstremistskikh Materialov [Federal List of Extremist Materials]." Ministry of Justice of the Russian Federation. http://minjust.ru/ extremist-materials (accessed July 25, 2016).

13. Miriam Cooke and Bruce B. Lawrence, eds. *Muslim Networks from Hajj to Hip Hop*. Chapel Hill: University of North Carolina, 2005, p. 1.

14. Gabrielle Glaser. "A Gay Muslim Filmmaker Goes Inside the Hajj." *New York Times*. September 24, 2015. www.nytimes.com/2015/09/27/nyregion/ parvez-sharma-a-sinner-in-mecca.html (accessed November 12, 2015).

6 REPERSONALIZATION

1. John C. Turner et al. *Rediscovering the Social Group: A Self-Categorization Theory*. Oxford: Blackwell 1987, 50.

2. S. Alexander Haslam, Stephen D. Reicher, and Michael J. Platow. *The New Psychology of Leadership: Identity, Influence and Power*. New York: Psychology Press, 2011; Craig McGarty. *Categorization in Social Psychology*. SAGE Publications: London, Thousand Oaks, CA, New Delhi, 1999.

3. Turner et al., *Rediscovering the Social Group*, p. 50.

4. Focus group with non-pilgrim Muslim men, April 30, 2010, Nalchik, Russia.

5. Focus group with elder Muslim men who performed the Hajj, April 27, 2010, Nalchik, Russia.
6. Said-Affandi Chirkavi. *Sokrovishnitsa Blagodatnykh Znanii [Treasures of Blessed Knowledge]*. Moscow: IKHLAS, 2002, pp. 75–76.
7. Mircea Eliade. *The Sacred and the Profane: The Nature of Religion*. New York: Harcourt, 1987, p. 100.
8. Ibid., p. 99.
9. Alexis de Tocqueville. *Democracy in America*. Translated by Gerald Bevan. London: Penguin Classics, (1835) 2003. Quoted in Robert A. Nisbet. *The Sociological Tradition*. New York: Basic Books, 1966, p. 236.
10. Focus group, Nalchik, Russia, April 27, 2010.
11. Interviewed by Sufian in Mecca during the Hajj, November 26, 2009.
12. The authors will provide upon request a methodological appendix containing the list of coded terms with respective word counts.
13. Social equality could be considered a non-diagnostic case, because the combined amount of time was about the same among the pilgrims and the non-pilgrims. However, because the distribution of time among the groups was skewed due to the topic being discussed only in one non-Hajj group, but in both Hajj groups, it is plausible that the pilgrimage effect on this topic was indeterminate.
14. Of the latter's work, see, in particular, Tariq Ramadan, *The Quest for Meaning: Developing a Philosophy of Pluralism*. London: Allen Lane, 2010; Tariq Ramadan, *Western Muslims and the Future of Islam*. New York: Oxford University Press, 2004.

7 ISLAM'S SOCIAL SPACES: EUROPE VERSUS THE UNITED STATES

1. Paul M. Barrett. "American Muslims and the Question of Assimilation." In Steffen Angenendt, Paul M. Barrett, Jonathan Laurence, Ceri Peach, Julianne Smith, and Tim Winter. *Muslim Integration: Challenging Conventional Wisdom in Europe and the United States*. Washington, DC: Center for Strategic and International Studies, 2007, p. 79.
2. Adam Nagourney, Jennifer Medina, Ian Lovett, and Julie Turkewitz. "As Bullets Flew, Urgent Prayers and Pure Panic." *New York Times*. December 6, 2015; Peter Baker and Eric Schmitt. "Rampage has U.S. Rethinking How to Stop Attacks." *New York Times*. December 6, 2015; Rukmini Callimachi. "ISIS Says 'Soldiers of Caliphate' Carried Out Rampage." *New York Times*. December 6, 2015.
3. Milton M. Gordon. *Assimilation in American Life: The Role of Race, Religion and National Origin*. New York: Oxford University Press, 1964; Richard Alba and Victor Nee. *Remaking the American Mainstream: Assimilation and Contemporary Immigration*. Cambridge, MA: Harvard University Press, 2003; Herbert J. Gans. "Acculturation, Assimilation and Mobility." *Ethnic and Racial Studies* 30(1) (January 2007): 152–164.

4. Joselyne Cesari. *When Islam and Democracy Meet: Muslims in Europe and the United States.* New York: Palgrave Macmillan, 2004.
5. Justin Gest and Richard Nielsen. "Is Cultural Integration Determined by Income and Education? Evidence from Surveys of Muslims in Britain, France and the United States." *MIT Working Papers* (version: July 19, 2015). www.mit.edu/~rnielsen/Gest%20and%20Nielsen%20-%20Muslim%20Integration.pdf (accessed December 5, 2015).
6. Justin Gest. *Apart: Alienated and Engaged Muslims in the West.* New York: Columbia University Press, 2010.
7. Pew Research Center. "Muslim Americans: No Sign of Growth in Alienation or Support for Extremism." Pew Research Center's Forum on Religion & Public Life. August 30, 2011. www.people-press.org/2011/08/30/muslim-americans-no-signs-of-growth-in-alienation-or-support-for-extremism/ (accessed November 19, 2015).
8. Ibid., p. 16.
9. Ceri Peach. "Muslim Population of Europe: A Brief Overview of Demographic Trends and Socioeconomic Integration, with Particular Reference to Britain." In Steffen Angenendt, Paul M. Barrett, Jonathan Laurence, Ceri Peach, Julianne Smith, and Tim Winter, eds. *Muslim Integration: Challenging Conventional Wisdom in Europe and the United States.* Washington, DC: Center for Strategic and International Studies, 2007, pp. 9–11.
10. "Placing Worship," *Architect: The Journal of the American Institute of Architects*, September 17, 2012. www.architectmagazine.com/projects/view/placing-worship/538/ (accessed November 19, 2015).
11. Ibid.
12. "Islamic, Yet Integrated." *The Economist.* September 6, 2014. www.economist.com/news/united-states/21615611-why-muslims-fare-better-america-europe-islamic-yet-integrated (accessed November 19, 2015).
13. "Placing Worship," *Architect.*
14. Ibid.
15. Ibid.
16. Shahed Saleem. "A History of Mosques in Britain." *Architects Journal.* April 19, 2012. www.architectsjournal.co.uk/a-history-of-mosques-in-britain/8629263.article (accessed on November 19, 2015).
17. Ibid.
18. "Placing Worship," *Architect.*
19. Shahed Saleem. "The British Mosque: A Social and Architectural History." *Muslim Institute.* www.musliminstitute.org/blogs/culture/british-mosque-social-and-architectural-history (accessed on November 19, 2015).
20. "Placing Worship," *Architect*; Saleem, "The British Mosque."
21. "Placing Worship," *Architect.*
22. Shariq A. Siddiqui. "Islamic Society of North America." In Edward E. Curtis, ed. *Encyclopedia of Muslim-American History.* Infobase Publishing, 2010, p. 296.
23. "Islamic, Yet Integrated," *The Economist.*

24. Siddiqui, "Islamic Society of North America," p. 298.
25. Ibid.
26. "ISNA Celebrates the 5th Annual Muslim-Jewish Weekend of Twinning." Islamic Society of America. December 25, 2013. www.isna.net/isna-cele brates-the-5th-annual-muslim-jewish-weekend-of-twinning.html (accessed November 19, 2015); The ISNA also posted a film trailer on YouTube about the campaign (http://youtu.be/PTXaVjJcQTg).
27. Berengere Massignon. "Islam in the EC System of Regulation." In Aziz Al-Azmeh and Effie Fokas, eds. *Islam in Europe: Diversity, Identity and Influence*. New York: Cambridge University Press, 2007, p. 135.
28. Ibid., p. 138.
29. The Report by the High-Level Advisory Group to the President of the European Commission, "Dialogue between Peoples and Cultures in the Euro-Mediterranean Area" (September 8, 2003), p. 10, quoted in Berengere Massignon. "Islam in the EC System of Regulation." In Aziz Al-Azmeh and Effie Fokas, eds. *Islam in Europe: Diversity, Identity and Influence*. New York: Cambridge University Press, 2007, p. 138.
30. Parveen Akhtar. *British Muslim Politics: Examining Pakistani Biraderi Networks*. New York: Palgrave Macmillan, 2013.
31. Abida Malik. "Identities, Islamophobia, and the State: Diverse Perspectives and Experiences of Muslim Civic Actors from Islamic Organizations in the UK." In Matthias Kortmann and Kerstin Rosenow-Williams, eds. *Islamic Organizations in Europe and the USA: A Multidisciplinary Perspective*. New York: Palgrave Macmillan, 2013, chapter 12.
32. Ibid.
33. Anne-Laure Zwilling. "France." In Jørgen Schøler Nielsen, Samim Akgönül, Ahmet Alibašić, Brigitte Maréchal, and Christian Moe. *Yearbook of Muslims in Europe*, vol. 1. Leiden: BRILL, 2009, quote on p. 131.
34. Zeyno Baran. *Citizen Islam: The Future of Muslim Integration in the West*. New York: Bloomsbury Academy, 2011, pp. 82–83.
35. Tom Heneghan. "Uncertain Future for France's Muslim Council." Reuters. May 5, 2008. http://blogs.reuters.com/faithworld/2008/05/05/un certain-future-for-frances-muslim-council/ (accessed on November 19, 2015).
36. Peter Skerry. "The Muslim-American Muddle." *National Affairs*, 9 (Fall 2011): 14–37.
37. Herbert J. Gans. "Acculturation, Assimilation and Mobility." *Ethnic and Racial Studies* 30(1) (January 2007): 152–164.
38. Alejandro Portes and Min Zhou. "The New Second Generation: Segmented Assimilation and Its Variants." *The Annals of the American Academy of Political and Social Science*, 530(1) (November 1993): 74–96; Ronald Inglehart and Christopher Welzel. *Modernization, Cultural Change and Democracy: The Human Development Sequence*. New York: Cambridge University Press, 2005; Rahsaan Maxwell. "Evaluating Migrant Integration: Political Attitudes across Generations in Europe." *International Migration Review*, 44(1) (2010): 25–52.

39. "Muslim Americans: Middle Class and Mostly Mainstream." Pew Research Center. May 22, 2007. www.pewresearch.org/2007/05/22/muslim-americans-middle-class-and-mostly-mainstream/ (accessed on November 19, 2015), p. 3.
40. Ibid.
41. Ibid., pp. 51, 53.
42. Ibid.
43. Mary C. Waters and Tomas R. Jimenez, "Assessing Immigrant Assimilation: New Empirical and Theoretical Challenges," *Annual Review of Sociology* 31 (2005): 105–125.
44. Claire L. Adida, David D. Laitin, and Marie-Anne Valfort. "Identifying Barriers to Muslim Integration in France." *Proceedings of National Academy of Sciences* (PNAS) 107(52) (2010): 22384–22390.
45. Alessandro Acquisti and Christina M. Fong, "An Experiment in Hiring Discrimination Via Online Social Networks." Social Science Research Network. http://papers.ssrn.com/sol3/papers.cfm?abstract_id=2031979 (accessed November 12, 2015).
46. "Muslim Americans: Middle Class and Mostly Mainstream," Pew Research Center, p. 19.
47. Toni Johnson. "Europe: Integrating Islam." Council on Foreign Relations, July 25, 2011. www.cfr.org/religion/europe-integrating-islam/p8252 (accessed November 19, 2015).

8 THE LA RAZA AXIS: HISPANIC INTEGRATION IN NORTH AMERICA

1. Mircea Eliade. *The Sacred and the Profane: The Nature of Religion*. New York: Harcourt, 1987, p. 26.
2. Ibid., p. 25.
3. Ibid., pp. 23–24.
4. Morris Janowitz. *The Reconstruction of Patriotism: Education for Civic Consciousness*. Chicago: University of Chicago Press, 1983, pp. 128–129.
5. Samuel P. Huntington. *Who Are We? The Challenges to America's National Identity*. New York: Simon & Schuster, 2004, pp. 223–256; Samuel P. Huntington. "The Hispanic Challenge." *Foreign Policy* (March/April 2004), quote on p. 38.
6. Rodolfo O. de la Garza. "Latino Politics." *Annual Review of Political Science*, 7 (2004): 91–123.
7. Matt A. Barreto and Francisco I. Pedraza. "The Renewal and Persistence of Group Identification in American Politics." *Electoral Studies*, 28 (2009): 595–605. The survey data came from Luis R. Fraga, John A. Garcia, Rodney Hero, Michael Jones-Correa, Valerie Martinez-Ebers, and Gary M. Segura, Latino National Survey (LNS), 2006 [Computer File]. ICPSR20862-v1. Geoscape International [Producer], Miami, FL. Ann Arbor, MI: Inter-university Consortium for Political and Social Research [Distributor] www.icpsr.umich.edu/icpsrweb/RCMD/studies/20862/version/1 (accessed April 17, 2016).

8. Jose Angel Gutierrez. "The Chicano Movement: Paths to Power." *The Social Studies*, 102(1) (2011): 25–32, quoted on p. 28.

9. Matt A. Barreto and Stephen A. Nuno. "The Effectiveness of Coethnic Contact on Latino Political Recruitment," *Political Research Quarterly*, 64 (2) (2011): 448–459.

10. Luis Fraga, John Garcia, Rodney Hero, Michael Jones-Correa, Valerie Martinez-Ebers, and Gary M. Segura. "*Su Casa es Nuestra Casa*: Latino Politics Research and the Development of American Political Science." *American Political Science Review*, 100(4) (November 2006): 515–521. The principal exemplars of the argument among the works cited therein are Michael R. Alvarez and Tara L. Butterfield. "The Resurgence of Nativism in California? The Case of Proposition 187 and Illegal Immigration." *Social Science Quarterly*, 81 (March 2000): 167–179; Adrian D. Pantoja, Ricardo Ramirez, and Gary M. Segura. "Citizens by Choice, Voters by Necessity: Patterns in Political Mobilization by Naturalized Latinos." *Political Research Quarterly*, 54 (December), 729–750; Adrian D. Pantoja and Gary M. Segura. "Fear and Loathing in California: Contextual Threat and Political Sophistication among Latino Voters." *Political Behavior*, 25(3) (September 2003): 265–286; Matt A. Barreto. "Latino Immigrants at the Polls: Foreign Born Voter Turnout in the 2002 Election." *Political Research Quarterly*, 58 (1) (March 2005): 79–86; and Shaun Bowler, Stephen P. Nicholson, and Gary M. Segura. "Earthquakes and Aftershocks: Tracking Partisan Identification amid California's Changing Political Environment." *American Journal of Political Science*, 50 (January 2006): 146–159.

11. Matt A. Barreto, Gary M. Segura, and Ali A. Valenzuela. "Latino Attitudes and Support for Barack Obama: Three Windows into a (Nearly) Baseless Myth." American Political Science Association (APSA) 2010 Annual Meeting Paper, September 1–4, 2010, Washington, DC. Measures of prejudice comprised racial stereotypes, resentment (symbolic racism), and affect misattribution procedures.

12. Both *Hispanic* and *Latino* are considered appropriate terms describing populations of Mexican as well as Central and Latin American heritage (with the exception of Brazilians, who may be considered Latino, but not Hispanic, even though Portuguese and Spanish are closely related languages).

13. Deirdre Martinez. *Who Speaks for Hispanics?: Hispanic Interest Groups in Washington*. Albany: State University of New York Press, 2009, p. 33 (ProQuest ebrary, accessed October 16, 2014).

14. Margo Gutierrez and Matt S. Meier. *Encyclopedia of the Mexican American Civil Rights Movement*. Westport, CT: Greenwood Press, 2000, p. 130 (ProQuest ebrary, accessed October 16, 2014).

15. Benjamin Marquez. *Constructing Identities in Mexican-American Political Organizations: Choosing Issues, Taking Sides*. Austin: University of Texas Press, 2003, p. 54.

16. Ibid., pp. 3–15.

17. Martinez, *Who Speaks for Hispanics?*, p. 57.

18. LULAC. "History: LULAC's Milestones," http://lulac.org/about/history/mile stones/ (accessed November 19, 2015).

19. Martinez, *Who Speaks for Hispanics?*, p. 57.
20. Latino Leadership. "National Council of La Raza: NCLR." http://latino-lea
    dership.org/partners-affiliations/ (accessed November 12, 2015).
21. Marguerite Casey Foundation. "National Council of La Raza." http://casey
    grants.org/grantees/national-council-of-la-raza/ (accessed November 12,
    2015).
22. Ibid.
23. Joanna Campbell. "National Council of La Raza." *Learning to Give*. A
    public philanthropy website. http://learningtogive.org/papers/paper261.html
    (accessed November 19, 2015).
24. Martinez, *Who Speaks for Hispanics?*, p. 68.
25. Ibid.

CONCLUSION

1. Bernard Lewis. *Faith and Power: Religion and Politics in the Middle East*. New
   York: Oxford University Press, 2010; for counterarguments, see Ahmet T.
   Kuru. "Authoritarianism and Democracy in Muslim Countries: Rentier
   States and Regional Diffusion." *Political Science Quarterly*, 129(3) (2014):
   399–427.
2. Reza Aslan. *No God but God: The Origins, Evolution, and Future of Islam*.
   New York: Random House, 2005.
3. John O. Voll and John L. Esposito. *Islam and Democracy*. New York: Oxford
   University Press, 1996; Armando Salvatore and Mark Levine, eds. *Religion,
   Social Practice, and Contested Hegemonies: Reconstructing the Public Sphere
   in Muslim Majority Societies*. New York: Palgrave Macmillan, 2005, p. 2.
4. John Bunyan. *The Pilgrim's Progress*. New York: Pocket Books, Inc., 1957,
   p. vi.

Bibliography

Acquisti, Alessandro, and Christina M. Fong. "An Experiment in Hiring Discrimination Via Online Social Networks." *Social Science Research Network*, http://papers.ssrn.com/sol3/papers.cfm?abstract_id=2031979 (accessed November 12, 2015).

Adida, Claire L., David D. Laitin, and Marie-Anne Valfort. "Identifying Barriers to Muslim Integration in France." *Proceedings of the National Academy of Sciences (PNAS)*, 107(52) (2010): 22384–22390.

Akhmadulin, V'iachslav. "Deiatel'nost Sovetskogo Gosudarstva Po Organizatsii Hadzha Sovetskikh Musul'man V 1944–1991 gg [Soviet State's Management of Organizing of Soviet Muslims' Hajj in 1944–1991]." *Khadzh Rossiiskikh Musulman: Ezhegodnyi Sbornik Putevykh Zametok o Khadzhe [Russian Muslims' Hajj: Annual Journal of Travel Notes about Hajj]*, 5 (2013). N. Novgorod, Russia: Medina Publishing House, 2013.

Akhtar, Parveen. *British Muslim Politics: Examining Pakistani Biraderi Networks.* New York: Palgrave Macmillan, 2013.

Al-Ken, Akeel Ibrahim. "The Hajj: Past, Present, and Future. The Communication Aspect." PhD, Leeds: The University of Leeds, 1995. http://etheses.whiterose .ac.uk/523/1/uk_bl_ethos_341805.pdf (accessed February 17, 2017).

Alba, Richard, and Victor Nee. *Remaking the American Mainstream: Assimilation and Contemporary Immigration.* Cambridge, MA: Harvard University Press, 2003.

Alcorta, Candace S., and Richard Sosis. "Ritual, Religion, and Violence: An Evolutionary Perspective." In Mark Juergensmeyer, Margo Kitts, and Michael Jerryson, eds. *The Oxford Handbook of Religion and Violence.* New York: Oxford University Press, 2013, 571–596.

Alenova, Olga, and Zaur Farniev. "Poeticheskii Krizis [Poetic Crisis]." *Kommersant*, June 23, 2011, www.kommersant.ru/doc/1655370 (accessed November 12, 2015).

Alexanderson, Kris. "A Dark State of Affairs: Hajj Networks, Pan-Islamism, and Dutch Colonial Surveillance during the Interwar Period." *Journal of Social History*, 47(4) (2014): 1021–1041.

Alexseev, Mikhail A. "Local vs. Transcendent Insurgencies: Why Economic Aid Helps Lower Violence in Dagestan, but Not in Kabardino-Balkaria." In

William Ascher, Natalia Mirovitskaya, and Jay Heffron, eds. *Economic Development Strategies and Inter-group Violence*. New York: Palgrave/MacMillan, 2013, 277–314.

Alexseev, Mikhail A. "Russia's 'Cold Peace' Consensus: Transcending the Presidential Election." *Fletcher Forum of World Affairs*, 21(1) (Winter/Spring 1997): 33–50.

Alexseev, Mikhail A., and Sufian N. Zhemukhov. "From Mecca with Tolerance: Religion, Social Recategorisation and Social Capital." *Religion, State, and Society*, 44(1) (2016): 371–391.

Allport, Gordon W., and John M. Ross. "Personal Religious Orientation and Prejudice." *Journal of Personality and Social Psychology*, 5 (1967): 432–443.

Altemeyer, Bob, and Bruce Hunsberger. "Authoritarianism, Religious Fundamentalism, Quest and Prejudice." *International Journal for the Psychology of Religion*, 2 (1992): 113–133.

Alvarez, Michael R., and Tara L. Butterfield. "The Resurgence of Nativism in California? The Case of Proposition 187 and Illegal Immigration." *Social Science Quarterly*, 81 (March 2000): 167–179.

Ammerman, Nancy Tatom. "Organized Religion in a Voluntaristic Society." *Sociology of Religion*, 58 (1997): 203–215.

Architect: The Journal of the American Institute of Architects. "Placing Worship." September 17, 2012, www.architectmagazine.com/projects/view/placing-worship/538/ (accessed November 19, 2015).

Aslan, Reza. *No God but God: The Origins, Evolution, and Future of Islam*. New York: Random House, 2005.

Baker, Peter, and Eric Schmitt. "Rampage Has U.S. Rethinking How to Stop Attacks." *New York Times*, December 6, 2015.

Baran, Zeyno. *Citizen Islam: The Future of Muslim Integration in the West*. New York: Bloomsbury Academic, 2011.

Barreto, Matt A. "Latino Immigrants at the Polls: Foreign Born Voter Turnout in the 2002 Election." *Political Research Quarterly*, 58(1) (March 2005): 79–86.

Barreto, Matt A., and Stephen A. Nuno. "The Effectiveness of Coethnic Contact on Latino Political Recruitment," *Political Research Quarterly*, 64(2) (2011): 448–459.

Barreto, Matt A., and Francisco I. Pedraza. "The Renewal and Persistence of Group Identification in American Politics." *Electoral Studies*, 28 (2009): 595–605.

Barreto, Matt A., Gary M. Segura, and Ali A. Valenzuela. "Latino Attitudes and Support for Barack Obama: Three Windows into a (Nearly) Baseless Myth." American Political Science Association (APSA) Washington, DC: Annual Meeting Paper, September 1–4, 2010.

Barrett, Paul M. "American Muslims and the Question of Assimilation." In Steffen Angenendt, Paul M. Barrett, Jonathan Laurence, Ceri Peach, Julianne Smith, and Tim Winter. eds. *Muslim Integration: Challenging Conventional Wisdom in Europe and the United States*. Washington, DC: Center for Strategic and International Studies, 2007, 75–82.

Barrett, Thomas M. "The Remaking of the Lion of Dagestan: Shamil in Captivity." *The Russian Review*, 53 (3) (1994): 353–366.

Basedau, Matthias, Birte Pfeiffer, and Johannes Vüllers. "Bad Religion? Religion, Collective Action, and the Onset of Armed Conflict in Developing Countries." *Journal of Conflict Resolution*, 60(2) (2016): 226–255.

Bettencourt, Ann, Kelly Chapman, Nancy Dorr, and Deborah Hume. "Status Differences and In-Group Bias: A Meta-analytic Examination of the Effects of Status Stability, Status Legitimacy, and Group Permeability." *Psychological Bulletin*, 126(3) (2001): 1411–1445.

Bianchi, Robert R. *Guests of God: Pilgrimage and Politics in the Islamic World.* New York: Oxford University Press, 2004.

Bianchi, Robert R. *Islamic Globalization: Pilgrimage, Capitalism, Democracy, and Diplomacy.* Singapore: World Scientific, 2013.

Bowler, Shaun, Stephen P. Nicholson, and Gary M. Segura. "Earthquakes and Aftershocks: Tracking Partisan Identification Amid California's Changing Political Environment." *American Journal of Political Science*, 50 (January 2006): 146–159.

Bram, Chen, and Moshe Gammer. "Radical Islamism, Traditional Islam and Ethno-nationalism in the Northern Caucasus." *Middle Eastern Studies*, 49(2) (2013): 296–337.

Brown, Jonathan. *The Canonization of Al-Bukhari and Muslim: The Formation and Function of the Suni Hadith Canon.* Leiden, The Netherlands: Koninklijke Brill NV, 2007.

Bullough, Oliver. *Let Our Fame Be Great: Journeys among the Defiant People of the Caucasus.* New York: Basic Books, 2010.

Bunyan, John. *The Pilgrim's Progress.* New York: Pocket Books, Inc., 1957.

Burton, Fred, and Scott Steward. "The Hajj: Challenges and Opportunities." *Security Weekly*, Stratfor, December 5, 2007, www.stratfor.com/weekly/haj ji_challenges_and_opportunities (accessed November 19, 2015).

Callimachi, Rukmini. "ISIS Says 'Soldiers of Caliphate' Carried Out Rampage." *New York Times*, December 6, 2015.

Campbell, David E. "Acts of Faith: Churches and Political Engagement." *Political Behavior* 26(2) (2004): 155–180.

Campbell, Joanna. "National Council of La Raza." *Learning to Give*, http://lear ningtogive.org/papers/paper261.html (accessed November 19, 2015).

Campo, Juan E., ed. *Encyclopedia of Islam.* New York: Infobase Publishing, 2009.

Cesari, Joselyne. *When Islam and Democracy Meet: Muslims in Europe and the United States.* New York: Palgrave Macmillan, 2004.

Chirkavi, Said-Affandi. *Sokrovishnitsa Blagodatnykh Znanii [Treasures of Blessed Knowledge].* Moscow: IKHLAS, 2002.

Clingingsmith, David, Asim Ijaz Khwaja, and Michael Kremer. "Estimating the Impact of the Hajj: Religion and Tolerance in Islam's Global Gathering." *The Quarterly Journal of Economics*, 124(3) (2009): 1133–1170.

Collier, Paul, and Anke Hoeffler. "Greed and Grievance in Civil War." *Oxford Economic Papers*, 56(4) (2004): 563–595.

Cole, Juan. *Engaging the Muslim World.* New York: Palgrave Macmillan, 2009.

Cole, Juan. *The New Arabs: How the Millennial Generation Is Changing the Middle East.* New York: Simon and Schuster, 2014.

Coleman, Simon, and John Elsner, eds. *Pilgrimage: Past and Present in the World Religions.* Cambridge, MA: Harvard University Press, 1995.

Cooke, Miriam, and Bruce B. Lawrence, eds. *Muslim Networks from Hajj to Hip Hop.* Chapel Hill: University of North Carolina, 2005.

Curtis IV, Edward E. *Encyclopedia of Muslim-American History.* New York: Facts On File, 2010.

Davletshin, Abrul-Gaziz. "Otchet Stabs-Kapitana Davletshina o Komandirovke v Khidzhaz [Captain Davletshin's Report about his Trip to Khijaz]." *Khadzh Rossiiskikh Musulman: Ezhegodnyi Sbornik Putevykh Zametok o Khadzhe [Russian Muslims' Hajj: Annual Journal of Travel Notes about Hajj]*, vol. 2. N. Novgorod, Russia: Medina Publishing House, 2009. www.idmedina.ru/ books/history_culture/hadjj/2/glava-5.htm (accessed November 12, 2015).

DeHanas, Daniel Nilsson. "Of Hajj and Home: Roots Visits to Mecca and Bangladesh in Everyday Belonging." *Ethnicities*, 13(4) (2013): 457–474.

Delaney, Carol. "The 'Hajj': Sacred and Secular." *American Ethnologist*, 17(3) (August 1990): 513–530.

Derluguian, Georgi M. *Bourdieu's Secret Admirer in the Caucasus: A World-Systems Biography.* Chicago: University of Chicago Press, 2005.

D'jakonov, Igor M. *Kniga Vospominanii.* Saint-Petersburg, Russia: Evropeiskii Dom, 1995.

Doktorov, Timur, "KBR: 'Politicheskii Kotel' Nagrelsia do Predela ['Political Cauldron' Got Hot to the Maximum Degree]." *Vek*, September 9, 2010. https://wek.ru/kbr-politicheskij-kotel-nagrelsya-do-predela.

Dovidio, John F., Samuel L. Gaertner, Nurit Shnabel, Tamar Saguy, and James Johnson. "Recategorization and Prosocial Behavior: Group Processes, Ingroup Relations, and Helping." In Stefan Sturmer and Mark Snyder, eds. *The Psychology of Prosocial Behavior: Group Processes, Intergroup Relations.* Oxford: Wiley-Blackwell, 2009.

Durkheim, Emile. *The Elementary Forms of the Religious Life.* New York: Free Press, (1912) 1947.

Dzhigkayev, Shamil. "Edut Volchata Na Khadzh [Little Wolves Perform Hajj]." *Makh Dug*, 7 (2008).

The Economist. "Islamic, Yet Integrated." September 6, 2014, www.economist .com/news/united-states/21615611-why-muslims-fare-better-america-eur ope-islamic-yet-integrated (accessed November 19, 2015).

Eliade, Mircea. *The Sacred and the Profane: The Nature of Religion.* New York: Harcourt, 1987.

Esposito, John L. *Future of Islam.* New York: Oxford University Press, 2010.

Esposito, John L. *Islam: The Straight Path*, revised 3rd edition. New York: Oxford University Press, 2005.

Esposito, John L. *Who Speaks for Islam: What a Billion Muslims Really Think.* New York: Gallup Press, 2007.

Falomir-Pichastor, Juan M., and Natasha S. Frederic. "The Dark Side of Heterogeneous Ingroup Identities: National Identification, Perceived

Threat, and Prejudice against Immigrants." *Journal of Experimental Social Psychology*, 49(1) (2013): 72–79.

Fearon, James D., and David D. Laitin. "Ethnicity, Insurgency, and Civil War." *American Political Science Review*, 97 (2003): 75–90.

Federal Bureau of Investigation (FBI). "Most Wanted Terrorists: Usama Bin Laden." September 29, 2010, www.fbi.gov/a-z-index/wanted/wanted_terror ists/usama-bin-laden (accessed November 19, 2015).

Fish, M. Steven, Francesca R. Jensenius, and Katherine E. Michel. "Islam and Large-Scale Political Violence: Is There a Connection?" *Comparative Political Studies*, 43(11) (November 2010): 1327–1362.

Fox, Jonathan. *Religion, Civilization, and Civil War. 1945 through the New Millennium*. Oxford: Lexington, 2004.

Fox, Jonathan. "World Separation of Religion and State into the 21st Century." *Comparative Political Studies*, 39(5) (2006): 537–569.

Fraga, Luis R., John A. Garcia, Rodney Hero, Michael Jones-Correa, Valerie Martinez-Ebers, and Gary M. Segura, Latino National Survey (LNS), 2006 [Computer File]. ICPSR20862-v1. Geoscape International [Producer], Miami, FL. Ann Arbor, MI: Inter-University Consortium for Political and Social Research [Distributor], www.icpsr.umich.edu/icpsrweb/RCMD/stu dies/20862/version/1 (accessed April 17, 2016).

Fraga, Luis R., John A. Garcia, Rodney Hero, Michael Jones-Correa, Valerie Martinez-Ebers, and Gary M. Segura. "*Su Casa Es Nuestra Casa*: Latino Politics Research and the Development of American Political Science." *American Political Science Review*, 100(4) (November 2006): 515–521.

Friedmann, Johanan. *Tolerance and Coercion in Islam: Interfaith Relations in the Muslim Tradition*. Cambridge: Cambridge University Press, 2003.

Fullerton, J. Timothy, and Bruce Hunsberger. "A Unidimensional Measure of Christian Orthodoxy." *Journal for the Scientific Study of Religion*, 21 (1982): 317–326.

Gaertner, Samuel L., and John F. Dovidio. *Reducing Intergroup Bias: The Common Ingroup Identity Model*. Philadelphia, PA: Psychology Press, 2000.

Gall, Carlotta, and Thomas de Waal. *Chechnya. Calamity in the Caucasus*. New York: New York University Press, 1998.

Gans, Herbert J. "Acculturation, Assimilation and Mobility." *Ethnic and Racial Studies* 30(1) (January 2007): 152–164.

Garza, Rodolfo O. de la. "Latino Politics." *Annual Review of Political Science*, 7 (2004): 91–123.

Gerges, Fawaz A. "The Islamist Moment: From Islamic State to Civil Islam?" *Political Science Quarterly*, 128(3) (2013): 389–426.

Gest, Justin. *Apart: Alienated and Engaged Muslims in the West*. New York: Columbia University Press, 2010.

Gest, Justin, and Richard Nielsen. "Is Cultural Integration Determined by Income and Education? Evidence from Surveys of Muslims in Britain, France and the United States." *MIT Working Papers* (version: July 19, 2015), www.mit.edu/ ~rnielsen/Gest%20and%20Nielsen%20-%20Muslim%20Integration.pdf (accessed December 5, 2015).

Gill, Anthony. "Religion and Comparative Politics." *Annual Review of Political Science*, 4 (2001): 117–138.

Glaser, Gabrielle. "A Gay Muslim Filmmaker Goes Inside the Hajj." *New York Times*, September 24, 2015, www.nytimes.com/2015/09/27/nyregion/par vez-sharma-a-sinner-in-mecca.html (accessed November 12, 2015).

Gordon, Milton M. *Assimilation in American Life: The Role of Race, Religion and National Origin.* New York: Oxford University Press, 1964.

Gradirovski, Sergei, and Neli Esipova. "Russian Muslims: Religious Leaven in a Secular Society." *Harvard International Review*, 30 (Spring 2008): 58–62.

Greeley, Andrew. "Coleman Revisited: Religious Structures as a Source of Social Capital." *American Behavioral Scientist*, 40(5) (1997): 587–594.

Gubler, Joshua, and Joel S. Selway. "Horizontal Inequality, Crosscutting Cleavages, and Civil War." *Journal of Conflict Resolution*, 56(2) (2012): 206–232.

Gutierrez, Jose Angel. "The Chicano Movement: Paths to Power." *The Social Studies*, 102(1) (2011): 25–32.

Gutierrez, Margo, and Matt S. Meier. *Encyclopedia of the Mexican American Civil Rights Movement.* Westport, CT: Greenwood Press, 2000.

Habyarimana, James, Macartan Humphreys, Daniel N. Posner, and Jeremy Weinstein. "Why Does Ethnic Diversity Undermine Public Goods Provision?" *American Political Science Review*, 101(4) (2007): 709–725.

Hale, Henry E. *Patronal Politics: Eurasian Regime Dynamics in Comparative Perspective.* New York: Cambridge University Press, 2015.

Halemba, Agnieszka. "National, Transnational or Cosmopolitan Heroine?: The Virgin Mary's Apparitions in Contemporary Europe." *Ethnic and Racial Studies*, 34(3) (2011): 454–470.

Hall, Deborah L., David C. Matz, and Wendy Wood. "Why Don't We Practice What We Preach? A Meta-analytic Review of Religious Racism." *Personality and Social Psychology Review*, 14(1) (2010): 126–139.

Hanson, Stephen E. *Post-imperial Democracies: Ideology and Party Formation in Third Republic France, Weimer Germany, and Post-Soviet Russia.* New York: Cambridge University Press, 2010.

Haslam, Alexander S. *Psychology in Organizations.* London: SAGE Publications, 2001.

Haslam, S. Alexander, Stephen D. Reicher, and Michael J. Platow. *The New Psychology of Leadership: Identity, Influence and Power.* New York: Psychology Press, 2011.

Hefner, Robert W. *Civil Islam: Muslims and Democratization in Indonesia.* Princeton, NJ: Princeton University Press, 2000.

Helbardt, Sascha, Dagmar Hellmann-Rajanayagam, and Rudiger Korff. "Religionization of Politics in Sri Lanka, Thailand, and Myanmar." *Politics, Religion & Ideology*, 14(1) (2013): 36–58.

Heneghan, Tom. "Uncertain Future for France's Muslim Council." Reuters, May 5, 2008, http://blogs.reuters.com/faithworld/2008/05/05/uncertain-future-for-fr ances-muslim-council/ (accessed November 19, 2015).

Horowitz, Donald L. *Ethnic Groups in Conflict.* Berkeley: University of California Press, 1986.

Huntington, Samuel P. *The Clash of Civilizations and the Remaking of World Order*. New York: Simon & Schuster, 1996.

Huntington, Samuel P. "The Hispanic Challenge." *Foreign Policy* (March/April 2004): 30–39.

Huntington, Samuel P. *Who Are We? The Challenges to America's National Identity*. New York: Simon & Schuster, 2004.

Ibrahim, Mir Muhammad. *Sociology of Religions: Perspectives of Ali Shariati*. New Delhi, India: Prentice-Hall, 2008.

Inglehart, Ronald, and Christopher Welzel. *Modernization, Cultural Change and Democracy: The Human Development Sequence*. New York: Cambridge University Press, 2005.

Islamic Society of North America (ISNA). "ISNA Celebrates the 5th Annual Muslim-Jewish Weekend of Twinning." December 25, 2013. www.isna.net/isna-celebrates-the-5th-annual-muslim-jewish-weekend-of-twinning.html (accessed November 19, 2015).

Janowitz, Morris. *The Reconstruction of Patriotism: Education for Civic Consciousness*. Chicago: University of Chicago Press, 1983.

Johnson, Toni. "Europe: Integrating Islam." Council on Foreign Relations. July 25, 2011. www.cfr.org/religion/europe-integrating-islam/p8252 (accessed November 19, 2015).

Kane, Eileen. *Russian Hajj: Empire and the Pilgrimage to Mecca*. Ithaca, NY: Cornell University Press, 2015.

Kanokov, Arsen, "President Kabardino-Balkarii Arsen Kanokov – 'Gazete' [President of Kabardino-Balkaria, Arsen Kanokov's Interview to 'Gazeta']." *SK-News*. October 13, 2006. https://sk-news.ru/news/analitic/7428/.

Kantner, John, and Kevin J. Vaughn. "Pilgrimage as Costly Signal: Religiously Motivated Cooperation in Chaco and Nasca." *Journal of Anthropological Archaeology*, 31 (2012): 66–82.

Karpov, Vyacheslav. "Religiosity and Tolerance in the United States and Poland." *Journal for the Scientific Study of Religion*, 41(2) (2002): 267–288.

Kavkazskiy Uzel. "V Kabardino-Balkarii Vzorvan Avtomobil' S Militsionerami [In Kabardino-Balkaria a Police Car Has Been Blown Up]." April 30, 2010. www.kavkaz-uzel.ru/articles/168269/ (accessed November 19, 2015).

Kavkazskiy Uzel. "Kabardino-Balkariia: Khronika Vzryvov, Obstrelov I Teraktov [Kabardino-Balkaria: The Chronicle of Explosions, Shootings, and Terrorist Acts]." November 10, 2015. www.kavkaz-uzel.ru/articles/172027/ (accessed November 19, 2015).

Khodarkovsky, Michael. *Bitter Choices: Loyalty and Betrayal in the Russian Conquest of the North Caucasus*. Ithaca, NY: Cornell University Press, 2011.

King, Charles. *The Ghost of Freedom: A History of the Caucasus*. New York: Oxford University Press, 2008.

Kippenberg, Hans G. "Searching for the Link between Religion and Violence by Means of the Thomas-Theorem." *Method and Theory in the Study of Religion*, 22 (2010): 97–115.

Kumykov, Tugan, ed. *Problemy Kavkazskoi voiny i vyselenie cherkesov v predely Osmanskoi imperii (20–70-ye gg. XIX v.). Sbornik arkhivnykh dokumentov [Problems of the Caucasus War and the Deportation of the Circassians to the*

Ottoman Empire (from the 1820s to the 1870s). Compilation of Archival Documents]. Nalchik, Russia: Elbrus, 2001.

Kunovich, Robert M., and Randy Hodson. "Conflict, Religious Identity, and Ethnic Intolerance in Croatia." *Social Forces*, 78(2) (December 1999): 643–668.

Kuru, Ahmet T. "Authoritarianism and Democracy in Muslim Countries: Rentier States and Regional Diffusion." *Political Science Quarterly*, 129(3) (2014): 399–427.

Kurzman, Charles. *The Missing Martyrs: Why There Are so Few Muslim Terrorists*. New York: Oxford University Press, 2011.

Kurzman, Charles, David Schanzer, and Ebrahim Moosa. "Muslim American Terrorism since 9/11: Why so Rare?" *The Muslim World*, 101(3) (July 2011): 464–483.

Lam, Pui-Yan. "As the Flocks Gather: How Religion Affects Voluntary Association Participation." *Journal for the Scientific Study of Religion*, 41 (3) (2002): 405–422.

Latino Leadership. "National Council of La Raza: NCLR." http://latino-leadership.org/partners-affiliations/ (accessed November 12, 2015).

League of United Latin American Citizens (LULAC). "History: LULAC's Milestones." http://lulac.org/about/history/milestones/ (accessed November 19, 2015).

Levine, Robert A., and Donald T. Campbell. *Ethnocentrism: Theories of Conflict, Ethnic Attitudes, and Group Behavior*. Oxford: Wiley, 1972.

Lewis, Bernard. *Faith and Power: Religion and Politics in the Middle East*. New York: Oxford University Press, 2010.

Lewis, Bernard, and Dominique Schapper, eds. *Muslims in Europe: Social Change in Western Europe*. London: Pinter, 1994.

Low, Michael Christopher. "Empire and the Hajj: Pilgrims, Plagues, and Pan-Islam under British Surveillance, 1865–908." *International Journal of Middle East Studies*, 40(2) (2008): 269–290.

Malcolm X, and Alex Haley. *The Autobiography of Malcolm X*. New York: Grove Press, 1965.

Malik, Abida. "Identities, Islamophobia, and the State: Diverse Perspectives and Experiences of Muslim Civic Actors from Islamic Organizations in the UK." In Matthias Kortmann and Kerstin Rosenow-Williams, eds. *Islamic Organizations in Europe and the USA: A Multidisciplinary Perspective*. New York: Palgrave Macmillan, 2013.

Mandaville, Peter. *Global Political Islam*. New York: Routledge, 2007.

Marguerite Casey Foundation. "National Council of La Raza." http://casey grants.org/grantees/national-council-of-la-raza/ (accessed November 12, 2015).

Marquez, Benjamin. *Constructing Identities in Mexican-American Political Organizations: Choosing Issues, Taking Sides*. Austin: University of Texas Press, 2003.

Martinez, Deirdre. *Who Speaks for Hispanics?: Hispanic Interest Groups in Washington*. Albany: State University of New York Press, 2009.

Massignon, Berengere. "Islam in the EC System of Regulation." In Aziz Al-Azmeh and Effie Fokas, eds. *Islam in Europe: Diversity, Identity and Influence.* New York: Cambridge University Press, 2007.

Maxwell, Rahsaan. "Evaluating Migrant Integration: Political Attitudes across Generations in Europe." *International Migration Review,* 44(1) (2010): 25–52.

Mayer, Tamar, and Suleiman A. Mourad, eds. *Jerusalem: Idea and Reality,* New York: Routledge, 2008.

McGarty, Craig. *Categorization in Social Psychology.* London, Thousand Oaks, CA, New Delhi, India: SAGE Publications, 1999.

McGlinchey, Eric. *Chaos, Violence, Dynasty: Politics and Islam in Central Asia.* Pittsburgh PA: University of Pittsburgh Press, 2011.

McKenzie, Brian D. "Religious Social Networks, Indirect Mobilization, and African-American Political Participation." *Political Research Quarterly,* 57(4) (2004): 621–632.

"Mikhail Babich: 'My Budem Vyzhigat Terrorizm Kalenym Zhelezom' [Mikhail Babich: 'We Will Burn Out Terrorism with a Hot Iron']." *Polnomochnii Predstavitel' Prezidenta Rossiiskoi Federatsii v Privolzhskom Federalnom Okruge [The Full Representative of the President of the Russian Federation in Volga Federal District].* July 20, 2012, www.pfo.ru/?id=56137.

Minahan, James. *One Europe, Many Nations: A Historical Dictionary of European National Groups,* Westport, CT: Greenwood, 2000.

Ministry of Justice of the Russian Federation. "Federal'nyi Spisok Ekstremistskikh Materialov [Federal List of Extremist Materials]." http://minjust.ru/extremist-materials (accessed July 25, 2016).

Moberg, David O. *The Church as a Social Institution: The Sociology of American Religion.* Englewood Cliffs, NJ: Prentice-Hall, 1962.

Mohammed-Marzouk, Methal R. "Knowledge, Culture, and Positionality: Analysis of Three Medieval Muslim Travel Accounts." *Cross-Cultural Communication,* 8(6) (2012): 1–10.

Mummendey, Amélie, and Michael Wenzel. "Social Discrimination and Tolerance in Intergroup Relations: Reactions to Intergroup Difference." *Personality and Social Psychology Review,* 3 (1999): 158–174.

Murphy, Paul J. *The Wolves of Islam: Russia and the Faces of Chechen Terror.* Dulles, VA: Brasseay's Inc., 2005.

Nagourney, Adam, Jennifer Medina, Ian Lovett, and Julie Turkewitz. "As Bullets Flew, Urgent Prayers and Pure Panic." *New York Times,* December 6, 2015.

Neuberg, Steven L., Carolyn M. Warner, Stephen A. Mistler, Anna Berlin, Eric D. Hill, Jordan D. Johnson, Gabrielle Filip-Crawford, Roger E. Millsap, George Thomas, Michael Winkelman, Benjamin J. Broome, Thomas J. Taylor, and Juliane Schober. "Religion and Intergroup Conflict: Findings from the Global Group Relations Project." *Psychological Science,* 25(1) (2014): 198–206.

Nisbet, Robert A. *The Sociological Tradition.* New York: Basic Books, 1966.

Norris, Pippa, and Ronald Inglehart. *Sacred and Secular: Religion and Politics Worldwide.* Cambridge: Cambridge University Press, 2004.

Nursing Schools. "15 Fascinating Scientific Facts about Siblings." May 15, 2011. www.nursingschools.net/blog/2011/05/15-fascinating-scientific-facts-about-siblings/ (accessed November 19, 2015).

O'Brien, Susan. "Pilgrimage, Power, and Identity: The Role of the Hajj in the Lives of Nigerian Hausa Bori Adepts." *Africa Today*, 46 (Summer 1999): 11–40.

Pantoja, Adrian D., Ricardo Ramirez, and Gary M. Segura. "Citizens by Choice, Voters by Necessity: Patterns in Political Mobilization by Naturalized Latinos." *Political Research Quarterly*, 54 (December): 729–750.

Pantoja, Adrian D., and Gary M. Segura. "Fear and Loathing in California: Contextual Threat and Political Sophistication among Latino Voters." *Political Behavior*, 25(3) (September 2003): 265–286.

Papas, Alexandre, Thomas Welsford, and Thierry Zarcone, eds. *Central Asian Pilgrims: Hajj Routes and Pious Visits between Central Asia and the Hijaz.* Berlin: Klaus Schwartz Verlag, 2012.

Pape, Robert A. *Dying to Win: The Strategic Logic of Suicide Terrorism.* New York: Random House, 2005.

Patterson, Eric. "Religious Activity and Political Participation: The Brazilian and Chilean Cases." *Latin American Politics and Society*, 47(1) (2005): 1–29.

Peach, Ceri. "Muslim Population of Europe: A Brief Overview of Demographic Trends and Socioeconomic Integration, with Particular Reference to Britain." In Steffen Angenendt, Paul M. Barrett, Jonathan Laurence, Ceri Peach, Julianne Smith, and Tim Winter. *Muslim Integration: Challenging Conventional Wisdom in Europe and the United States.* Washington, DC: Center for Strategic and International Studies, 2007.

Pearce, Susanna. "Religious Rage: A Quantitative Analysis of the Intensity of Religious Conflicts." *Terrorism and Political Violence*, 17(3) (2005): 333–352.

Penny Magazine. "Circassia and the Circassians." London: Charles Knight & Co, April 14, 1838, pp. 137–139.

Peters, Francis E. *The Hajj: The Muslim Pilgrimage to Mecca and the Holy Places.* Princeton, NJ: Princeton University Press, 1994.

Pettigrew, Thomas F., and Linda R. Tropp. "A Meta-analytic Test of Intergroup Contact Theory." *Journal of Personality and Social Psychology*, 90(5) (2006): 751–783.

Pew Research Center. "The Global Religious Landscape." *Pew Research Center's Forum on Religion & Public Life.* December 18, 2012. www.pewforum.org/2012/12/18/global-religious-landscape-muslim/ (accessed November 19, 2015).

Pew Research Center. "Muslim Americans: Middle Class and Mostly Mainstream." May 22, 2007. www.pewresearch.org/2007/05/22/muslim-americans-middle-class-and-mostly-mainstream/ (accessed November 19, 2015).

Pew Research Center. "Muslim Americans: No Sign of Growth in Alienation or Support for Extremism." *Pew Research Center's Forum on Religion & Public Life.* August 30, 2011. www.people-press.org/2011/08/30/muslim-americans-no-signs-of-growth-in-alienation-or-support-for-extremism/ (accessed November 19, 2015).

Plomin, Robert. "Commentary: Why Are Children in the Same Family so Different? Non-shared Environment Three Decades Later." *International Journal of Epidemiology*, 40(3) (June 2011): 582–592.

Porter, Venetia, ed. *Hajj: Journey to the Heart of Islam*. Cambridge, MA: Harvard University Press, 2012.

Portes, Alejandro, and Min Zhou. "The New Second Generation: Segmented Assimilation and Its Variants." *The Annals of the American Academy of Political and Social Science*, 530(1) (November 1993): 74–96.

Postmes, Tom, and Nyla R. Branscombe, eds. *Rediscovering Social Identity*. New York: Psychology Press, 2010.

Putnam, Robert D. *Bowling Alone: The Collapse and Revival of American Community*. New York: Touchstone, 2000.

Putnam, Robert D. *Making Democracy Work: Civic Traditions in Modern Italy*. Princeton, NJ: Princeton University Press, 1993.

Putnam, Robert D., and David E. Campbell. *American Grace: How Religion Divides and Unites Us*. New York: Simon & Schuster, 2010.

Radio Free Europe (RFE/RL). "Russia: Chechen Official Puts Death Toll for 2 Wars at up to 160,000." August 16, 2005. www.rferl.org/content/article/10 60708.html (accessed November 19, 2015).

Radio Free Europe (RFE/RL). "Russia: Nalchik Raid Leaves a Painful Legacy." October 12, 2006, www.rferl.org/content/article/1071996.html (accessed November 19, 2015).

Ramadan, Tariq. *The Quest for Meaning: Developing a Philosophy of Pluralism*. London: Allen Lane, 2010.

Ramadan, Tariq. *Western Muslims and the Future of Islam*. New York: Oxford University Press, 2004.

Regnum. "Imam Musulmanskoi Obshiny Vladikavkaza Provedet Poltora Goda V Kolonii-Poselenii [Imam of the Vladikavkaz Muslim Community Is Sentenced to a Year and a Half in a Colony]." October 4, 2011. http://regn um.ru/news/1452287.html (accessed November 19, 2015).

Regnum. "Imama Nal'chika Uvolili, Vosstanovili Na Rabote, Ob'avili Blagodarnost' I Snova Uvolili [The Imam of Nalchik Was Fired, Restored in His Position, Commended for Good Service, and Let Go Again]." August 8, 2008. www.regnum.ru/news/cultura/1042786.html (accessed November 19, 2015).

Regnum. "Rais-imam Nalchika: Mufti Kabardino-Balkarii Prenebregaet MVeruyuschikh [Nalchik Rais-Imam: The Mufti of Kabardino-Balkaria Dismisses the Opinion of Muslims]." April 23, 2008. http://regnum.ru/new s/991435.html (accessed November 19, 2015).

Robinson, Adam. *Bin Laden: The Inside Story of the Rise and Fall of the Most Notorious Terrorist in History*. New York: Arcade Publishing, 2011.

Roccas, Sonia. "Religion and Value Systems." *Journal of Social Issues*, 61(4): 747–759.

Roy, Olivier. *Globalized Islam: The Search for a New Ummah*. New York: Columbia University Press, 2004.

Royal Embassy of Saudi Arabia. "1,379,531 Pilgrims from 188 Countries Arrived for Hajj." October 13, 2013. www.saudiembassy.net/latest_news/new s10131302.aspx. (accessed July 14, 2015).

Royal Embassy of Saudi Arabia. "1,384,941 Foreign Pilgrims Participated in Hajj." September 22, 2015. www.saudiembassy.net/latest_news/new s09221501.aspx. (accessed July 14, 2015).

Royal Embassy of Saudi Arabia. "2,521,000 Pilgrims Participated in Hajj 1430." November 29, 2009. www.saudiembassy.net/latest_news/news11290904.aspx. (accessed July 14, 2015).

Royal Embassy of Saudi Arabia. "2.8 Million Pilgrims Participated in Hajj 1431." November 18, 2010. www.saudiembassy.or.jp/En/PressReleases/2010/2010 1118.htm. (accessed July 14, 2015).

Royal Embassy of Saudi Arabia. "2,927,717 Pilgrims Performed Hajj This Year." November 6, 2011. www.saudiembassy.net/latest_news/news11061102.aspx. (accessed July 14, 2015).

Royal Embassy of Saudi Arabia. "3,161,573 Pilgrims Perform Hajj This Year." October 27, 2012. www.saudiembassy.net/latest_news/news10271201.aspx. (accessed July 14, 2015).

Royal Embassy of Saudi Arabia. "Record Number of Pilgrims Arrive for Hajj." December 6, 2008. www.saudiembassy.net/affairs/recent-news/new s12060801.aspx. (accessed July 14, 2015).

Royal Embassy of Saudi Arabia. "Small Increase in Foreign Pilgrims." October 2, 2014. www.saudiembassy.net/latest_news/news10021401.aspx. (accessed July 14, 2015).

Saleem, Shahed. "The British Mosque: A Social and Architectural History." *Muslim Institute.* www.musliminstitute.org/blogs/culture/british-mosque-so cial-and-architectural-history (accessed November 19, 2015).

Saleem, Shahed. "A History of Mosques in Britain." *Architects Journal.* April 19, 2012. www.architectsjournal.co.uk/a-history-of-mosques-in-britain/8629263 .article (accessed November 19, 2015).

Salvatore, Armando, and Mark Levine, eds. *Religion, Social Practice, and Contested Hegemonies: Reconstructing the Public Sphere in Muslim Majority Societies.* New York: Palgrave Macmillan, 2005.

Sarkissian, Ani. "Religion and Civic Engagement in Muslim Countries." *Journal for the Scientific Study of Religion,* 51(4) (2012): 607–622.

Selway, Joel Sawat. "Cross-Cuttingness, Cleavage Structures and Civil War Onset." *British Journal of Political Science,* 41(1) (2011): 111–138.

Sergeev, Nikolai, "V Raslpedelenii Khadzh-Turov Nashli Priznaki Extremizma [Signs of Terrorism Have Been Found in Distribution of Hajj Tours]." *Kommersant,* July 20, 2012. www.kommersant.ru/doc/1984193 (accessed November 19, 2015).

Seul, Jeffrey R. "'Ours Is the Way of God': Religion, Identity, and Intergroup Conflict." *Journal of Peace Research,* 36(5) (1999): 553–569.

Shadueva, Larisa. "Interview with the Head of the Spiritual Directorate in Kabardino-Balkaria, A. M. Pshikhachev." *Kabardino-Balkarskaia Pravda,* February 11, 2006.

Shterin, Marat, and Akhmet Yarlykapov. "Reconsidering Radicalisation and Terrorism: The New Muslims Movement in Kabardino-Balkaria and Its Path to Violence." *Religion, State and Society,* 39(2–3) (2011): 303–325.

Siddiqui, Shariq A. "Islamic Society of North America." In Edward E. Curtis, ed. *Encyclopedia of Muslim-American History*. New York: Infobase Publishing, 2010.

Sidel, John T. *Riots, Pogroms, Jihad: Religious Violence in Indonesia*. Ithaca, NY: Cornell University Press, 2006.

Skerry, Peter. "The Muslim-American Muddle." *National Affairs*, 9 (Fall 2011): 14–37.

Sokolov, Boris. *SSSR I Rossiia na Voine: Lyudskie Poteri XX veka [The USSR and Russia at War: People's Casualties in the Twentieth Century]*. Moscow: Yauza, 2014.

Stepan, Alfred. "Rituals of Respect: Sufis and Secularists in Senegal in Comparative Perspective." *Comparative Politics*, 44 (July 2012): 379–401.

Stewart, Frances. *Horizontal Inequalities and Conflict: Understanding Group Conflict in Multiethnic Societies*. Basingstoke: Palgrave Macmillan, 2008.

Svensson, Isak. "Fighting with Faith: Religion and Conflict Resolution in Civil Wars." *Journal of Conflict Resolution*, 51(6) (2007): 930–949.

Tajfel, Henri, and John C. Turner. "The Social Identity Theory of Inter-group Behavior." In Stephen Worchel and William G. Austin, eds. *Psychology of Intergroup Relations*. Chicago: Nelson-Hall, 1986, 7–24.

Telegraph. "Hajj Pilgrimage 2011: By Numbers." November 3, 2011, www.telegraph.co.uk/news/worldnews/middleeast/saudiarabia/8867639/Hajj-pilgrimage-2011-by-numbers.html (accessed November 19, 2015).

Tikaeva, Fatima. "Obschestvo na puti konsolidatsii [Society on Its Way to Consolidation]." *Islam v Evrazii*, January 23, 2009. http://islamvevrazii.ru/obsh274.php (accessed November 19, 2015).

Tishkov, Valery. *Chechnya: Life in a War-Torn Society*. Berkeley: University of California Press, 2004.

Tocqueville, Alexis de. *Democracy in America*. Translated by Gerald Bevan. London: Penguin Classics, (1835) 2003.

Toft, Monica Duffy. "Getting Religion? The Puzzling Case of Islam and Civil War." *International Security*, 31(4) (2007): 97–131.

Turner, John C., Michael A. Hogg, Penelope J. Oakes, Stephen D. Reicher, and Margaret S. Wetherell. *Rediscovering the Social Group: A Self-Categorization Theory*. Oxford: Blackwell, 1987.

Turner, John C., Penelope J. Oakes, Alexander S. Haslam, and Craig McGarty. "Self and Collective: Cognition and Social Context." *Personality and Social Psychology Bulletin*, 20(3) (1994): 454–463.

Verba, Sidney, Kay Lehman Scholzman, and Henry Brady. *Voice and Equality: Civic Volunteerism in American Politics*. Cambridge, MA: Harvard University Press, 1995.

Voll, John O., and John L. Esposito. *Islam and Democracy*. New York: Oxford University Press, 1996.

Waters, Mary C., and Tomas R. Jimenez. "Assessing Immigrant Assimilation: New Empirical and Theoretical Challenges." *Annual Review of Sociology*, 31 (2005): 105–125.

Watt, William Montgomery. *Muhammad: Prophet and Statesman*. New York: Oxford University Press, 1974.

Whitehouse, Harvey, and Brian McQuinn. "Ritual and Violence: Divergent Modes of Religiosity and Armed Struggle." In Mark Juergensmeyer, Margo Kitts, and Michael Jerryson, eds. *The Oxford Handbook of Religion and Violence.* New York: Oxford University Press, 2013.

Wikipedia. "Eid Al-Adha." https://en.wikipedia.org/wiki/Eid_al-Adha#cite_note-4 (accessed November 20, 2015).

Wilson, John, and Thomas Janoski. "The Contribution of Religion to Volunteer Work." *Sociology of Religion,* 56(2) (1995): 137–152.

Wilson, John, and Marc Musick. "Who Cares? Toward an Integrated Theory of Volunteer Work." *American Sociological Review,* 62(5) (1997): 694–713.

Wollebaek, Dag, and Per Selle. "Participation in Social Capital Formation: Norway in a Comparative Perspective." *Scandinavian Political Studies,* 26 (1) (2003): 67–91.

Wuthnow, Robert. "Mobilizing Civic Engagement: The Changing Impact of Religious Involvement." In Theda Skocpol and Morris P. Fiorina, eds. *Civic Engagement in American Democracy.* Washington, DC: Brookings Institution Press, 1999.

Zhemukhov, Sufian N. "The Birth of Modern Circassian Nationalism." *Nationalities Papers,* 40 (Spring 2012): 502–524.

Zhemukhov, Sufian N. "One Thousand Years of Islam in Kabarda: An Experiment in Periodization." *Anthropology and Archaeology of Eurasia,* 49(4) (2011): 54–71.

Zwilling, Anne-Laure. "France." In Jørgen Schøler Nielsen, Samim Akgönül, Ahmet Alibašić, Brigitte Maréchal, and Christian Moe, eds. *Yearbook of Muslims in Europe,* vol. 1. Leiden: BRILL, 2009.

Index

Central Council for Muslims in Germany (ZMD), 163, 165
Cesari, Joselyne, 152
Chechens, 28, 29, 31
Chechnya, Republic of, 15, 19, 28, 29, 30, 31, 57, 58, 105
Chirkavi, Said Affandi, 25, 129
Christian, Christianity, 6, 31, 52, 53, 54, 57, 71, 75, 81, 82, 111, 122, 128, 161, 169, 187
  Orthodox, 53, 54, 84
Circassians, 10, 13, 14, 16, 17, 18, 19, 20, 28, 29, 34, 40, 42, 46, 52, 53, 54, 64, 70, 71, 87, 122, 130, 148, 186
  genocide, nineteenth century, 19, 20
Cold War, 75
Cole, Juan, 3, 7, 185
common (in)group value, 94, 95, 108, 109, 119, 122, 123, 127, 131, 148, 155, 156, 159, 160, 178
Communism, 13, 25, 28, 130
Crimea, 17, 28, 53
Croatia, 85

Dagestan, Republic of, 18, 19, 25, 30, 54, 57, 58, 71, 122, 129
Davletshin, Abdul-Aziz, 21, 79, 114
democracy, 6, 150, 175, 183
Dickens, Charles, 188
Dovidio, John, 110

Egypt, 80, 101, 165, 184
Elbrus, Mt., xiii, 13
Eliade, Mircea, 1, 8, 9, 93, 96, 97, 101, 103, 109, 116, 122, 130, 172, 173, 174
Esposito, John, 3, 4, 6, 47, 73, 74, 75, 109, 144, 152, 185
ethnicity, 2, 16, 17, 20, 25, 26, 45, 46, 48, 52, 53, 54, 55, 76, 83, 108, 122, 130, 174, 176, 181, 186
  and race, 80, 101, 131, 177
  and religion, 57, 66, 71, 75, 85, 94, 101, 110, 112, 131, 152, 153, 157
  ethnic conflict, 27, 30
  ethnic relations, 34, 46, 54, 94, 112, 149, 150, 158, 164, 176, 180
ethnicization, 26
Europe, 5, 9, 47, 77, 80, 86, 90, 101, 150, 151, 152, 153, 154, 155, 159, 160, 162, 165, 171, 172, 176, 182
European Union (EU), 162, 163

Fardh, 50
Fearon, James, 5
Federation Nationale des Musulmans de France (FNMF), 164
Fish, Steven, 3, 5, 6
France, 112, 152, 154, 164, 166, 169
Freud, Sigmund, 85

Gaertner, Samuel, 110
Garza, Rodolfo de la, 175
Georgia, 34, 35, 53
Gerges, Fawaz A., 3, 80
Germany, 154, 163, 166, 169
glasnost, 25
Gorbachev, Mikhail, 25

Hadith, 105, 136
Hajj
  age of pilgrims, 45, 103, 110, 122, 134, 135, 139, 140, 141, 142
  and equality, 44, 68, 69, 131, 133, 134, 135, 139, 144
  and money (income), 16, 46, 47, 50, 52, 68, 69, 85, 89, 99, 109, 134
  and race, 90, 101, 102, 153
  as a Pillar of Islam, 1, 24, 26, 49, 50, 60, 97, 129, 147, 184
  diversity, 75, 81, 101, 102, 103, 104, 123, 130, 134, 137, 138, 144, 153
  gender of pilgrims, 3, 45, 48, 81, 103, 110, 122, 134, 135, 139, 140, 141, 142
  Hajji and Hajjiah title, 16, 23, 38, 51, 74, 85, 99, 111
  Hajj-Ifrad, 57
  Hajj-Tamattu, 57
  Ihram robes, 57, 132, 133
  in post-Soviet Russia, 17, 25, 27
  in the Russian Empire, 16, 17, 18, 19, 21, 87
  in the Soviet Union, 22, 23, 24, 25
  Tawaf, walking around Ka'aba, 58, 71, 82, 87, 103
  tourism and business, 25, 26, 85, 88, 90
  ZamZam, holy water, 26, 51
  ziyarat, secondary pilgrimage, 108
halal, 104
haram, 54, 115
Hefner, Robert, 3, 80
hijab, headscarf, 61, 62, 71, 122
Hijra, 19, 63
Hinduism, 84